Presented to

Sanborn Regional High School
Kingston, New Hampshire

by
The Boston Globe

in honor of
Jeremy James Bowers, Grade 11

Winner of
The Boston Globe
1987 Constitution Essay Contest

December, 1987

READ ALL ABOUT IT!

READ ALL ABOUT IT!
A DAY IN THE LIFE OF A
METROPOLITAN NEWSPAPER

by Jane T. Harrigan

photographs by Suzanne Kreiter

The Globe Pequot Press

Chester, Connecticut 06412

Excerpt from *It Came from the Swamp* by Susan Trausch.
Copyright © 1986 by Susan Trausch. Reprinted by
permission of Houghton Mifflin Company.

Library of Congress Cataloging-in-Publication Data

Harrigan, Jane T.
    Read all about it!

    Includes index.
    1. Boston globe. 2. Newspaper publishing—
Massachusetts—Boston. I. Title.
PN4899.B65B64 1987   071.44′61   87-17798
ISBN 0-87106-760-9

Manufactured in the United States of America
First Edition / First Printing

Contents

Photographs follow page 158

To D.

Preface

No American bombs fell on foreign nations on June 4, 1986. No jets were hijacked, no superpower summits were held, no Olympic gold medals were awarded. In short, it seemed an average news day, the kind from which most newspapers are made.

The events that would form the *Boston Globe* happened that Wednesday in the halls of the U.S. Capitol and the Massachusetts State House; on the streets of Cape Town, South Africa, and Santiago, Chile; in courtrooms and classrooms and all the large and small spaces where humans act out their daily drama. As this drama unfolded, 2,500 people at the *Globe* watched it, recorded it, made room for it. They would face a million small decisions before the presses rolled that night, and one large one: whether to withhold a story at the government's request.

But as the day began, none of them knew what lay ahead. Neither did I. I chose this day at random as a way to show the process, to find out what these people do that causes a folded newspaper to land with a thud on hundreds of thousands of doorsteps each morning. How does it happen? I asked the people at the *Globe* that question, and many of them answered this way: "When you find out, let me know." This book is an account of how the *Boston Globe* of June 5, 1986, came to be. But it's not just about the events of June 4, the day covered in that newspaper, and it's not just about the *Globe*. The threads from which one day's paper is woven stretch back weeks and months into the past, and forward as far into the future. As I write this nine months later, some of the stories that were on the front page that day in June are still making news. And some of the stories the editors and reporters discussed that day still have not been written.

Though the subject here is the *Globe*, it might be any newspaper. The kinds of decisions made on that day in that place are faced, in one form or another, by everyone who has found an occupation in the addiction to daily journalism. They're faced at large papers and small, chain papers and independents, big-city papers and country weeklies. The book tells the story of newspapers through the work of one group of people, much as a reporter might tell the story of a national trend through the eyes of a single family. To quote a newsroom adage: The more specific the information, the more universal the message.

Newspaper people are reluctant to talk about what they do. They like to ask questions, not answer them, and they worry that their dedication to informing the public and keeping the press free will sound corny if they put it into words. Maybe it does. But the book's intent is not to glorify the people who make newspapers; after ten years as a journalist, I'd hardly be inclined to do that. Neither is it the book's intent to judge whether these particular people did things right or wrong on this particular day. Like a newspaper, the book simply presents the information.

Like a newspaper, too, the book cannot cover everything that happened. The people who appear in these pages are not necessarily the most important people at the *Globe*. They're some, but not all, of the people who played a role on the day in question, and who had the time and the inclination to talk about it. A few of them have left the paper since then, but the jobs they did are still being performed much as they're described here. Sadly, one person who figures in these pages has left journalism forever. Bob Anglin died March 20, 1987, at the age of fifty-three. As David Nyhan wrote in his farewell column, "he was one of those born-to-be-a-newspaperman guys." I'll always remember something he said to me and to so many other people: "Show me a reporter with a respect for authority, and I'll show you a lousy reporter."

No preface would be complete without acknowledgments, and these acknowledgments would not be complete without my thanks to the people at the *Globe*. They let me, a stranger, into their world, and then they did something more difficult: They left me alone. Not once did anyone try to tell me what to write. Not once did anyone even ask what I'd be writing. Thanks especially to Cheeb Everitt for showing me around, and to Jack Driscoll and Tom Mulvoy for straightening out all the confusions I encountered.

Thanks, too, to the eighty people who wrote memos describing their activities on June 4. The book wouldn't have been possible without them, since I couldn't be everywhere at once. I did, however, deploy two extra sets of eyes and ears in the *Globe* building that day. One set belonged to Scot French, who drove to Boston on short notice and spent the night at the *Globe*, then drove back to New Hampshire in time to start work in his own newsroom. His memos helped incalculably. Sue Hertz, my teaching colleague at the University of New Hampshire, was the other observer that day. She deserves two thank yous—one for her note-taking at the *Globe*, and one for the 10,000 times she listened to my obsessive ramblings about this project. Sympathetic silence and constructive suggestions also came from two other colleagues in the journalism program at UNH, Andy Merton and Don Murray. This assignment is a hand-me-down from Don, and I'm proud to admit it.

A special expression of gratitude goes to Suzanne Kreiter, able photographer and friend. Her enthusiasm for the book rekindled my own. Eric Newman faced the unenviable task of editing an editor, and he handled it with aplomb. The friends and relatives who have helped me with their patience in the last year are too numerous to list here. Perhaps now they can greet me with "Hello" instead of "Is it finished yet?"

Finally, I thank my husband, Dave. Night after night, in the face of all evidence to the contrary, he assured me that I could write my first book and survive my first year of teaching at the same time. He didn't complain when he had to take his vacation alone, and I didn't complain (much) when he took up the clarinet.

As a crusader for more women in journalism, I feel compelled to add one more note. Although I have tried any number of strategies to avoid using the pronoun *he* when referring to a single, generic newspaper employee, in some cases good grammar left me no alternative. There is no job in this book that can't be performed equally well by a man or a woman.

One last acknowledgment: Thanks to the people of Boston, who have made me a much more aggressive driver.

6:00 A.M.

There's a soul that makes the machine go.
—Tom Mulvoy, managing editor

"Was anybody hurt? What did the guy get away with? No one saw a car at all?"

In the murky morning light of the *Boston Globe* newsroom, Paul Feeney is pulling the first nugget of news from an hour of telephoning police departments. The three robberies aren't much—at best, they might rate a news brief in the Metro section—but right now they're the only breaking story he's got. With nearly eighteen hours to go before the presses roll for the first edition, something more compelling is bound to happen.

"Quincy," he whispers across the desk to Gerry Weidmann, the other morning reporter, without breaking the flow of questions into the phone.

"Did anyone see a second man at any point? How about a description of the one fellow? Twenties, brown curly hair, blue windbreaker, green pants. Nobody injured? Okay. Beautiful."

Feeney and Weidmann and four other people—two overnight editors, an editorial assistant, and a switchboard operator—sit at the center of a sea of empty desks in the blue-carpeted newsroom. The screens of hundreds of computer terminals protrude like periscopes above desk level, staring blankly. When the deadline crunch hits late this afternoon, the space that dwarfs the six of them will hold more than 400 people.

"Quincy police are seeking a young gunman who went on a mini crime spree, holding up three businesses in the city." The blinking green cursor clicks quickly across the screen of his terminal as Feeney writes.

1

Weidmann continues his cop calls. The numbers of the thirty departments he checks each morning are programmed into his phone so that he punches only one button for each.

"A reporter is only as good as his contacts," he says between punches. "In this job, I know people on the phone. If they walked in here I wouldn't know them, and they wouldn't know me. One time, though, I walked into a police station and said two words—'Good morning'—and the guy behind the desk said, 'You're Gerry Weidmann.' "

He hits another button and begins the chant again. "Good morning. Gerry Weidmann at the *Globe*. Anything happening?"

• • •

Twenty-five miles north, in suburban Topsfield, executive editor Jack Driscoll wakes up in time to beat his three daughters to the shower. As he takes a leisurely walk to pick up the *Globe* and its chief competitor, the *Boston Herald*, from the tubes at the end of the driveway, the sun sneaks over the roof of the church across the street. The pheasant that's been screeching its mating call around his yard all week is making itself scarce this morning.

Driscoll, the top authority in the newsroom, thinks of himself as a symphony conductor. His role is to blend the disparate parts of the news operation, synchronize their efforts, cue in the right section at the right time. Three months ago, when he took charge after editor Michael Janeway's abrupt resignation (Driscoll was already executive editor, but now the title of "editor" has been retired), he used the conductor analogy during a news conference. Shortly thereafter, the staff presented him with a gift that now hangs on the wall of his corner office in the newsroom. It is a conductor's baton, mounted and framed, with three words in headline type: Music, Maestro, Please.

After twenty-eight years at the *Globe*, Driscoll has learned not to expect long, uninterrupted moments for thinking big thoughts at the office. He does most of his planning, and all reading of anything longer than a page, at home.

This morning he's thinking about something that will push the Quincy robberies even farther inside the paper. The

Globe's national staff is about to wrap up a story on the secrets that Ronald Pelton, a former communications expert for the National Security Agency, is charged with selling to the Soviets. Pelton is being tried in Baltimore, and the CIA has threatened court action against news organizations that reveal any information other than what comes out at the trial.

For the last week, the *Globe*'s Washington bureau chief and two of the bureau's eight writers have been involved in thrust-and-parry negotiations with Lieutenant General William Odom, director of the NSA. Odom wants to know what the reporters have found out, and they want to know how much they can print without endangering national security. The government would prefer that the paper print nothing. The paper maintains that although it does not want to damage national security, most of the information in the story is already public record.

Driscoll knows that his reporters have put together almost an A-to-Z primer on how the United States tracks Soviet subs. He also knows that the paper won't print all of it. But the question remains: Who should draw the line, and where? He hasn't talked to Odom since Friday, though the Washington staff talked to him yesterday. The story will receive its final editing today, and it will run tomorrow. He wonders what will happen after that.

· · ·

Pressmen with folded papers under their arms are walking out of the *Globe* building as Godfrey Kauffmann is walking in. He pauses in the doorway long enough to hear his favorite sound: silence. If the presses were still rolling, he'd have to start bracing for the worst.

Getting a newspaper to its readers requires a complex chain reaction, and Kauffmann, the circulation director, is at the end of the chain. His department lives and dies by the "off time," the time the last paper rolls out and the presses shut down. All kinds of things can delay a paper: late-breaking news or sports, any of a thousand people screwing up, any of a hundred machines breaking down. Whatever the cause, the effect is the same. The dominoes start falling on the circulation department's heads.

3

The *Globe* usually gets out on time, or close enough to keep the first domino upright. In the last few weeks, however, a new commitment to running "live" sports color—color photos taken at a game on deadline, then rushed back in time for the first edition—has stretched the system thin. The costs of late papers—the readers and distributors who complain, the paperboys who quit, the commuters who can't buy the paper on their way to the train and so won't look for it tomorrow— are too depressing to think about on a clear spring morning.

Kauffmann pushes through the doorway into the silence. Maybe the Wednesday paper got out on time. Maybe it will be a good day in the circulation department.

•   •   •

In Santiago, Chile, Pam Constable awakens to the rumbling of trucks. The nightly cordon of the area around the presidential palace has been lifted. Outside her hotel window, green-uniformed soldiers guard the palace plaza. Pedestrians hurry past, bundled against the bone-chilling damp of early winter.

Over tea, she checks the papers. A car bomb exploded downtown. Two hundred and fifty students were arrested in protests. Good, she didn't miss anything yesterday. She was at both scenes.

Constable is one of six full-time foreign correspondents who cover the globe for the *Globe*. Based in Boston, she travels for three or four weeks at a time through South America, visiting two or three countries on each trip. Then she returns to the States for two weeks to regroup, catch up on her sleep, see her fiancé, and plan her next trip. The paper also uses a roving Boston-based correspondent to cover Africa. It has permanent correspondents in London, covering Europe; Tokyo, covering Asia; Jerusalem, covering the Middle East; and Mexico City. Phil Bennett, the reporter in Mexico City, focuses mainly on Central America while Constable concentrates on South America and the Caribbean, but sometimes they help each other out.

To supplement the foreign staff's work, the paper uses part-time writers known as stringers. (The name lingers from the days when part-time writers' pay was based on the length of their stories, which were measured in the office with a piece of string.) Neither the correspondents nor their editors at the *Globe* pretend that six people, even with stringers' help, can be everywhere in the world that news happens. They cover as many of the big stories as they can, use the wire services (Associated Press, United Press International, Reuters, and a few others whose stories come through the *Globe*'s computers) for the rest, and spend as much time as possible on more thoughtful, explanatory pieces, hoping to convey to readers what "their" part of the world is really like.

Today, for example, Constable plans to work on a story about the student protests. The government of President Augusto Pinochet has been turning over administration of public high schools to the local mayors, whom he appointed. Pinochet says the move will save money, but many Chileans see it as one more attempt to curtail their freedom. Every afternoon this week, students in high school uniforms have marched through the streets, demanding that their schools remain independent. The police have met them with tear gas and water cannons.

Constable could write a story each day describing the previous day's protests and enumerating the arrests. If the demonstrations were happening near Boston, readers would expect daily coverage. But she knows that a story from Santiago, no matter how well she writes it, can't have that kind of immediacy. Instead of simply relating the facts, she wants to explain what the student protests mean, why they matter.

She'll need to talk to more people today, and to follow the action on the downtown streets. But she's already done enough reporting to have a good idea of what's happening. The protests, she thinks, show that Chile's thirteen-year military dictatorship has failed to create an apolitical generation. The country's teenagers are joining the opposition.

•   •   •

The worry, the one that woke her at 4:00 A.M., is there waiting when Marilyn Won's alarm goes off in the south end of Boston. Today is her last chance to make sure everything's perfect with the Guide to Art Galleries.

5

When Won proposed selling ads to local art galleries and grouping them together in Calendar, the tabloid of local events that runs in the Thursday *Globe*, her bosses told her to go for it. She appreciated their enthusiasm almost as much as she appreciated their restraint in not pointing out what she already knew: The gallery guide had been tried before, and it had failed. She thinks she can make it work.

Years ago, when she was a psychiatric social worker coordinating a welfare hotel in New York, Won would have scoffed at the idea that anyone could enjoy selling advertising space for a living. Now she loves it. She loves making the rounds of downtown Boston stores in a conservative business suit and brown running shoes. She's fascinated by the people she meets. She doesn't even mind—not usually, anyway— when they hold her personally accountable for the paper's editorial policies.

Take that guy in the art gallery, one of the first days she went out selling the gallery guide. He started screaming almost as soon as she walked in. "I'm purple with rage!" he yelled, waving his arms theatrically. "The *Boston Globe* hates art! We can't get coverage no matter what we do."

Over and over she told him calmly, "I really do empathize, but you have to understand that advertising and editorial are totally separate." She gave him names of people to call at the paper, urged him to write a letter to the editor. He responded with more dramatic diatribes. By this time, both of them had started to enjoy his performance. She left smiling, then treated herself to shrimp-flavored popcorn at her favorite place down the block.

Needless to say, he didn't buy an ad. Eleven other galleries did. Oh please, she thinks as she gets out of bed, let the guide be perfect.

• • •

Back in the newsroom, overnight editor (or, officially, assistant metropolitan editor) Bob Ward is smoking his last Pall Mall and cleaning up the debris of an eight-hour shift. The opening credits of "Good Morning America" flash on the TV suspended from the ceiling, but the only sound is coded chatter from the police scanners on his desk. On the 11:00-to-

7:00 shift, Ward carries a portable scanner with him even when he goes upstairs for coffee. Plenty of nights he hears something that makes him drop the coffee and run back down.

Not last night, though. It wasn't one of those nights when he sits and counts the holes in the ceiling, but neither was it the kind that gets the adrenaline pumping. Feeney and Weidmann haven't found much this morning, either, but you never know. Two mornings ago, a woman called at about this time and said she'd been raped. She wanted to talk to the paper, she said, because three other women had been raped in her neighborhood in recent months, and the police hadn't done anything to warn residents.

"We could have taken more caution in our own houses if we knew he was out there," the woman said. The reporters felt bad for her; she sobbed when she talked about the rape. But she was determined to spread the word, and it was a good story. It made page one of yesterday's paper.

"The whole complexion of the day can change in a minute," Ward says as he heads for the door. "That's why this job is such a pain, and so interesting."

7:00 A.M.

You've got to keep your sneakers on. You never know where you'll be running off to.
—Stan Grossfeld, chief photographer

Tom Landers keeps the engine running as he sits in his weathered tan Datsun in the parking lot of the Dough Boy doughnut shop. Static and wailing sirens crackle from the four radios he uses to monitor police, fire, and ambulance frequencies. If he hears anything interesting, he's ready to tear out and take pictures.

The Datsun, 125,000 miles on the odometer, overflows with the paraphernalia of a roving photographer. Two of the police radios are mounted under the dashboard, along with the two-way radio that ties him to the *Globe* photo department. Two more are in back, in a plastic milk crate wedged there by a wastebasket, towels, Windex ("I'm fanatic about clean windows"), and shoes and clothing for every conceivable climate change. Although the car isn't messy, chaos is never more than a few sharp turns away.

A bag nestled in the pile of clothes holds a camera or two, but most of his equipment is locked in a blue metal box in the trunk. In nineteen years at the *Globe* he's been chased, mugged, and shot at, but the times his cameras have been stolen rankle most.

Landers' father was a *Globe* photographer for thirty-seven years. His brother is photo editor of the *Boston Herald*. Photography is his inheritance, and the car and the parking lot feel like home. In recent months he's covered a volcano in Colombia and a memorial service in Houston for the seven *Challenger* astronauts. But on most working days, for at least a few hours, he sits at the Dough Boy, waiting.

He's rarely alone. The cruising photographer for the *Herald* uses the Dough Boy as a staging area too, as do police officers and ambulance crews between calls. The newsmen and the city workers know one another from years of showing up at the same disaster scenes, and their conversation is streaked with the black humor of people who have seen it all. Between the technical jargon and their private shorthand— "the island for dogs," for instance, means the group has decided to meet for a hot dog lunch on Castle Island, a peninsula jutting into Dorchester Bay—they sound like a grownup version of a teenage clique, hanging out in a parking lot.

Landers and his *Herald* counterpart are both friends and competitors. If one of them is out of earshot when an important-sounding call comes over the radio, the other will alert him. But the minute their wheels hit the street, they're on their own. Landers puts it this way: "The competition is in your ability when you get there."

Driving in Boston is torture, and the need for speed compounds the pain. When he's stuck in traffic trying to reach a fire or accident (the cement truck that hit the thoroughbred the other day, or the crowded morning commuter train that crashed), Landers' mind races like a taxi meter: What other route could I take? Can I get there before the burning building is just a cellar hole? And what's that they're saying on the radios?

The radios. He says they drive him crazier than the traffic. He says the noise regularly sends him digging for the Excedrin. He says all that, but sometimes when he's sitting in the Datsun and the dispatchers' voices sound calm, he turns on a fifth radio and listens to music.

•   •   •

The clamp truck picks its way among the cylindrical stacks like a George Lucas spacecraft zipping through a forest of towering newsprint. It passes bay after bay of brown-wrapped rolls, the wrappings striped and coded to show the paper's pedigree, then angles to a stop beside the yawning door of a red railroad car. This is the *Globe* warehouse, where freight cars full of newsprint pull into the building, bringing fodder for the hungry presses.

Newspaper presses are insatiable consumers of paper. They gobble it, they inhale it, they digest it by the ton, and always they want more, more. Like the narrator of a National Geographic special on some exotic animal, the keepers of the presses spout numbers to describe the machines' voracious appetites.

Each year the *Globe* uses nearly 150,000 tons of newsprint, the product of about 2 million trees. Paper cost the company more than $70 million last year, ink an additional $1.5 million. By contrast, the quarters that 514,000 readers plunked down to buy the daily paper, and the dollar bills that 811,000 people spent for the Sunday paper, added up to less than $69 million. The readers literally don't pay for the paper the *Globe* is printed on. Advertising revenue, of course, more than makes up the difference.

An average roll of newsprint weighs 1,800 pounds. If given a push down the street and unrolled to its cardboard core, it would create a paper path seven miles long. The *Globe*'s ten presses use between 300 and 400 rolls a night, depending on the number of pages in the paper. When the presses are running at full speed, printing 1,000 copies a minute, the newsprint moves through each press at a rate of more than twenty-five miles per hour.

Although newsprint is hardly high-class stuff ("It's the lousiest paper you can buy," says pressroom superintendent Bob Godfrey), it can behave as temperamentally as the princess who felt the pea beneath a pile of mattresses. A single stone on the floor of a freight car can inflict a gash that renders an 1,800-pound roll useless. Usually the damage can't be spotted until the paper has been loaded onto the press and started running, only to rip and bring everything to a halt.

Keeping track of the paper, making sure it's in the right place when the pressmen need it, requires six men and a computer. Last night, for example, seven carloads of paper arrived in the freight yard of the *Globe*'s headquarters in Dorchester, a few miles south of downtown Boston. One car was unloaded immediately, its contents sent to the pressroom.

The clamp truck, a forklift with arm-like clamps instead of a fork, is unloading three more cars this morning. The driver grabs the round sides of each roll with the clamps, flips the roll from vertical to horizontal, and delivers it to the appropriate bay like a robotic butler. When he reaches the right neighborhood, inhabited by rolls of similar size and type, he flips the roll vertical again and carefully sets it down. The rolls are stacked two high in the freight cars, three high in the warehouse.

The other three carloads of paper, seventy to ninety rolls per car, will wait in the freight yard until they're needed. Although the *Globe* expanded its warehouse in 1974 and built a new satellite printing plant in Billerica, twenty-two miles to the north, in 1983, it doesn't have enough indoor space to store the four-week supply of paper it likes to keep on hand.

Four weeks' worth may be more of a cushion than he really needs, warehouse superintendent Frank Pritchard says, but no one can forget the last time a big paper mill went on strike. He'd get to work and find not a single roll of paper in the building. So the company plays it safe. It buys from nine different suppliers, one of which recycles unsold *Globe*s, and it keeps as many as thirty-six carloads of paper waiting outside.

They can't wait long. Newsprint has a life span of only about six months before it dries out and becomes brittle. Within those six months, it might freeze in the winter or absorb too much moisture in the summer. In any weather, as anyone who has ever hung a clipping on the refrigerator can verify, newsprint starts to discolor almost as soon as it's exposed to light. That trait traces to its beginnings as groundwood, the fir and spruce trees ground into pulp to form the paper's furnish, or base. To make high-quality paper, a mill chemically treats the pulp and then cooks it down, so that the paper uses only about half of what was originally in the tree. Newsprint, however, is simply ground-up trees minus bark. It

11

can include up to 98 percent of the tree's original content, and the tree's original content includes sugars and resins that yellow in the sun.

To fight the first enemy, time, the warehouse rotates its entire paper supply every three months. To fight the second enemy, light, it leaves the paper wrapped until the last possible moment. Other variables must also be juggled. The *Globe* needs six different sizes of paper—three sizes for the older presses, which use fifty-three-inch rolls, and three for the newer ones, which use fifty-five-inch rolls. Long rolls (which print sixteen pages), three-quarter rolls (twelve pages), and half rolls (eight pages) must be available in each width.

This morning Bill Burnand, Pritchard's assistant in the warehouse, is doing the juggling. The people upstairs haven't yet calculated how big tomorrow's paper will be, but Burnand knows that Sports will run a color photo of tonight's Red Sox game against the Cleveland Indians. The pressroom has already asked for a certain brand of paper because it reproduces color the most clearly. He'll have to make sure the rolls from that manufacturer aren't blocked in by others.

Burnand checks the green and pink cards stuffed into the slots of the gray metal board outside his office. Now that he knows what's in each bay, it's time to enter the inventory information into the computer. Out of luck. The computer is down.

· · ·

If this meeting ends soon, Tom Ashbrook is thinking, I can catch the subway home in time to have a beer with Danielle and watch the news. In Tokyo, the CNN morning report from Atlanta airs at 11:00 P.M. It took some getting used to, but sometimes the fourteen-hour time difference works to his advantage; last night's Celtics–Rockets game, for instance, made great breakfast company this morning on Armed Forces Radio.

Today has been one of those rare days that allowed Ashbrook to catch up and look ahead. If he were in Boston, an enterprising editor would have spotted him the minute he drew a clear breath and shipped him out on some story. No matter how many reporters an editor has, there are never enough working on tomorrow's paper.

12

But in Tokyo, Ashbrook is pretty much his own boss. Today he started researching a story on family dynasties in Japanese politics, an idea that germinated when the prime minister's son announced a run for office. Already he's found quite a few family relationships in the Diet, the Japanese parliament. He hopes the story will tug a little on the curtain that hides Japan's power elite.

He also did some preliminary reading today on the country's quest to build a "thinking computer," and he and his assistant put together information on AIDS in Japan for a story a *Globe* medical reporter is doing in Boston. Then he headed for the annual meeting of the Correspondents Club, where he sits now, admiring the view of the Imperial Palace grounds from the twentieth-floor window.

Because the club has proved a real asset in Ashbrook's two and a half years of covering Asia, coming tonight was a pleasant duty. He's half-listening to the business meeting when something unexpected happens: He is nominated to serve on the board of directors. It's an honor, but his schedule keeps him out of Tokyo so much that he couldn't do the job justice. He starts plotting his own defeat.

• • •

"I'll make it easy for you," Paul Deveine tells the customer who stands squinting at the menu over the grill. "We've got eggs, eggs, and eggs."

Actually, the *Globe* cafeteria has more than eggs, including full-course dinners in the middle of the night. Manager Barbara Smith says that *Globe* tastes run heavily to salad, fish, and "anything with spaghetti sauce on it." The night crew in the composing room, where the pages are pasted up, is especially fond of spaghetti and chicken Parmesan at 5:00 A.M.

When the paper left the area of Boston once known as Newspaper Row and moved to Morrissey Boulevard in 1958 (it moved overnight, putting out one day's issue downtown and the next day's in Dorchester), it gained expansion space but lost, among other things, convenience to downtown restaurants. There are no restaurants within walking distance of the building, and few that can be driven to without letting

13

lunch consume most of the afternoon. So the *Globe* provides food for its captive audience, just as it provides a barber for employees who can't get to their regular shop, and check-cashing services for those who can't get to the bank.

Almost everyone who works in the building can remember a day when he or she was there long enough to eat all three meals in the cafeteria. On an average day, the cashiers in the cafeteria and the two coffee shops can ring up 1,300 more meals than the company has employees. Pressed for the truth, most people at the *Globe* will admit to liking something that the cafeteria offers—the salad bar or the made-to-order cheeseburgers, or the big bowl of strawberries that's set out even in winter. But like cafeteria customers everywhere, they often complain about the food.

The man standing at Paul Deveine's grill this morning isn't complaining; he isn't saying anything. Deveine tries to be patient. He rearranges the home fries, restacks the bacon, pulls out another package of bagels. Still the man doesn't order. Deveine gives it one last shot. "We got eggs," he tells the customer again. "You want them my way, I cook them. You want them your way, you cook them."

·   ·   ·

As the flight from Washington touches down in Boston, the end of Steve Kurkjian's wrangles with the government over the Ronald Pelton secrets story seems to be in sight. Of course, the end seemed to be in sight last week, too, when the story was scheduled to run Sunday. But he thinks it really will go this time. Kurkjian, the *Globe*'s Washington bureau chief, has met with National Security Agency officials several times in the last few days, talking endlessly about why they want the paper to withhold much of its information about Pelton's alleged spying when he worked for the agency. Now Kurkjian has come to Boston to usher the story through its final steps: editing the latest version, checking again with the lawyers, and, he'd be willing to bet, negotiating one more time with the government.

In some ways, journalists are like children. The more they're told to stay away from something, the more interested in it they become. Their motive is more than childish curiosity. They know that the person or group warning the media away must consider the information important, and if it's important, it's probably something the public should know.

So when the *Washington Post*, in a story published a few weeks ago, said it was being pressured by the CIA not to report what it knew about the Pelton case, the case immediately took on new interest for every journalist in the country. They had become almost numb to the parade of spies and accused spies in the last year, but now one case stood out. Ronald Pelton's information must be special.

Then the CIA upped the ante. It said that the *Post* and NBC News had damaged national security with their reporting on the Pelton case, and they could be prosecuted under a 1950 law. Now the agency really had reporters' attention. The *Post* and NBC had reported only that Pelton was charged with telling the Soviets about eavesdropping involving American submarines. That wasn't much detail, reporters thought, to provoke such an extreme response. What was so crucial about the operations Pelton had supposedly compromised?

Kurkjian wanted to know. When the *Post* story ran in mid-May, he'd been in Washington five months. He was enjoying his new job as bureau chief, but he missed the reporting he'd done as head of the *Globe*'s Spotlight investigative team. Although coordinating the work of the Washington bureau's eight writers took most of his time, he tried to get out and do his own stories as often as possible. He decided to go to Baltimore and write about the start of the Pelton trial.

In his story, Kurkjian dealt not only with the secrecy issues raised by the case (one senator told him that the administration "ought to be putting its own house in order before going after the press"), but also with the question of why it took the government so long to catch Pelton. Pelton's first anonymous calls to the Soviet embassy in Washington were intercepted and taped by U.S. agents, but it was five years before they arrested him.

While Kurkjian was in Baltimore, Fred Kaplan, who covers defense issues, and Walter Robinson, who covers the White House, started digging. They weren't sure they'd find much about the U.S. intelligence operations that were being

15

only obliquely referred to at Pelton's trial, but soon they had compiled an impressive stack of information. Even more surprising, some of it was already public record, having been published in arcane scientific journals, other newspapers, and a 1984 novel, *The Hunt for Red October.*

No one who worked on the story will say much about where the information came from. Kurkjian says that each piece had more than one source, and some of it had many sources. He and Robinson agree that most of the reporting credit belongs to Kaplan.

So Kurkjian's position in late May was this: His reporters had obtained considerable detail on several intelligence operations run by the U.S. government. Now they faced two questions. First, were the projects they knew about the same projects Pelton had allegedly compromised? And second, would the information, if published, endanger national security?

The beginnings of an answer came from the government. On May 28, William Casey, director of the CIA, and Lieutenant General William Odom, director of the National Security Agency, met with Associated Press reporters. In the interview, they downplayed the earlier threats to take news organizations to court, but they warned that recent leaks of sensitive information had already damaged the nation's intelligence-gathering capabilities and cost taxpayers billions of dollars.

The two men issued a further warning about the Pelton case, asking journalists not to speculate on information not specifically covered at the trial. If you're doing a story on intelligence-gathering techniques, they told the media, come to us and we'll help you decide what should and shouldn't be printed.

Clearing a story with someone in advance is anathema to journalists. Walter Robinson puts it this way, not entirely in jest: "It's bad enough having editors who get *Globe* paychecks, without giving outside people a role in our editorial process." He says he was "sort of horrified" when he heard that the *Post* had withheld information after President Ronald Reagan contacted board chairman Katharine Graham. But Robinson knew, as Kurkjian and Kaplan did, that intelligence stories are different from other stories. The three of them might not buy the government's whole argument, but certain facts were indisputable. The *Globe* couldn't just publish what it had found without considering the possible consequences.

So the paper decided to accept Odom and Casey's invitation. It would go to them with the story, ask whether the information might be dangerous, and see what happened. What happened was a series of meetings that reached no conclusive result. By Monday's meeting, however, Kurkjian thought he had heard enough to know what the paper should and shouldn't publish. So, he thinks impatiently as he grabs a cab to the *Globe*, let's get this show on the road.

8:00 A.M.

Those advertising guys are paying for all our groceries.

—Godfrey Kauffmann, circulation director

In a windowless cubicle off the *Globe* atrium, on a white counter bristling with eraser shavings, Marianne Hyland is mapping everyone's fate. She is deciding where the ads in tomorrow's paper will run, thus determining how much space will be available for news, sports, and features. In a company where 900 terminals feed on forty high-powered mini-computers and a few hundred smaller ones, she scrawls her calculations on legal pads and scraps of green paper, all the while talking ferociously to herself.

If journalists ruled the world, newspapers would swell and shrink with the volume of news. Editors would add pages at the last minute if stories turned out longer than expected, or subtract pages if nothing much was happening. But in the real world, the size of a newspaper—not to mention its financial health—is determined by the amount of advertising it sells. Because the ratio of news to ads must remain constant so that neither dominates, more ads means more space for news. The timing can be complicated. At Christmas time, for example, news tends to be slow because many of the traditional sources of stories—governments, courts, educational institutions—are on a holiday schedule. But ads pour in to a newspaper during Christmas, forcing reporters and editors to shift into overdrive to fill gigantic amounts of space. In summer, when ad sales traditionally dwindle, a major news event can swallow up the meager space, pushing less immediate stories off the edge and into another day.

Like most papers, the *Globe* has guidelines prescribing the ideal number of columns of space each department should get each day. Hyland and her colleagues on the display desk try to work within those guidelines, but circumstances can conspire against them. For one thing, the number of pages in a paper usually can increase or decrease only in increments of four; the four surfaces of a folded sheet of newsprint form four separate pages. It's possible to increase the size by only two pages, but that creates a "dinky," a single sheet that's guaranteed to fall to the floor—much like the ubiquitous subscription cards in magazines—as soon as a reader carefully folds his newspaper on the subway. The *Globe* tries to avoid dinkies.

If the ad count leaves the news space, known as "news hole," just a few columns short of its ideal size, the managers who check Hyland's work each morning aren't likely to recommend adding four pages. Ink and paper are expensive, as is the time of the people who would have to fill the space and the people who would do the extra printing.

Because of this delicate balance, tension between news people and advertising people is inevitable. No matter how much they enjoy one another's company, no matter how clearly they understand that the paper needs both groups to survive, each side is occasionally consumed by the conviction that the other is running the show. On a night when the news hole is tight, a copy editor will curse advertising's dominance as she trims yet another inch from a story whose author, she knows, will spew coffee in a rage when he sees the paper in the morning.

For their part, advertising people will forever bemoan the policy that excludes ads from the first three pages of the paper, and rail against the limits that keep a certain amount of space ad-free on other pages. A few months ago, when a new feature called Neighborhoods reduced available ad space on the second page of the Metro section, some advertising people groused. They knew that the *Globe* needed to be more consistent in its coverage of local communities, and they knew that the Neighborhoods stories would help. "But I need that page," Hyland said, without much hope.

Although ad count forms the basis for laying out the paper, the top editors can request extra space for special projects. Today, for example, they want two facing pages in the front section left at least half empty to handle the runover of the Ronald Pelton story. The runover, also known as the jump or carryover, is the remainder of a story that begins on the front page. Readers are led to it by the runover line, the line that tells them to turn to page so-and-so. The runover line labels the story with a slug, or one-word description, that is often the same word used to identify the story in the newsroom computer system. The slug of the Pelton story is SECRETS.

In addition to special news requests, human nature and the limitations of the presses complicate Hyland's work. Color ads or news photos can be printed only on certain pages, and sections can be divided only in certain ways, without requiring an expensive press setup called a bar sheet. On the human side, she tries to protect both the companies that buy the ads and the *Globe* employees who sell them—or, as she puts it, "I have to take everyone's pet peeves into account." Two stores selling similar furniture, for example, would not be pleased to find their ads on the same page, or on facing pages. And if an advertiser is not pleased, it can make life miserable for the sales rep who handles its account.

For that reason, Hyland's desk is a popular morning checkpoint. As she scribbles and erases and calculates and mutters to herself ("No, I can't bury this guy's ad twice"), sales reps and managers file through the tiny cubicle she shares with two other people. The reps peer at her legal pads, check the positions of their most important ads, kid around endlessly, offer to buy her coffee. Because the door from the advertising department has no window, each person who enters to consult the oracle risks being hit in the rear by the next.

The people on the display desk never actually see the ads they're laying out; they work with printouts that list the amount of space each advertiser has bought. The measure of their success is the clarity with which they remember their failures. Months after it happened, Hyland can still convulse her colleagues in embarrassed laughter recalling the day they put the Nieman-Marcus ad opposite the Filene's Basement ad. What Filene's Basement was advertising, they discovered when they saw the paper, was Nieman-Marcus merchandise at huge markdowns. Then there was the day that, having exhausted every other possible layout, they scheduled part of the arts section for the obituary page. That, of course, was the day the rock reviewer reported on a Grateful Dead concert.

.   .   .

Attleboro. East Milton. Brewster. Waltham. Winchester. The State House. Millbridge, Maine. Fenway Park. Jim Henson's Muppet studio. The U.S. House of Representatives.

Bill Ryerson is listing the places the photographers are supposed to go today. Already the list has twenty-seven assignments on it, not counting the two photographers and one technician who have been in Houston all week for the National Basketball Association playoffs. The staff is going to be spread pretty thin. Ryerson, assistant chief of the photo staff, decides to send Tom Landers on the first assignment, checking on pickets at the electric company.

"*Globe* 8, come in *Globe* 8." The two-way radio in Landers' Datsun crackles to life, and he heads downtown at Ryerson's instruction. A block from the Boston Edison office, he can see the classic choreography of confrontation. The pickets block a driveway. The police move in. The pickets scatter. A few minutes later they regroup and block another driveway. The police move in. Landers pulls a little closer but stays in his car. He knows from experience that if he jumped out with cameras in hand, his presence might incite one side or the other to action.

Photographers are often affected by what they photograph; Landers, for instance, cringes whenever he sees an injured child. But although events may affect photographers, their creed forbids them from affecting events. It's easy to start an argument in a group of news photographers by asking how much manipulation of a subject is fair. Some will insist on none at all; others will say it depends on the type of picture.

Chief photographer Stan Grossfeld, who has won Pulitzer Prizes for his work in Ethiopia and Lebanon, says a pho-

21

tographer should never interfere with news. "If there's a guy lying in the road and an ambulance attendant's bag is blocking my only shot, I won't move the bag," he says. "But if you've got a beautiful feature scene and a person is passing by, it's okay to put the person in for scale. Or if the president is speaking at a city hall rally and you're behind him, you can yell so he'll turn around and you can get both him and the crowd. You can make a picture better, but you've got to keep your integrity."

Landers takes a hard line on questions of manipulation. He believes that his job is to show the paper's readers how a situation was, not how he wanted it to be. After watching the striking Edison workers for a while, he quietly gets out of his car. Using a telephoto lens (lenses to a photographer, he says, are like brushes and paint to an artist), he shoots a few frames without moving much closer to the action. "Sometimes I wish I'd gone to college, so I could teach history," he had mused a few weeks earlier, during an unusually quiet afternoon in the doughnut shop parking lot. "But then I think, in a way I'm living history."

.   .   .

Fingers of sunlight are starting to reach through the "glass houses," the offices of the top editors, which define the irregular edges of the newsroom the way crust outlines a slice of bread. Unlike the denizens of the glass houses, who have walls and windows, most reporters and copy editors work face to face, at desks clustered by department. So far, newsrooms have proved sterile territory for salesmen promoting the free-standing partitions that add pseudo-privacy to nearly every other kind of modern office. Today, as ever, being a reporter means learning to tune out the people whose desks touch yours on two sides, maybe three.

Paul Feeney and Gerry Weidmann still occupy the center of the room, but now their horizon is dotted in almost every direction with small clumps of people, logging onto the computer and flipping through the papers. Everywhere, the talk is of last night's Celtics victory.

Across the room in Living, the *Globe*'s features section, Nathan Cobb and Linda Matchan are using the Celtics as a shield against the moment of truth, the moment when each must type a code word into the computer, call up a half-written story, and finish it. Cobb's story, part of his occasional American Pop series on popular culture, is about bowling banquets. It will run on tomorrow's Living page—probably, if he matches his usual record, as the lead story. To research it, he has attended six bowling banquets in the last two weeks. He hopes he never sees another plate of roast beef.

Matchan's story is not for Living but for the Spotlight team's latest investigative project, a series on medical malpractice. The series will run five consecutive days, with shorter stories called sidebars accompanying each day's main piece. She has interviewed four or five doctors, and now she is writing a sidebar about the stress doctors experience when they are sued for malpractice. One doctor described a malpractice suit as "really equivalent to professional rape, in the most demeaning and humiliating way." Although she can't use this doctor's name, she thinks that his quotes powerfully convey the emotional toll that lawsuits can take. She has decided to lead the story with him.

The usual reporter's day runs from 10:00 to 6:00, but few days are usual. While Matchan and Cobb have come in early to snatch some quiet writing time, Diane Lewis always arrives at 8:00. She's ready in case Bob Anglin, the editor who takes charge when the overnight man leaves, needs to send someone out on assignment. ("Should we send?" is a perennial editors' question, meaning, "Is this event worth covering?" or "Might it be over by the time we get there?" or "Will a wire story be enough?")

So far, no shouts have come from Anglin's direction, so Lewis picks up where she left off yesterday. She has been assigned to write a story marking the anniversary of the hijacking of TWA Flight 847, but she's not sure what the story should say. She stares at her terminal, hoping for computerized inspiration.

On the screen is a list of the headlines and dates of all the stories the *Globe* has run about the hijacking. Because the newsroom computer and the library computer have been hooked together for only a few weeks, the list's very appearance on her screen is a novelty. Until now, reporters who wanted information from the library had to call or walk downstairs, then wait at their desks for a reply. In the afternoons, when hundreds of people are making simultaneous demands on the computer, sometimes it's still quicker to do it that way.

Lewis chooses a year-old news story from the list, opens it on the screen, and starts to read. "The problem is that this has been done to death," she says. "But I have to try." She has the passenger list from the hijacked flight, and she plans to call every passenger until she reaches a few who will talk. Already she's found one interesting sidelight. Uli Derickson, the flight attendant many hailed as a hero after the hijacking, is still flying, although TWA's flight attendants are on strike. When Lewis asked for her phone number, the people at the union said they wouldn't give out the numbers of scabs.

Anglin glances across the room at Lewis and wishes he had somewhere to send her. No news may be good news, but it doesn't make good newspapers. Like Feeney and Weidmann and Bob Ward, Anglin has been at the *Globe* long enough to remember, wistfully, when the paper put out eight editions a day. Now *that* was a pressure cooker—constantly updating, revising, grabbing as much information as you could and running with it. With four editions of the morning paper and four of the afternoon, the newsroom could get news into the paper almost as soon as it happened.

Today the *Globe* publishes four editions, all in the morning. Most events that happen after midnight won't make it into the paper for almost twenty-four hours—unless, like the space shuttle *Challenger* explosion, they're momentous enough to justify a special edition. Anglin knows that reporters today, because they have more time, often do a more thorough job. They're expected to tell readers not just what happened, but what it means. Still, he misses the sense of urgency that used to propel them all toward deadline like a slingshot. On glum days he sums up the present this way: "I'm city editor of a paper that doesn't exist any more."

Years ago, the *Globe* had a whole room full of radios and a man who sat there all day, listening. The two scanners on Anglin's desk have replaced all that. He keeps one ear trained on them as he looks through five other newspapers and checks the date box, a set of drawers where press releases and other material that might yield a story have been filed by date. After hearing a syllable or two on the scanner, he can tell who's talking. "That's health and hospitals," he says of one voice. Then, in rapid succession, "That's the detectives on the street; Boston fire; Newton fire control." It's not like the old immediacy, but if he hears something on the scanner and gets a reporter out right away, the reporter can often get information that wouldn't be available later.

A few desks away, Feeney and Weidmann are marveling over yesterday's newsroom debate about whether a certain neighborhood is in Roxbury or Dorchester. Anglin joins in. Imagine those young reporters not knowing that police district boundaries are different from the ones set up by the courts, the post office, and the city map.

"I guess after we go, nobody will know this stuff," Weidmann says.

· · ·

How loyal can you get, David Cohen asks himself. An hour ago he was mentally revising the table of contents for the June 29 Sunday magazine while swimming laps at the Gloucester YMCA. Now he's editing page proofs while drinking coffee in a roadside pancake house. The proofs are for a story about a wacky discount store chain that will run June 22; as production editor of the magazine, Cohen usually deals with three weeks' editions at once. His plans for today didn't call for editing on this greasy table, but he pulled in to the restaurant after hearing one too many radio reports about stalled traffic downtown. He'll just have to wait it out.

It's early for editors, many of whom stay until 7:00 or 8:00 P.M., to be at work, but a few have had more luck than Cohen. The lights are on in the big corner office with the conductor's baton on the wall, and Jack Driscoll is reading through the messages people have sent him since last night. In addition to making stories easier to write and edit, computers have reduced the noise level in the newsroom by giving people a new way to "talk" to one another. When a reporter or editor sits down at any terminal and types in his six-letter computer name (JDRISC, in Driscoll's case) and secret password, the words *message pending* will flash if someone has been trying to reach him. Unlike telephone messages, these messages can't be lost, copied down incorrectly, or picked up by the wrong person. They wait patiently in the system for their intended recipient.

For reporters and editors, many of whom feel more comfortable writing than speaking, computerized messaging is a godsend. They can set forth a carefully thought-out argument for a story, or for a day off, without having to wait for their supervisor to be free—and without having to look him in the eye. Bob Anglin calls it "the greatest dodge ever invented."

Some mornings Driscoll hits the "read" button and finds messages by the screenful. Today's not too bad. A couple of people are asking for a few minutes of his time, someone is reminding him about a speech he promised to give, and managing editor Tom Mulvoy has sent him copies of messages Mulvoy wrote yesterday to various reporters. There are no messages about the Pelton story, which promises to occupy most of the day, but Driscoll knows that Steve Kurkjian is coming from Washington. They can negotiate in person.

Outside Driscoll's office, a few desk clusters away, Fletcher Roberts is doing what a dozen other editors will soon be doing. He has made a list of his reporters and is trying to figure out, from notes in the computer and various messages on his desk, what each one is working on today—and, more important, whether he or she is likely to have a story for tomorrow's paper.

Roberts handles the reporters known as specialists: four education writers, two environment writers, three medical reporters, the three-person "urban team," a legal affairs writer, a religion writer, and another reporter whose job he kiddingly describes as "left-wing-causes writer." He and his assistant usually edit six to ten stories a day. Editing, Roberts likes to point out, does not just mean looking for mistakes in

26

a story when it's done. At its best, editing begins with the assignment, when the editor and reporter decide which of many possible projects to tackle first. Then the two discuss what sources the reporter might turn to, what questions the reporter might ask, what direction the story might take.

Ideally, Roberts likes to "question the reporters after they question their sources," so that they can decide together whether they have enough information and, if so, what kind of story to write. That reduces, for both sides, the risk that he'll receive a story on deadline that isn't at all what he had in mind. People who study such things have christened this process "consultive editing." It's every good editor's ideal and, as Roberts freely admits, every good editor's frustration. There's never enough time to do it right. Since he moved into this job from another editing job three months ago, he says, his editing hasn't been so much consultive as harried.

As he starts the morning roundup, Roberts already knows a little about today. For one thing, it's Wednesday, and Wednesday is *New England Journal of Medicine* day. The medical writers have had advance copies of the journal for a few days, but the information is embargoed until tomorrow's paper. Before the embargo was agreed upon, reporters at the many newspapers and broadcast stations that study the journal would often write a story on some medical discovery before doctors had had time to read about it. Patients would see newspaper accounts of the breakthrough and quickly call their doctors, who wouldn't be able to answer their questions.

Journalists generally oppose embargoes; their job is to publish the news, not sit on it. But in this case they could see the validity of the doctors' concerns, and they welcomed the extra time to understand and simplify the complex scientific stories the journal runs. Today, for example, Roberts knows that medical writer Judy Foreman is planning a story on streptokinase, an enzyme that gobbles up blood clots in heart attack victims. Or something like that—he didn't entirely understand the process when Foreman told him about it yesterday.

Let's see, what else has he got? Peggy Hernandez, who covers the Boston School Department, has told him that the school bus drivers might sign their contract today. The drivers struck three months ago, and although they returned to work after twelve days, they still haven't signed a contract. Another old story might be back in the news as well: Reporter Jean Dietz has heard that a ruling might be handed down today in the Behavior Research Institute case. A few months ago the state ordered the institute to stop using physical punishment as therapy for its residents, who are severely emotionally disturbed. The institute then asked a judge to overrule the state order, and, interestingly, many of the residents' parents joined in the request. Punishment, they said, is the only thing that might help their children.

That's a potential front-page candidate, Roberts thinks. So is the story that Jim Franklin, nicknamed "Father Franklin" because he writes about religion, is doing on the Paulist Center. The center, a Catholic chapel downtown, has been allowing women to preach at Mass, but the Boston archdiocese has apparently warned the Paulist fathers to adhere to the letter of the liturgical law. In an area with so many Catholics, and so many feminists, the story could spark a lot of interest. Roberts will advocate it for the front. He believes that one of his most important functions as an editor is getting his reporters' best work on the front page. Of course, all the other assistant metro editors are trying to do the same thing. He'll see what they have to offer when the group meets at 10:30.

• • •

As a young man, William O. Taylor II thought about becoming a doctor, or a minister or a teacher or a lawyer. If he were choosing today, he might do something in conservation. But he made his choice thirty years ago, when he followed generations of Taylor footprints to the door of the *Boston Globe*. He worked in production, personnel, finance, advertising, and, for a short time, in the newsroom. During the two-year construction of the plant on Morrissey Boulevard, he very nearly lived there, assimilating every detail of the building.

Today, like his father and grandfather and great-grandfather before him, Bill Taylor is the *Globe*'s publisher. Except for its first shaky year, before Charles H. Taylor took over, the paper has always had a publisher named Taylor. There have been only four of them in 113 years.

History has affixed a label to each Taylor's legacy. Charles H. Taylor, known as the General, marched into a failing enterprise at age twenty-seven and, during his forty-eight-year tenure, pushed and pulled and cajoled it to the largest circulation in New England. His son William O. Taylor quietly held the paper together through years of economic depression and fierce competition. W.O.'s son William Davis, known as Davis, cut the *Globe* loose from its inhibitions and gave it a shove into the modern world. Though his innovations were legion, the favorite Davis Taylor story among the staff involves something he did very quietly. At the height of racial unrest in the South, he slipped away to Selma, Alabama, and, without a word to anyone, took part in a protest march.

Not every Taylor was a publisher. The General had two other sons besides William: Charles Jr. was treasurer and manager of the *Globe* for forty-four years, and John I. worked in classified advertising for a short time before becoming president of the Red Sox in 1904. Charles Jr.'s son, Charles H. Taylor III, served as assistant to both W.O. and Davis Taylor when each was publisher, and his son, Charles H. Taylor IV, became a director of the company in 1970, a position he retains today.

John Ingalls Taylor, grandson of the General and son of John I., was president of the *Globe* from 1963 to 1975. He and his cousin Davis Taylor still share an office at the paper and are directors of the company. The other Taylor kin in evidence on Morrissey Boulevard today include Alexander Hawes, assistant managing editor for administration, who is a grandson of the General's daughter Grace; Steve Taylor, manager of the *Globe*'s computer network, who is the son of Charles Taylor IV; and Ben Taylor, assistant managing editor for local news, who is John Ingalls Taylor's son.

Although the *Globe*'s parent company, Affiliated Publications, went public in 1973 and invested in radio, cable television, book publishing, and cellular telephones, it is still strongly identified with the Taylors, and with Boston. "The company doesn't build boats or sell real estate," executive editor Jack Driscoll says. "The paper is always number one. That has personalized the *Globe* and made it very much an extension of the Taylor family."

That view, shared by many, makes Bill Taylor uncomfortable. He doesn't *want* the paper to reflect his family, at least not in any way its readers can identify. "I don't think that makes much sense anymore," he says. Taylor isn't sure yet how history will define his stamp as publisher. He hopes he'll be remembered, among other things, for expanding the *Globe*'s community involvement; he spends nearly half his time on community and charitable work. Today, for example, his early-morning identity is not so much *Globe* publisher as vice chairman of this year's area United Way campaign. Trying to ignore a miserable head cold, he is discussing the campaign at a meeting in the offices of the Jordan Marsh department store chain, a company that played an important part in *Globe* history.

Eben Jordan, who started Jordan Marsh in 1851, was the only one of the *Globe*'s original incorporators who stuck with the paper through the near-bankruptcy of its early years. In 1877 he and the General devised a plan for a new company to buy out Globe Publishing Company and pay its debts. Jordan put up the money for the new Globe Newspaper Company. Within ten years, the *Globe* was the dominant paper in the region.

When Eben Jordan died in 1895, the General wrote an editorial brimming with gratitude to the man who had saved his company. "He alone believed that I would win, and stood by me even when the battle seemed almost hopeless," Taylor wrote. "No amount of debt or trouble could shake his confidence." Eben Jordan's son and grandson later became directors of the newspaper, and the Jordan Trust still owns 28 percent of the stock of the *Globe*'s parent company, Affiliated Publications Inc.

When no outside duties beckon, most mornings find Bill Taylor ensconced by 7:15 in his large office, with its Oriental rugs and den-like atmosphere, sipping coffee and reading the *Globe*, the *Herald*, the *New York Times*, and the *Wall Street*

Journal. He never reads them as thoroughly as he'd like, mostly because of the stream of phone calls from "people who know I'm in early and want to bend my ear." When his secretary arrives at 8:30, the two of them begin plowing through the mail, a never-ending pile of invitations to various functions, inquiries from groups that want to hold some sort of function at the *Globe* building, and requests for money from the company's charitable foundation, which made grants of $2.3 million last year to organizations ranging from hospitals to summer camps. He passes the requests along to the foundation's director.

Then it's on to other concerns, chief among them making sure the right people are in the right jobs, doing the right sorts of planning. Taylor hopes his years as publisher will be remembered as a time when the *Globe* became a better place to work. An independent, family-run paper can't offer ambitious employees as many opportunities at the top as they would find at a big chain—but then, in his opinion, "with a lot of chains, you're getting homogenized milk." The *Globe* has a quirkiness he cherishes. He stresses its uniqueness when he talks to new employees.

"I've tried to make this a place where a person can come in and give it a lifetime shot," he says. "I want people to feel they've been challenged all the way along; they can muddle through a midlife crisis and still stay. I want people to feel that once they're here, it's not just a job but an opportunity. Women and blacks have as good a shot here, or better, as in any other place. I want it to be a fun place to work, but with a very professional atmosphere."

After a pause, he adds, "The jury's still out on some of those scores."

•   •   •

Back at the display desk, Marianne Hyland breathes a sigh of relief. She's finally found an arrangement that will work: an eight-section, 104-page paper. She could have done it in four sections, a more economical arrangement, but that wouldn't have provided enough section fronts for everyone who wants one.

31

As it is, Business won't have the front page of a section, but at least it will get its second-choice spot, immediately behind Sports. Living will get a section front, which isn't always possible, and the Arts pages and amusement ads will run in that section. Ideally, she'd complete this "soft package" by putting the comics and TV listings in the Living section, but there isn't room. They'll have to go in the second half of the Metro section.

In condensed form, the procedure Hyland follows to arrive at the size of a section goes like this: First, using the printout she gets every morning from the advertising department, she adds up the number of inches of advertising sold for a particular section—for example, the business section. Say the total is eighty-four inches of ads.

She divides that by twenty-one inches, the depth of a newspaper page. The resulting number, four, tells her that if all the ads in the business section were run together, they would take up four full columns. To the four columns of advertising she adds the number of columns of news space the section wants that day, say thirty-eight. The total is forty-two. Now she knows that the news and advertising content of the business section will take up forty-two columns. Since each page is six columns wide, that means the business section needs seven pages. Because a section can't be seven pages long (the total must be divisible by four), she makes it eight. Editors can always find enough stories to fill the space.

Today, after doing these calculations for each section, she's ended up with 104 pages. That's what the pressroom calls a twenty by eight by eight by sixteen paper, meaning it will have two sections in each of those sizes. Hyland's next task is to pull out a long yellow sheet printed with page numbers and write down what will go on each page. Pages one through twenty and twenty-one through twenty-eight will be "main news," the front news section. Pages twenty-nine through thirty-six and thirty-seven through fifty-two will be Metro/Region, today including comics, TV listings, and classified ads. Pages fifty-three through seventy-two and seventy-three through eighty will be Sports and Business. Pages eighty-one through eighty-eight will be the Living and Arts

32

sections, and the last sixteen pages, printed as a tabloid with page numbers starting at one, will be Calendar.

Phew. Once the managers have come by and approved the lineup, Hyland starts "drawing the book." She decides where each ad will run, then outlines its size on a dummy, a standard-sized piece of white paper ruled into six columns to represent a newspaper page. The ads range from a one-by-one, one inch deep and one column wide, to a six-by-twenty-one, which is a full page. Drawing the book, Hyland relies on her mental file of dos and don'ts. If the list says one women's clothing store is advertising a coat sale, she won't put another store's coat ad near it. If two ads contain coupons, she can't put them front to back. Even as she fills up the dummy sheets, she knows she might have to redo them all later. A new full-page ad could somehow sneak in past the deadline, or an existing ad could drop out. A big news event could add pages to the paper and require redummying the whole thing. A plane crash or hijacking could cause the airlines to pull their ads (most airlines buy ads with the understanding that they won't run in a paper that reports on an air disaster).

Today, though, she's on schedule and not pulling out any more hair than usual. Bob Godfrey comes up from the pressroom to look at the layout. "The nuns didn't hit you hard enough," he jokes as he tries to read her handwriting. Then he begins his own version of layout, drawing cryptic symbols and numbers on a diagram of the pressroom to ensure that the presses will be able to print color on the necessary pages. Tomorrow's paper will have one color ad, plus color photos and graphics on the Sports front, and a single color on the cover of Calendar. The shoe store that bought the color ad originally wanted yellow, but it settled for orange because Calendar is using red, and the red ink might have contaminated the yellow.

Hyland holds her breath as Godfrey draws, but within minutes he looks up, satisfied. Now he'll post the diagram in the pressroom so that the 9:00 crew can start "make ready," setting up the presses for tonight's run. He'll also inform the warehouse, which must arrange to have the proper number of full and half rolls of newsprint available. Hyland will send a copy of "the book" to the newsroom, to let them know how much space they'll have. It's a big paper; she doubts that anyone will complain.

9:00 A.M.

It's an amazing thing, the way a newspaper gets news.

—Steve Kurkjian, Washington bureau chief

A mysterious package is sitting on Larry Tye's desk when he arrives in the newsroom. Opening it, he gingerly takes out two, three, a dozen gruesome models of corroding teeth. Some sets are wearing traditional dentures; others have individual false teeth screwed into their plastic gums. Reaching into the box again, he pulls out descriptions and diagrams. Apparently the people at Harvard Dental School want to make very sure he and the illustrator understand how dental implants work.

On some stories a reporter struggles for the slightest bit of cooperation. On this one, Tye is being deluged. Early this morning the *Globe* message center called him at home to tell him he'd received an urgent message from Harvard. When he called there, the director of the implant program gave him the names of twelve people who had had dental implants. That's about eleven more names than he needs, but maybe some toothy humans will breathe life into this scientific story. He knows that news about the implant process, which involves drilling holes into the jawbone and inserting screws to hold the false teeth, could be important to the 50 million Americans with gaps in their bites. Still, it's a little early in the day to share his desk with a dozen decaying Cheshire cats.

Tye heads downstairs to bring the teeth to Holly Nixholm in the design department. Maybe she can decorate her office with them while she's thinking about a drawing. At any rate, this could be his last chance to walk around. The editor of the Sci-Tech section says he needs the story first thing tomorrow. Considering the amount of reporting he still has to do, Tye doubts he can finish before midnight.

• • •

Raccoons are going to be a recurring theme today, but David Mehegan doesn't know it yet. At 9:00 A.M. he's at the New England Wildlife Center in Hingham, interviewing the director for a story on the effects of suburban development on wildlife. He's heard that raccoons, possums, and skunks are growing increasingly numerous and bold in some neighborhoods because the building boom has driven them out of their natural habitat.

It's an interesting subject, but he can't afford to spend much time on it right now. Soon his editor will be going into the morning meeting and telling the other editors about the terrific real estate story Mehegan is doing for tomorrow. The story is about people who, squeezed out of the Boston housing market by high prices and low availability, move farther and farther from the city and spend hours commuting to and from work. Trouble is, he hasn't done any terrific interviews yet. Everybody claims to know people who commute from the ends of the earth, but it's hard to find home buyers who fit the bill, can be reached during working hours, and are willing to talk. Mehegan leaves Hingham and drives toward Dorchester, mentally listing the places where he might be able to track down a few more potential sources this morning.

• • •

Walking into the newsroom, which he left only eight hours ago, Tom Oliphant feels like the magician's assistant who's about to be sawed in half. He doesn't like days when he has to work on two stories at once, though at least today he has a head start on both of them. A newspaper story deserves the full attention of a writer for a day, he thinks for the millionth time. One's job is writer and reporter, not typist. Then, briefly, another thought: I'd never have a day like this at the *New York Times*.

Usually when Oliphant mentions the *Times*, it's to compare it unfavorably with the *Globe*, his employer since he arrived as a college intern twenty years ago. For the last fifteen years he's been a political writer in Washington, where he hopes to return tonight. But first there's the matter of the two stories.

The first story is the reason he's in Boston. Nine states held primaries yesterday, and Oliphant flew north to write a roundup for today's paper. Because of all the wire services that feed into the *Globe*'s computers, he has access to much more information in Boston than he would if he stayed in the Washington bureau. He wrote and rewrote until 1:00 A.M., adding the latest election results each time the presses were replated for a new edition. (The first edition goes to readers farthest from the city, the second closer in, and so on until the final replate, which circulates downtown.) The process wasn't easy; everyone's replating attention was focused on another late-breaking story, the Celtics' playoff victory. Oliphant didn't really mind. Hard as he worked on the election story, he knows it "hasn't got a heck of a lot of real interest to anyone but political junkies."

Still, the junkies—and they're numerous in these parts—deserve the whole story, and he couldn't give it to them last night because the primary results from western time zones were too sketchy. So he needs to write another story for tomorrow's paper. Actually, he's looking forward to it. Because he'll be writing about news many people will already have heard, he can play with the structure and style. He can write a more feature-y lead, try to grab readers who don't usually follow politics.

The story he wrote last night bordered on the type Oliphant calls *pro forma*, meaning, basically, "just the facts, ma'am." If he worked at the *Times*, he likes to say, he'd have to write that kind of story every day. (On the other hand, if he worked at the *Times*, he'd probably never have to split his day in half.) It's not that he doesn't like the *Times*; he's simply glad that the *Globe* doesn't try to be a paper of record, making sure everything that happens gets its inch of print. With its smaller presence, especially in Washington, the *Globe* couldn't do that even if it wanted to. The result is that Oliphant can choose his arenas and have a little fun. Reporters have to stay at the *Globe* awhile to win that kind of freedom, but once they do, the freedom tends to keep them there. Some writers who don't get that far, or who want a more traditional kind of prestige, see their *Globe* days as training camp for the *Times* or the *Washington Post*.

Oliphant checks the paper to refresh his memory about today's story, which ran on page ten. His lead reads: "One of the Republican senators swept into office six years ago on the coattails of Ronald Reagan survived a surprisingly close race last night in a state deeply affected by the depression in agriculture." A fairly straight news lead. When writing it, he delayed naming the subject, James Abdnor of South Dakota, because Abdnor is not a familiar figure in New England. The senator's identification with Reagan, and his state's problems, indicated the story's significance better than his name.

Oliphant had decided to lead with the South Dakota race because the closeness seemed to show the fragility of the Republicans' hold. Abdnor's seat is one of the important ones the Democrats are counting on to try to win back control of the Senate in November.

He wrote four grafs about Abdnor. (*Graf* is the journalist's word for paragraph. When used in instructions to the typesetters or pasteup people, it is purposely misspelled, as is *hed* for headline and *lede* for lead. That way, no one will consider those words part of the story and accidentally put them into the paper.) After that beginning, Oliphant needed a transition from South Dakota to the other states. He wrote, "Elsewhere in a crowded national primary calendar, voters in eight other states went to the polls, with these principal developments."

Then he wrote long paragraphs about each state, each preceded by a bullet, or heavy black dot, to let readers know they were reading a list. Most of the rest of the story was background about the campaigns, which he'd written in advance. With the results coming in as fast as he could type them—and deadlines coming faster still—there wasn't time to do much else.

That was an obligatory story, not particularly exciting to write. On the other hand, it was delicate work. Because the results were incomplete, he had to make a long series of judgments about who was likely to win. If he jumped to conclusions too early, he'd look foolish and so would the paper.

Today Oliphant has fewer obligations. News about the winners in the West will be twenty-four hours old by the time his next story comes out tomorrow morning. The political junkies will want more than the facts; they'll want him to explain the impact of what happened. He'll still have to round up the nine states' results, but he already knows he wants to start with California. The guy who won out there was exactly the kind of guy—a moderate Republican from the northern part of the state, rather than a conservative from the south—who'd be expected to lose if you believed all the textbook predictions. Maybe that should be his lead—contrasting what happened with what was "supposed" to happen. He could use a sort of refrain to debunk the theories: "But then along came Ed Zschau."

Oliphant sits at a copy editor's terminal and begins to write. He has no terminal of his own in Boston because his office is in Washington. Anyway, the copy desk is the quietest place to work at this hour; the copy editors don't arrive until late afternoon, when stories are finished and ready to edit. "It wasn't supposed to be possible," he writes. "Moderates don't win Republican primaries in California in the age of Ronald Reagan; conservatives do. But then along came Ed Zschau."

This is going to be fun. Then he remembers the magician with the saw. He'd better go talk with his editor about his second story, an assessment of tax reform's prospects in the Senate. He collected a notebook full of quotes on the subject before he left Washington yesterday. The Senate debate begins today, but there's no way he's going to write a *pro forma* story on this one.

•   •   •

Tom Mulvoy's job is exactly what he had in mind thirty years ago, when he told the bishop at his confirmation that he wanted to be a newspaperman. He was a little scared to say it. The year before, when his brother Mark had told Cardinal Cushing he wanted to be a sportswriter, one of the nuns had whacked him across the head. But when his year came, Tom sang it out. He didn't know the title, he didn't know the specifics, but this job—this molding and planning in his glass office, two miles from the house where he was born and right across the street from his alma mater, Boston College High School—this job as managing editor is exactly what he was talking about. (Mark got what he wanted, too; he is managing editor of *Sports Illustrated*.)

If Jack Driscoll is conductor of the newsroom symphony, Tom Mulvoy is concert master. He is both manager and editor, dealing with everything from budgets to headlines to hiring. This morning he had breakfast with a friend who works for the city of Boston. They chatted about the latest city happenings, and, as usual, Mulvoy came away with a few thoughts that might someday become stories. The friend has always been a good source. Now Mulvoy is in his office, reading the production report and the night editor's report. No disasters there; the night seems to have gone pretty well.

He read most of the front-page stories before he left last night, but he skims them again (things look different in print, somehow, from the way they look twenty lines at a time on a computer screen), then reads through the rest of the paper. One of his favorite morning tasks is sending congratulatory messages to reporters who have done a particularly good job. He sends notes that aren't so complimentary, too, but he tries to make sure that the congratulations outnumber the complaints.

Mulvoy and Driscoll sit at the top of a purposely strong system of newsroom department heads—Metro, Business, Living, Sports, and all the subdivisions in between. Each department head knows his or her field and reporters, and each aims, in Mulvoy's words, "to deliver with a great deal of energy more stories than could ever fit in the paper." On good days, these editors will offer ten or fifteen or twenty stories for page one. That's where Mulvoy asserts his authority. He listens to the editors' descriptions, he reads as many stories as he can, and then, at 6:15 each day, he announces which six stories will go on the front. People can argue, and sometimes he'll change his mind, but the choice is his. They've all learned from experience that, at least on this score, group decision making doesn't work.

His other duties are less concrete. He serves as interlocutor among the various departments in the newsroom, and between the newsroom and the other departments in the building. He "reassures, redirects, straightens out" whatever, and whoever, needs straightening. Sometimes he's called on to reassert a decision that's already been made. "A person can get the same answer all the way up the chain of command," he says, "but sometimes they won't really accept it until they hear it from me."

He also does a great deal of planning. So do the department heads, of course, but Mulvoy focuses on the areas where those separate plans intersect. His attention volleys back and forth between short-term planning and long-range commitments. At a newspaper, "long range" means anything beyond tomorrow. "You never can take your eye off tomorrow's paper," he says, "but at the same time you've got to be thinking about Sunday, and next week, and the next big event, and wait—are we going to do polling for the November election?"

It is, as Mulvoy tells anyone who asks, a fabulously interesting job. It dovetails with his lifelong curiosity about what makes people tick, and with his "unrelenting concern about the right words." After almost twenty years at the *Globe*, he's realized he's going to be unrelenting until the day he turns in his parking sticker, because the paper will never achieve perfection. Once in a while the planets align to produce a perfect story—perfectly written, perfectly edited, perfectly played, with a perfect headline and a perfect photo with a perfect cutline (caption). One perfect story, once in a while. But it's a big paper.

Nothing quite reached perfection this morning, but he sees a few stories worth complimentary notes. Before he can write anything, though, he'll have to contend with the "message pending" flashing on his screen. When he hits the "read" button, 150 lines of messages unfold. By the time he's finished reading and answering them, he has to leave for a meeting with some people downtown who are trying to publicize a multiple sclerosis benefit. He can't actually go to work for them, as they seem to want, but he can give them advice on getting their message into the paper.

On his way to the parking lot, Mulvoy sees Steve Kurkjian heading for the office of the national editor, Royal Ford.
He knows they'll be talking about the secrets story. The latest
installment of the to-print-or-not-to-print debate will be waiting when he comes back.

. . .

They've been over and over and over it, and now they're going
over it again. What have we got? What doesn't the government want us to print? Why not? What should we do? If the
Soviets already know this stuff because of spying, why the
secrecy? Each day they answer the questions. The next day
they ask them again.

Kurkjian, the Washington bureau chief, and Ford, his
editor in Boston, are sure they want to run the story tomorrow. The lawyers have looked at it, the government has seen
parts of it, everybody and his third cousin has said his piece.
But the story is, as Mulvoy describes it in his Boston accent,
"a hot podaduh." It can't hurt to talk about it some more. It
can't hurt to be sure.

Kurkjian is explaining what he expected last week as he
went into his first meeting with the National Security Agency,
the agency for which Ronald Pelton was working when he
allegedly sold intelligence secrets to the Soviets. Walter Robinson and Fred Kaplan, who did the reporting, would have
needed the agency's comment on the story anyway, for balance, but last week they were looking for something more.
CIA director William Casey had told journalists that if they
wanted to write about national security without damaging it,
"we will work with you on that line."

Kurkjian, Robinson, and Kaplan each had different expectations going into the meetings with the NSA director,
Lieutenant General William Odom, just as each now has a
different assessment of what happened. Sitting in Ford's office
this morning, Kurkjian speaks only for himself. He remembers thinking three things as he went to meet Odom: that the
government people would treat the journalists with respect,
that they would err on the side of caution, and that they
might lie.

That last expectation sprang not so much from cynicism as from an experience with bureaucratic thinking. Since threatening legal action against the *Post* and NBC for their reporting on the Pelton case, the CIA and NSA had faced both scathing criticism and escalating inquiries from reporters newly interested in the story. That, Kurkjian reasoned, put the agencies in an entrenched position, and their directors were bound to feel that they were under siege. "And when people are under siege," he says, "they may play with the truth."

At their first meeting, in a CIA-owned house in downtown Washington, Odom himself alluded to the siege mentality when he told the *Globe* group that his agency always operates as if the nation were at war. "Other operations of the government are at peace, but we're at war," Kurkjian remembers him saying.

A woman from the NSA and a man from the Department of Defense came with Odom to that meeting. Kaplan began with a three-minute summary of what he had found out about the intelligence operations called Project A and Project B, which he believed Pelton had compromised. Then, as he would at every subsequent meeting, Odom responded not by detailing objections to specific information but by listing the reasons he thought national security would be jeopardized if the *Globe* published anything at all. The reasons fell into three main categories.

First, Odom said that the United States couldn't be sure exactly what Pelton might or might not have told the Soviets about certain intelligence operations. Although the Soviets probably knew about pieces of a particular system, he said, they might not have the full analysis they needed to see how it all fit together. The *Globe* people didn't find this argument particularly persuasive because they had been told, and the *Post* had already printed, that the Soviets had in fact seized an American communications-interception device based on information they received from Pelton. But maybe parts of Project A were still going on, in which case publication might allow the Soviets to install counter-measures. Was Project A still in progress? they asked. Odom wouldn't say.

43

The NSA's next argument was that other governments did not know that the United States was conducting the types of operations the reporters had found out about. Friendly or unfriendly governments? the *Globe* people asked. Odom wouldn't say.

His third set of arguments had to do with the media. By printing even small morsels of information, Odom said, the *Globe* would open the floodgates. More and more reporters would dive into the story, each trying to outdo the others. And if the *Globe* printed information that the *Post* had withheld, the *Post* might consider the embargo broken and print everything it had. (Hmmm, the *Globe* people wondered, what else did the *Post* have?) Another story in the *Post*, Odom said, would be like flypaper for the media hordes.

Unusual as the procedure was, the NSA had decided that it would have to divulge some national security information at Pelton's trial if it wanted him convicted. Odom said that the testimony had been carefully selected to minimize the damage, but reporters could negate all that care by speculating on information other than what came out in the courtroom in Baltimore.

Kurkjian, Kaplan, and Robinson didn't leave that first meeting as converts to the government line, but Odom had given them a lot to think about. Since then Kurkjian, especially, has often reviewed not just the general's words but also what he calls "telepathy," the messages behind the words. Years as an investigative reporter have given Kurkjian confidence that he can read a glance or a movement of the shoulders, or hear a change in tone that makes one negative answer different from the others. He thinks he's picked up enough telepathy from Odom—though certainly not many concrete answers—to know where the gravest dangers lie.

From the beginning, the *Globe* people knew they'd have to tread most lightly when dealing with matters of technology. They couldn't just go around telling foreign governments, along with ordinary readers of the paper, how U.S. intelligence hardware works. So they tried to get specific responses from the NSA on specific pieces of hardware. That, Kurkjian says, is where "telepathy" came in.

For example, the reporters would describe what they knew, and one of the government people would say something like "There may be some details in what you said that wouldn't be damaging." Then the reporters would try to break that answer down. If the conversation revolved around a particular four-part system, the reporters might ask, "Do the Soviets know about part one?" Maybe they'd get a flat "No" as a response. When they asked about another part, the response might be "We can't discuss that." The two answers were different, and the reporters knew they were different for a reason. Their job was to figure out what that reason was.

They've been debating telepathy, along with every other aspect of the story, for a week. A few decisions remain to be made, but Kurkjian feels ready to go. Kaplan and Robinson sent a few of the trickiest paragraphs to the NSA by courier on Monday. Now, having reviewed the agency's objections and done some rewriting ("Sanitizing," Robinson calls it), they're sending the paragraphs back today. Kurkjian has told the two reporters to stay near the phone in Washington. Maybe in a few hours they can all cut the cord and send the story on its way.

•   •   •

Everyone thinks Israel is so modern, Curtis Wilkie is telling Kathy Tolbert. Why, then, haven't I had any water in my apartment for two days? Why are the phones screwed up? And did the Celtics win last night?

It's 9:45 A.M. in Boston and 4:45 P.M. in Jerusalem, where Wilkie is Mideast correspondent for the *Globe*. Tolbert, the foreign editor, has called to check on a Sunday story he's doing, and generally to see what he's up to. Even if Wilkie spends the whole time complaining, the call will be an improvement on her morning.

As always, she read the *Globe* at home first thing, before checking the *Times* and listening to the radio news. As soon as she opened the paper, she found a mistake in a cutline on page three. The photo, from the Associated Press, ran with a *Globe* stringer's story on the Crossroads squatter camp in South Africa. The cutline said, "Squatters' shacks burn last night near Cape Town." Shacks were definitely burning, and they were near Cape Town, but Tolbert knew the picture hadn't been taken last night. She knew she'd seen it around the office before—probably last week, maybe earlier. Sure enough, when she got to work and found the photo, the AP cutline indicated that it had been taken more than two weeks before. A layout person probably had a jumble of wire photos on his desk last night, picked this one because it fit the hole best, and, not reading the cutline carefully, figured the shacks must have burned yesterday if the story was running today.

Nothing in the photo dates it; she can be almost positive that no one reading the paper noticed the mistake. Still, it's an error, and newspapers aren't in the business of selling untruths for a quarter. The paper will have to run a correction tomorrow, in the "For the Record" column on page two. In its corrections, the *Globe* tries to explain how the mistake happened, and correct it without repeating it. The correction for tomorrow will read: "Because of an editing error, the caption with a photograph accompanying a story in yesterday's U.S./ World section about the Crossroads squatter camp in South Africa was incorrect. The photo showed shacks burning on May 20."

The error gets Tolbert's day off to a discouraging start. Everybody works so hard, she thinks, and then one person's attention wavers for half a second and *poof*, the whole paper's credibility is on the line. Worse still, that one person can be anyone, even the best reporter or editor. Even one of the big bosses. Even me. Deadline pressure gives birth to all manner of monsters.

Frustrating as this train of thought is, she's glad to have time to pursue it. As foreign editor, Tolbert feels as if the last year has yanked her through one overwhelming news event after another: the TWA and *Achille Lauro* hijackings, the Mexican earthquake and Colombian volcano, the Geneva summit, the terrorist attacks at the Rome and Vienna airports, the U.S. raids on Libya, the fall of Duvalier in Haiti and Marcos in the Philippines, the Chernobyl accident . . . . Each time, she was responsible for coordinating the paper's coverage, getting the right reporters to the right places at the right times, figuring out when to "send" and when a wire

46

story would be enough. Now that the craziness finally seems to have calmed a bit, she has time to think and plan.

She wants to make sure that the foreign reporters are planning, too. When her call to Wilkie gets through, he's in rare form, describing how he trooped seven flights down to get the *Jerusalem Post* this morning, then seven flights back up to read it, then back to the fourth floor to get water, then back to the seventh to make coffee and attempt a cold-water splash bath. He has no idea why the water in his flat has been out for two days. In the abbreviated language of journalistic memos (eliminating all forms of the verb *to be*), which reporters sometimes borrow for speech as well, he says, "Situation getting funky."

Wilkie, who was a Washington reporter before moving to Jerusalem a year and a half ago, usually writes more daily news stories than the *Globe*'s other foreign correspondents. That's partly because more conflict happens from day to day in his area, partly because, like news from Ireland, news from the Mideast has a natural constituency among *Globe* readers. Today, however, Wilkie has been working on a more reflective piece that will look at how the 1982 invasion of Lebanon has changed Israel.

He got up this morning at 7:00 (midnight, Boston time) and listened to the English-language newscast before going out in search of news and water. Coffee helped, but, lacking a shower, he was in a grim mood as he walked to the building in West Jerusalem where the *Globe* and other Western papers and agencies have their offices. He began by reading through the notes of the dozen interviews he'd done for the war story, with every good intention of starting to write this morning. The "resident hacks," however, had other ideas. They drew him into a discussion on how somebody might be able to get to Lebanon, where the exchange rate had risen overnight to thirty-nine Lebanese pounds per U.S. dollar. Like the others, Wilkie holds many increasingly worthless Lebanese pounds.

Soon the jabbering congregation had outgrown the room. After observing a moment of silence in honor of the 1:00 English newscast, the group adjourned to a restaurant for a noisy lunch that, Wilkie admits with some embarrassment, ended not long before Tolbert's 4:45 call. Long lunches are a Mideast tradition, he says, and reporters do not wish to disturb tradition. Anyway, he's got three hours to get his Sunday story started before he and his son, who's visiting, go off to dinner at the UPI correspondent's house.

As Mideast days go, this was an easy one. Or, as Wilkie puts it in memo-speak: "It not always this pleasant."

. . .

The good news, Vince Doria knows when he arrives, is that the final Celtics score made it into the first edition. The bad news is that the color on the Celtics photo wasn't the greatest, and the Red Sox color was worse. And chief photographer Stan Grossfeld doesn't like the photo of his that was chosen for the front page. And because the Celtics lost the other day, they won't be coming home triumphant tonight on the flight they booked last week, and neither will Doria's five sportswriters.

Okay. Slow down and take them one at a time. The good news is really good. Here's a message from the New Hampshire bureau, funneled through Jack Driscoll, saying that because the first edition was held for the Celtics, the *Globe* that reached New Hampshire had a final score and a live photo, whereas the local morning paper had only a game-in-progress story and a photo of Larry Bird in a warmup jacket.

Holding an edition is risky business. Most of the complaints that Doria hears as sports editor are from readers who live far from the city and therefore get the first or second editions. We're not getting our quarters' worth, these readers say. We want the late scores. But waiting for the late scores usually means making the paper late, which screws up the distribution system and, in the end, costs the *Globe* readers. Damned if you do, damned if you don't.

Last night, though, the seesaw almost balanced. The presses rolled on the first edition at midnight instead of 11:30, allowing the final score to get in without making the paper *too* late. Of course, first-edition readers didn't get a perfect story, just a running game story with the score sort of shoved into the lead. But at least they could read as much in the paper as they could hear on the radio. Bob Ryan, writing and rewriting constantly, had time to get a little fancier by the third edition. Instead of simply starting with the fact that the Celtics had won, he began his story this way: "It's more fun playing in the best final series game in a decade (yup, the best since the Phoenix Triple OT) when you win it."

At any rate, the first-edition triumph was a decisive skirmish in the *Globe*'s battle to get more readers up north. Doria can be glad of that. Even the bad news doesn't seem so bad if he takes it piece by piece. Last night was the first time the sports department had ever tried to put "live" color photos from two different places—in this case, Fenway Park and the Summit in Houston—into the same paper. (Live photos are photos taken and processed at the last possible minute, as opposed to file photos, which the newspaper already has on hand.)

Doria didn't really expect perfection this first time. Like most of the department's forty-six writers and editors, he has mixed feelings about this push to use color four or five days a week. For the last three weeks they've been slaves to color; it's running their lives. One of his assistants, Don Skwar, has put in dozens of extra hours dealing with color and the layout and logistical problems it creates. Skwar has done almost nothing else, and he's tired. They're all tired. But the feedback from the street is terrific. Everybody loves color. Most of the time, Doria thinks it's worth all the work.

He'd been wanting to get into color in a big way for a long time, ever since the paper bought the necessary equipment. The top managers said they wanted it, too, but somehow it never seemed to happen. Sports was running color in its special Friday section, Sports Plus, but not live color from games. Finally, Doria decided that if he waited for a grand plan, he'd wait forever. The solution was simple: Just do it.

He ordered color on opening day at Fenway. The photographers shot good stuff. That evening the United States bombed Libya. The color was pulled. Next try, Boston Marathon. Again, great stuff, and this time the photos made it into the paper. They looked good, everybody got excited, and the color push had begun. Because of the Marathon color, something terrific happened, something he hadn't anticipated. The production people—composing, engraving, the pressroom—liked the color photos and got excited about having them in the paper. The prouder they felt, the more they didn't mind the extra work, the last-minute rushing. That's made things less torturous than they might have been.

Dealing with color makes a lot of people in a lot of departments feel like newspaper neophytes again. While the sports people worry about timing and layout, the photographers are experimenting with lighting and exposures to see what sort of picture reproduces best. The pressmen are working on keeping the colors lined up, a difficult process complicated by the pressroom's transitional state. Because $60 million in new equipment is being installed gradually, the pressroom now has four different types of presses, which print color with varying degrees of success. The quality of the color photo a reader sees, therefore, can depend on which press printed that particular paper, and how early or late in the run it was done.

Grossfeld has recently developed the theory that when he takes a color photo, someone in the pressroom carefully studies the first papers off the presses to find the one in which his picture looks absolutely the worst. That paper, the theory goes, is then put into a cab and rushed directly to his house. How else, he asks, could he so consistently find something horrible—orange skin, say, or a Celtics uniform in a putrid shade of green—when he opens his door in the morning?

Doria laughed when he heard that theory, but he knows Grossfeld won't laugh when he sees today's sports front. Still, Doria decides after staring at the page awhile, it could be worse. Well, maybe the Red Sox photo couldn't be *much* worse, but the Celtics shot didn't turn out half bad, especially considering that it had to be transmitted from Houston. Anyway, it's all part of the learning process; they get better results each time they try.

He's not too worried, either, by the message that Grossfeld is upset about the front-page photo choice. Grossfeld's battles over page-one photo play are a familiar story, and Doria—who oversees the photo department in addition to being sports editor—understands the chief photographer's

50

motivation. Unlike the other newsroom departments, photos is a service department; it helps everybody but doesn't have any guaranteed space of its own. So it's only fair that Grossfeld should stand up for his photographers' rights.

The arguments can get pretty ferocious sometimes, but Doria can probably defuse this one. He's pretty sure Grossfeld thinks the photo he was pushing for the front page didn't end up anywhere in the paper, but actually it did. On the final replate, the night people subbed it into the two-page Celtics spread inside the sports section, which already included two other Grossfeld photos. And Grossfeld's front-page photo, although not his first choice, got great play: a quarter page, above the fold.

Doria looks for the hotel number in Houston. He hopes the photographers' energy is holding up. The last time Grossfeld spent this many consecutive days shooting sports, he had nightmares about being chased by giant basketballs—this from a guy who keeps a basketball in his car so he can stop and shoot hoops when he gets frustrated hunting for feature pictures.

Playoff season seems to get longer every year, and, exciting as it is, it takes a heavy toll on the writers and photographers. One game after another after another, each more important than the last. Days like this, the off days between games, are in many ways the worst. Everyone wants to rest before they have to bang their heads against the brick wall of deadline again, but they can't. The pages still need to be filled with words and pictures about the Celtics and the Rockets. Doria's task this morning is to hook up with the five writers in Houston and plan tomorrow's stories. He also needs to distribute a few strategically placed nudges about the special Celtics championship section the paper is optimistically planning to run next week. An extra story assignment is the last thing the weary writers need, but now that ads have been sold for the section, there's no turning back.

Doria is ready to start his morning telephone rounds, but Grossfeld calls before he can pick up the phone. They talk through the photo problems, calmly, and plot their next moves. Next up, columnist Michael Madden. Doria reaches

51

him in his Houston hotel room. Skwar has already roughed out a layout for tomorrow's sports front that includes a large color Red Sox photo and a small color photo, a file shot, of Celtic Bill Walton. Walton has contributed a lot to the series, and tomorrow happens to be the ninth anniversary, to the day, of his NBA championship with the Portland Trail Blazers. How about a column on Walton, Doria asks. Great idea, Madden says.

Next call, Leigh Montville. Doria doesn't have a column idea for him, but he's sure Montville has several. It's almost 10:00 (9:00 in Houston), and the phone in Montville's room rings and rings. Finally it clatters off the hook, and Doria hears something that sounds like a cross between "hello" and "harumph," muffled by a pillow.

"Leigh?" he asks.

Grunt.

"It's Vince. Go back to sleep. I'll call you later."

10:00 A.M.

Sometimes I think you have to be half crazy to work here.

—Joan Venocchi, State House bureau chief

A casual observer might think Peggy Hernandez is goofing off. She is walking slowly from floor to floor in the eleven-story headquarters of the Boston School Department, stopping for a handshake here, a greeting there, a brief exchange about this and that. It all looks very informal, but actually she's performing one of the essential routines of the beat reporter: keeping in touch with her sources.

Hernandez calls this stage of the reporting process "working the building." The idea is to show her face, remind a lot of busy people of her existence, demonstrate that she's interested in what they do. Because keeping the press informed isn't tops on most people's office agendas, she must periodically inject herself into the consciousness of everyone from secretaries to the superintendent. Maybe they didn't think to call her about something that happened recently, or about a persistent rumor that's been roaming the halls. Her appearance at their desks could be just the cue they need. Anyway, she likes a lot of these people and likes to talk with them. She doesn't want them to think that she turns up only when there's a big story.

Hernandez has been able to turn up more often lately. She's been working across the street at the *Globe*'s City Hall bureau since one of the bureau's three reporters moved to the State House, leaving an empty desk. Though she can stay only temporarily, it's a much more convenient location than the newsroom on Morrissey Boulevard. In fact, she now goes to "the Boulevard" only after late-night School Committee

53

meetings, when City Hall is too spookily empty for comfortable writing.

Today she's following what's become her City Hall routine. She rolled in at about 9:30 and, having read the *Globe* at home, immediately picked up the *Herald*. She was looking for just one byline: Andrea Estes, the reporter who, like Hernandez, covers the School Department. Estes works in the office next door. Though the two are friendly—it's nearly impossible not to be, when you cover all the same meetings and news conferences—neither one likes to be scooped.

Reporters, especially reporters at the dominant newspaper in a city, don't talk much about competition, but it's never far from their minds. Nothing improves the quality of a story like finding out the other guys don't have it. Most reporters have learned to keep their competitiveness at socially acceptable levels, most of the time. But as photographer Stan Grossfeld likes to say, "You should see *Globe* people play basketball. Nobody wants to lose."

Hernandez hasn't lost today; Estes has no stories she missed. That established, she looks over some notes from yesterday and starts making calls to people who are plugged in to education happenings. It's the telephone equivalent of "working the building." She wants to telephone her editor, Fletcher Roberts, before she heads across the street to the School Department, but it's always safer to call an editor with a proposal ("Here's what I'm doing today") than a plea ("What should I do today?").

A few calls into the morning, she gets a good tip. A woman from a local education group tells Hernandez she's heard that nearly every teacher and principal in the Boston school system has received a positive job evaluation. That sounds odd, especially considering the 16 percent dropout rate and the recent announcement that fifty-one high school seniors won't be allowed to graduate this month because they can't read at an eighth-grade level. The woman has also heard that the superintendent is upset. Maybe there's something wrong with the review process, she suggests. Hernandez thanks her for the information and hangs up. She can't use anything the woman said because it's only hearsay, but now

54

that she's aware of the evaluations' existence, she can try to find them.

Hernandez calls Roberts, who agrees that the story is worth pursuing. He also reminds her to keep checking on whether the school bus drivers have signed a contract. She's been writing about the drivers off and on since they struck in January, and she's been checking on the contract every day for weeks. Although the constant fruitless calls are a pain, she knows that the one day she forgets to check will be the day the contract is signed.

Across the street, she begins her tour of the School Department on the fifth floor, which houses the offices of the superintendent and the administrators who make up his informal "cabinet." One of these officials has been especially good about providing her with off-the-record tips. Sure enough, that person comes through today, confirming that the teachers' and principals' job reviews are indeed overwhelmingly positive, and that the superintendent is upset. Now she has the background she needs to start hunting for on-the-record information.

But she doesn't leave yet. Because this official is such a good source, Hernandez always stays and chats as long as possible. After a few minutes of speaking generally about School Department events, the official says, "I expect we're going to get flak from the School Committee about the new pregnancy-prevention proposal because some members are going to think we're trying to push this on them." Immediately, excited questions fill Hernandez's mind. The pregnancy-prevention proposal is ready? What does it say? This could be big! What problems is this person talking about?

None of those questions come out of her mouth. She's learned that when interviewing a source, even one who's experienced at dealing with the media, it's never wise to pounce. If she said, "Wow!" or "*What* did you say?" the official might get nervous and change the subject. "I always try to act mildly interested in everything, and in nothing specifically, when people tell me things," Hernandez explains. So she responds with careful nonchalance. "Oh, you expect problems?" she asks.

The official holds up a memo—she can't have it, the official says—and begins describing the pregnancy-prevention proposal. Hernandez listens carefully but does not take notes. Because the official specified at the start that their discussion would be off the record, she can use the information only as background. If she started laboriously taking it down, she might strain the conversation to the point where the official would stop talking. Once she knows what the memo says, she can try to get the information from someone else.

The $75,000 pregnancy-prevention proposal for seventh-graders, the official tells her, was submitted yesterday. (That's a relief; it's not something she should have known weeks ago.) Although a citywide committee has recommended establishing health clinics that would distribute birth-control devices in some schools, the pregnancy-prevention proposal does not call for doing that. The official tells Hernandez that the memo was written by the deputy superintendent, and that it will be given to the School Committee later in the day. That's good news. Once a document goes upstairs to the School Committee, it's supposed to be available to any reporter who knows enough to ask for it.

Hernandez chats with the official for another minute or two before leaving the office. As soon as she steps into the hall, she pulls out her notebook and writes down all the details she can remember. If she can't get her hands on the memo later, at least she can try to find other people who will confirm its contents. She checks the time and sees that Roberts, her editor, is probably in his morning meeting with the other local news editors on Morrissey Boulevard. She'll call later and try to sell the pregnancy story as more interesting than the job evaluation story. But she knows she'll probably end up doing both.

• • •

"For a slow day, we sure did okay," Ben Taylor tells the six other editors arranged with varying degrees of alertness at one end of the long conference table. A few people smile. As often happens, the paper that readers picked up this morning bears little resemblance to the one the group envisioned when they sat around this table twenty-four hours ago. The biggest change came late yesterday afternoon, when Royall Switzler, the Republican candidate for governor, announced that he had lied about his military record. He had not, in fact, been a Green Beret, and he had not served in Vietnam. The story was an obvious choice to lead this morning's paper.

"Too bad they bumped the team police," somebody says. That story, about a proposal to cut police protection in public housing projects, was "bumped" from the front page to the front of the Metro section after the Switzler story broke.

"Yeah, and with a feature taking up a quarter of the page," Barbara Meltz says, pointing to a front-page story about a conflict over condominium development in nearby Revere. Murmurs of support come from the others. Because news judgment follows no set rules, second-guessing the night editors' choices is a favorite pastime on the "dayside." Actually, Meltz is pleased to see the condo story on the front page; it was written by one of "her" reporters. But she wonders if it should have been played so prominently.

Taylor, who is assistant managing editor for local news, leads this meeting of metro editors (some with the title senior assistant metro editor, others simply assistant metro editor) each morning, beginning anywhere from 10:00 to 10:30. They tie up loose ends from today's paper, and then each editor talks about what his or her reporters are working on for tomorrow's. Together, they can often generate ideas—a new angle on a story, an additional place to look for information, an unusual way to follow up on the news—that none of them had thought of alone. It's the first of five meetings Taylor attends every day, all with the same goal: molding a shapeless mass of information into a newspaper. The 10:00 meeting deals only with local and regional news; later, national, foreign, business, features, and sports will be added to the mix.

Reporters walk by the glass-walled conference room in a steady stream, arriving for the day or leaving on assignment or returning to their desks with coffee. A few glance in curiously. No matter how well a reporter gets along with an editor (and, as in any office, some relationships are better than others), he or she always wonders what "they" say when they get together and close the door. Editors talk about stories at their meetings, the reporters know, so they must talk about writers, too—the way reporters talk about editors when they get together in a bar or jogging along Dorchester Bay. On a bad day, it's easy to get paranoid, to see the newsroom as divided into hostile camps. Actually, however, almost every editor has been a reporter, and quite a few reporters have been editors. Most days, each group is too busy to worry much about the other's motives.

Today the reporters have a representative at the morning meeting. Marvin Pave is a "swing man." He's a reporter most of the time but swings over to become an editor on Sunday nights and whenever the desk is short-handed. At various times during his nineteen years at the *Globe*, he's also served as assistant city editor and high school sports editor. Today Pave and the newest senior assistant metro editor, Greg Moore, are filling in for the city editor, Kirk Scharfenberg, who's out.

The city editor coordinates local news coverage and supervises the "g.a.'s"—general assignment reporters, who cover whatever comes along, rather than a specific beat. When he's not attending meetings, Scharfenberg spends much of his time sitting at his terminal while reporters file by and offer updates on their stories' progress. If the reporters' dress and demeanor didn't vary so widely, the parade might look almost military: Each reporter halts in the same spot opposite Scharfenberg's desk, leans on the partition, and states his case. When there's a break in the flow, Scharfenberg prowls the newsroom, looking for g.a.'s to send out on assignment.

They're not easy to find. Stealing g.a.'s is a popular last-resort tactic among the editors who supervise beat reporters. Asked how many g.a.'s he has, Scharfenberg will say, "About a third as many as I'm supposed to." When a story needs doing and all his reporters are busy, he has no choice but to pull someone off a long-range project. Scharfenberg paints the picture this way: "The other editors can raid me, but I can only raid myself."

If there's any raiding to be done today, Pave and Moore will have to do it. But they'll probably have all the warm bodies they need; today is The Day of the Interns. Seventeen college students have arrived to spend the summer working as reporters. All morning they've been wandering into the newsroom looking both nervous and determined, hunting for their editors and a place to sit. Feature writer Linda Matchan, who's thirty-two, says that a new crop of interns always makes her feel old. Never mind that she's won awards and been nominated for a Pulitzer; the interns seem to get more confident and competent every year. Still, intern day offers one unbeatable form of amusement. The women reporters get to watch some of the men fall over themselves trying to impress the pretty young students.

The interns won't spend their first day sitting around; the editors are already planning their assignments. "We need Neighborhoods pieces," Pave says at the meeting. "If the page has room for three, I was thinking we could send interns to three housing projects as a follow to the team police." A "follow," as its name implies, is a story that further explores a subject in the news. This one had been mentioned earlier in the meeting by another editor, and Pave is expanding on the idea. Newspapers struggle to follow as many stories as possible, at least in part to counteract the stereotypes of "hit and run" journalism and "one-day wonder" stories. There's more to say about every story; no writer can get every last fact on deadline. For editors, however, the question becomes how much of their resources to devote to follows and how much to pursuing new stories. If the number of available reporters gets tight, breaking news always takes precedence.

Today's story about proposed cuts in team police patrols at housing projects creates an obvious follow-up question: How do the residents of the projects feel about the idea? That's the story Pave is proposing for the Neighborhoods page, the second page of the Metro section.

"I don't know," Taylor says. "We have a big BHA [Boston Housing Authority] package coming for Sunday, and I don't want to undercut that."

"Two different things," Pave replies, to general noises of agreement from the group.

Taylor concurs, and the matter is settled. "What else?" he asks.

"The State House [bureau] is going to follow Switzler," Dave Morrow says. The editor in charge of the City Hall bureau, Morrow is also listing the state government stories today because editor Dick Kindleberger is spending the morning at the State House. "What angle does anybody think?"

"The natural follow is the Republicans in disarray," Taylor says. "We were going to do something like that for Sunday, but now I don't think we should wait."

At the mention of Switzler's transgressions, the meeting temporarily dissolves into hoots. Switzler was nominated as the Republican gubernatorial candidate two months ago, after claims that his chief rival had performed poorly in a previous job and had indulged in some strange behavior—including, allegedly, nudity at work. People all over the state are marveling at the party's bad luck, and the editors are marveling along with them.

"What a mess!" somebody says with a laugh.

"The Republicans in this state are a disaster," someone else adds.

When editors or reporters get together, judgments often bubble to the surface so forcefully that they explode into noise. Such gatherings pop the cork that keeps journalists' opinions bottled up, where they can't show on the news pages. Among co-workers, they can let their feelings loose, then cork them up again and get back to work. No such strictures, of course, govern the editorial and op-ed pages. At that moment, a few offices away, columnist David Nyhan is writing an op-ed piece about the disasters that have beset the Massachusetts Republican party. He's calling the party "the Chernobyl of the national GOP, a meltdown area with the voters largely evacuated."

The conference room quiets as Taylor's voice turns serious. "Lincoln [Millstein, the business editor] suggests we use some interns as a team to check the records of every state rep and senator," he says.

"Maybe we could start with candidates for the six top offices," says Nils Bruzelius, editor of the Monday Sci-Tech section. "You might find someone . . ."

". . . living a lie," Meltz chimes in. "How about a survey of local Republicans?"

"What's anybody think?" Taylor asks.

"Nils's idea is the best," Morrow says. "Just do the constitutional officers."

"But I'd be nervous about using interns," Fletcher Roberts says.

"You've got to be careful," Bruzelius agrees. "Military records especially. It's easy to think someone doesn't have a medal they really have."

After several more minutes of discussion, they agree that using interns on such a sensitive project would be too risky. In fact, much as they all want to do it, they probably won't be able to find anyone who can devote such a huge block of time to an investigation that might yield nothing. The issue hangs unresolved as they wrap up the meeting with a quick accounting of stories in progress. The conversation proceeds in fits and starts.

"Jack [Driscoll] wants a couple grafs on the commencement at Essex Ag. He's the speaker, but he says don't mention his name."

"Okay, how about, 'An unidentified man delivered the commencement address'?"

"We'll have the long-awaited story about the expansion of the suburbs in all directions. You know, the people who commute 800 miles. I hope it'll be page one, with bells and lights."

"How about that story on the 1966 Grinnell College yearbook? It came out twenty years late because the administration thought there was too much illicit stuff in it."

"Yeah, but that one's lost some altitude because the 'Today' show did it last week."

"Chandler's chasing down the shuttle report. Maybe he should go to Washington."

"We've got to follow Tsongas. The *Herald* says his cancer is 95 percent cured."

"That's not a State House story. Get a medical reporter."

"The anti-apartheid shanties are still up, and the Harvard commencement is tomorrow. Hey, if homeless people are
living in them, that's a Neighborhoods piece."

"The new education commissioner is being sworn in today. Photo enough?"

"Mehegan's doing the population explosion of raccoons
and possums."

"Oh, God. The urbanization of raccoons is well-tilled
turf. Sci-Tech did it a couple months ago, and it was old
then."

"What's a possum, anyway?"

"Cross between a raccoon and a rat?"

"Ugly damn things," someone says.

•   •   •

What a lousy start for a day, Ron Rosenberg thinks as he
picks up his phone in the business department. First he had to
bring his car in for a new muffler. And now the people at
Apple Computer are calling from California, saying that the
only way he can interview company president John Sculley is
to do it for fifteen minutes—right now. Now? He hasn't prepared any questions. He's still annoyed that he couldn't see
the guy last week when he was in California. And anyway he's
in a rotten mood because his story in today's paper about the
new products that Honeywell announced yesterday was drastically cut—slashed, he might say. And then he got a note
from an editor who thought the story was overplayed (it ran
on the front page of the Business section) because it didn't
appear at all in the *Times* or the *Herald* or the *Wall Street
Journal*.

Lemmings, Rosenberg thinks. But there's no time to
complain. He tells the Apple public relations person he'll call
back in five minutes. Remembering that he saw a story about
the company in the *Journal* this morning, he finds it, scans it,
and scribbles some notes. After racking his brain for the questions he'd planned to ask Sculley last week, he dials California at 10:45. As Sculley talks, Rosenberg types his words into

the terminal, pausing occasionally to jot more questions in the margins of the *Journal* story. He wants to be ready when Sculley stops for a breath.

After fifteen minutes the p.r. person breaks in to say that Rosenberg's time is running out. Five minutes later, Sculley says goodbye. It wasn't as good as a face-to-face interview, but Rosenberg is satisfied that Sculley's comments will fill some holes in the Apple story he's writing. The next question is, when is he writing it for? He's got a couple of smaller stories to do, and he figures Apple will probably be for Sunday. But just after he hangs up the phone, Steve Bailey, an assistant business editor, comes by. He wants Rosenberg to do his Gene Amdahl story for Sunday. Amdahl developed IBM's first major mainframe computer and later started two other companies. Rosenberg has done interviews for that story but hasn't transcribed the tapes. He hopes he can meet the deadline.

First, however, he's got to open the mail. The pile is especially staggering because he's been out of the office for a while. He attacks it in order of importance: Federal Express envelopes first, then the packages, which usually contain catalogues or books. Next he opens the envelopes that are either handwritten or typed without a mailing label. Meanwhile, the phone is ringing with the usual complement of p.r. people wanting him to look at their companies' latest products, attend a technical conference, or meet some corporate honcho who's passing through Boston. He feels like a lion tamer, wielding a telephone receiver instead of a chair to keep the roaring p.r. people at bay. Sometimes they don't even bother with the phone. One day a few months ago, a young woman in a white leotard materialized in the middle of the business department. She slapped a piece of plywood onto the floor and loudly began to tap dance on it while singing a jingle to promote advertising in the Yellow Pages. Few people even looked up.

Before he can start transcribing the Amdahl tape, Lincoln Millstein, the business editor, changes Rosenberg's course again. He wants the Apple story for Sunday. The company's recent change in command from Steven Jobs to Sculley is news, Millstein says; the story should run soon. True enough, Rosenberg agrees. Problem is, he'd really like to be doing something else entirely. A "cute page-one story" has grabbed his imagination and won't let go. It started when he heard that the Smithsonian was going to open a new computer museum, and that IBM was donating money and equipment to the project. Boston already has a computer museum, which is heavily supported by Digital Equipment Corp. Rosenberg can envision fierce competition for old components. Boston against Washington. Digital against IBM. Great stuff.

Without really intending to, he starts writing about the museum war. Soon he has forty-five lines, and they look good. He prints them out and takes them over to Bailey, who reads the page and delivers the advice Rosenberg expected: Cut it out and get working on Apple. The *Globe* spent big bucks to send you to California, Bailey says. Maybe you'd better get your priorities straight.

Rosenberg sheepishly agrees. As he returns to his desk, Bailey softens the blow. "The museum story is good," he says. "You ought to do it soon."

. . .

Patti Doten is loading Richard Baker's outstretched arms with computer printouts and photos. They are the raw materials from which Baker will design the front page of tomorrow's Living section.

Living, which contains the *Globe*'s features, is the only section of the paper that is drawn every day by a full-time designer. For the other sections, copy editors who specialize in layout decide where to place the stories and photos. In Living, where the stories break free from the traditional confines of news, the design can break free as well. A person in a photograph might thrust his arm beyond the usual image area of the page, or the type might undulate around irregular margins, mirroring the shape of a drawing.

Doten, one of two assistant Living editors, is filling in today for editor Mike Larkin. Larkin describes the philosophy of the Living section this way: "The world is full of interesting individuals and ideas that don't fall into the neat categories the other departments of the paper are compartmentalized into. Our job is to find and expose them." He and his assistants juggle calls from press agents, supervise staffing, serve as backboards for writers who want to bounce story ideas. All in all, Larkin says, it's a lot like coordinating a talk show. "I answer the phone thinking, 'Let's see who today's guest will be.' "

Like most newspaper feature sections, Living evolved from the old concept of "women's pages." In the 1960s, when surveys showed that readers wanted newspapers to help them cope with a complex world, feature sections shifted their focus from fashion and recipes to service pieces for everyone: how to raise happy kids, how to eat healthy, where to get the best buys on designer suits.

Some of that orientation lingers, but Larkin believes that the section must do more if it wants to provide "relief from the perception that newspapers never tell anyone anything good." As a result, the sixty-person department now produces more stories about people and ideas, written in styles ranging from newsy-with-a-twist to thoroughly offbeat. It's an approach inspired by the *Washington Post*'s Style section, the first to raise feature writing to a level even hard-boiled news reporters could appreciate. Many of the *Globe*'s news reporters, in fact, like to write for Living. It lets them write longer (something every reporter is always trying to do), and they can put a "spin" on a story that wouldn't be appropriate in the news pages.

Despite improvements in the image of feature writing, Larkin acknowledges he still hears some snickers in the daily news meetings when he mentions that a writer is doing a story on, say, lettuce spinners, for the Wednesday food page. "It's easy to denigrate feature writing as 'not serious,' " he says. Then, pulling out a paper at random, he adds, "But I bet a lot more people read the story about this guy who photographs celebrities than read the story on the state budget."

In addition to the Wednesday food pages, the Living department handles the Thursday Calendar tabloid, the Friday At Home pages, and the book reviews and TV section for the Sunday paper. The Living and Arts pages run every day. Sometimes they're separate pages; other days, like tomorrow, they run together under a "flag" that says "Living/Arts." Doten has given Baker copies of the three main stories for tomorrow: Nathan Cobb's American Pop piece on bowling banquets, a review of the latest Boston-based detective novel in the Spenser series, and a fashion piece about a brand of athletic shoes with a two-part lacing system. "Goofy," Doten says. She and Baker study the photo, which shows a shoe with a few rows of laces ending in a bow at the arch, and another set of laces ending in a bow in the usual place. The shoes are all the rage on the West Coast, apparently, and they're just moving into Boston.

The shoe and bowling stories have staff photos, and the book review has a head shot of Spenser author Robert Parker. Bowling's your lead, Doten tells Baker. The off-lead or second lead, the story that runs in the upper left-hand corner, won't be done until late tonight. The Boston Pops is premiering the fanfare that conductor John Williams has written for the upcoming Liberty Weekend festivities, and one of the regular part-timers will do a review. Baker will have to design the page with a "plug," a wire story that can go in that spot for the first and maybe second edition, then be pulled when the Pops review is ready to plug in. An editor will choose the plug; Baker just needs to leave space for it, keeping in mind that the plug won't have a photo but the Pops story will.

Baker likes to read all the stories before he lets visions of possible layouts start flashing through his mind. Already he can see one bowling photo he particularly likes, but there's no use getting excited about it until he knows whether it conveys the story's message. He takes the pile of stories and photos and heads downstairs to the design department, shaking his head over the funny shoes.

     •   •   •

His Excellency El Sayed Abdel Raouf El Reedy, Egyptian ambassador to the United States, looks like Marcello Mastroianni—or at least he does at this moment to Marty Nolan, who stayed up until 2:00 A.M. watching the Angels defeat the Yankees in Anaheim. Sure sign of pennant fever. Now it's 10:30, and Reedy is charming the group assembled in the private dining room of Affiliated Publications, the *Globe*'s parent company. In addition to Nolan, the editorial page editor, there's Alan Berger, one of the six editorial writers; Jack Driscoll, the executive editor; Kathy Tolbert, the foreign editor; and Victor Lewis, an assistant foreign editor.

Reedy and his press secretary have come to the *Globe* just to talk. Policy makers in government and industry often make appointments to meet with newspaper editorial boards, or with individual editorial writers. The president of the American Petroleum Institute, for example, came in to see editorial writer Bruce Davidson this morning. The visitors see the meetings as a chance to feel out current opinion, answer questions, and make sure that their version of events is heard. The journalists see the meetings as good background (although with visitors less experienced than Reedy, the sessions can border on propaganda), a source of ideas, and a reminder that it's real people out there whom they're writing about.

For an hour, Reedy and the *Globe* group discuss everything from Cairo traffic to Syrian politics to PLO leader Yasir Arafat's future. Reedy tells Nolan he has the highest respect for Bill Beecher, the *Globe*'s diplomatic correspondent. Nolan says he agrees; they worked together for six of Nolan's thirteen years in Washington. Meanwhile, Nolan is admiring the ambassador's relaxed Mediterranean air. The Egyptians, he thinks, are the Californians of the Mideast. Supremely laid back.

At one point Reedy refers to an Egyptian belief that cats have seven souls. Do Americans, he asks, have a similar theory?

"Yes," Nolan tells him. "Cats have nine lives."

"Ah," the ambassador says with a shrug. "We're more modest."

11:00 A.M.

Better to offend a million readers than confuse one.
—Marty Nolan, editorial page editor

"Not another word on Star Wars," Marty Nolan warns. Groans rise from the editorial writers sprawled on the couch and chairs in his office. "And nobody write about the Celtics yet."

"C'mon, nothing could jinx them now, not even Alan," Bruce Davidson says with a glance at Alan Berger.

An hour late because of the Egyptian ambassador, the editorial department is shifting into meeting mode. The writers are doing what comes naturally: building arguments. Nolan has slipped into his usual role as devil's advocate.

Viola Osgood says she's angry that Laval Wilson, superintendent of Boston schools, has refused to grant diplomas to fifty-one high school seniors who failed an eighth-grade reading test. She believes that the students are being penalized for the system's failures.

"With the dropout problem, you'd think he'd help the kids, not punish them," she says.

Michael Kenney suggests that the students be allowed to attend graduation ceremonies and receive a blank paper instead of a diploma.

"Would the system be doing them a favor by hosting a charade?" Nolan asks. Osgood glares at him. He quickly apologizes, calling his own views on education "archaic."

Like story conferences in the newsroom, editorial meetings can unleash strong opinions. Unlike reporters, however, editorial writers are free to present those opinions to the readers. And unlike reporters, editorial writers don't get bylines. They exercise their power anonymously, in the name of the paper as a whole.

68

It would be easier to run a newspaper without editorials. The opinions expressed in larger type below the masthead can cause advertisers to pull out, news sources to dry up, readers to cancel their subscriptions. A few newspaper editors have argued that editorials are obsolete. How, these detractors ask, can a paper justify telling its readers, in effect, "On forty-nine pages we're giving you well-balanced stories untainted by personal points of view, but on the fiftieth page we're going to smash objectivity to smithereens and trumpet our opinions all over the place"?

That argument has few disciples at the *Globe*. Objectivity, first of all, does not shine as brightly as it once did in the firmament of journalistic ideals. Thomas Winship, whose twenty-year editorship of the *Globe* ended in 1984 (his father had been editor for ten years before him), may have applied the first coat of tarnish in 1971, when he surprised a national editor's convention by railing against objectivity.

"Objectivity is such a marvelous trip for an editor," he said. "Each morning he swallows his little objectivity pill" and then lords his superiority over the young activist reporters who cluster around the water cooler spouting opinions about Ralph Nader and Hanoi. Those kids, Winship told his fellow editors, "are intellectually more honest than we are. They're not in the business to be stenographers, nor should they be."

Winship ended by advising the editors to "forget about these silly code words—*objectivity, advocate journalism*—and worry instead about fairness, credibility, and professionalism. Worry a little more about digging out more of the truth."

Fifteen years later, Washington reporter Tom Oliphant puts it more bluntly: "There's no such thing as objectivity, so there's no use wasting time striving for it." The dictionary, he points out, defines *objective* as "expressing reality as it is apart from personal reflections or feelings." How can a reporter, or anyone else, view the world without looking through the filter of his feelings? The most he can hope to do, Oliphant says, is recognize that those feelings affect his perceptions, then work to make his story fair anyway.

Another of the *Globe*'s Washington reporters, John Robinson, faced just such a test when he was covering a long congressional debate over aid to the Nicaraguan *contras*. During his research on the issue, which included a trip to Nicaragua with a Congressional delegation, he developed the conviction that "we should arm those *contras* to the teeth" (the opposite view, not that it mattered to him, from the one the paper was advocating in editorials). One day, in a moment of candor in the back of a cab, he admitted his opinion to someone. As soon as it was out, he added quickly, "But I'm sure no one could tell that from my stories."

Oliphant sees pure objectivity as "some kind of automaton state." Reporters strive instead for thoroughness and fairness, the same ideals for which editorial writers aim. The difference is that when editorial writers have finished examining all sides of an issue, they choose one. Readers do much the same thing, Nolan points out, as they go through the paper. A reader might oppose a government policy reported on page one, support a committee recommendation on page two, scoff at one side's argument in a debate story on page three.

When he turns to the editorial page, Nolan says, that reader should find something he can't find on TV or in his home computer: informed opinion. Ideally, in the words of publisher Bill Taylor, the reader will find "editorials that promote discussion and thought, and sometimes action." Taylor's name heads the list of *Globe* executives that runs each day above the editorials. Most days, however, he sees the editorials no sooner than the other 514,000 people who read the paper. He says that the editorial department is free to write whatever it wants, with only two rules: Be accurate, and don't surprise me. His translation of the second rule is this: "If it's not going to fit the corporate culture, let me know."

Although Taylor retains formal veto power over editorials, he says he's never used it. "We work it out," he says. "Ninety-nine times out of a hundred we can develop a consensus." The hundredth time is likely to involve an election in which editorial board members disagree on endorsing a candidate. "We had quite a go-round over McGovern in '72 and

Carter in '80," Taylor recalls with a weary smile. In the end, he says, the editorials "backed into" the endorsements, expressing reservations about both candidates in each race before recommending one.

Nolan has his own two rules of editorial writing—be clear, and have a point—but he's well aware of Taylor's "no surprises" dictum (as is the newsroom, which has been keeping Taylor informed of the government's objections to the Pelton story). "Reading every single editorial would not be a good use of his talents and time," Nolan says of the publisher. "But I do show him some in advance that I think are appropriate. On the rest he just has to trust me, and I in turn have to trust the writers."

The department has six editorial writers in addition to Nolan and deputy editor Loretta McLaughlin. Material for the op-ed page—the page opposite the editorial page, where views other than the paper's official ones are expressed—comes from staff columnists and freelancers. Staff columnists Ellen Goodman, Bob Turner, and M. R. Montgomery write twice a week. They "write what they want and are very good writers and really don't need to be edited at all," says Thomas Gagen, who coordinates the op-ed page. Columnists David Nyhan and William V. Shannon write once a week, and others write less regularly.

In addition, Gagen can choose from a raft of syndicated material that comes over the wires—Mary McGrory and Art Buchwald are his most consistent choices from this crew—as well as columns, both solicited and unsolicited, that come in from readers and self-styled experts on various subjects. When reading unfamiliar contributors, Gagen asks himself two main questions: How well does this person write, and how much does he know about his subject? "If the writer doesn't have some expertise on Star Wars," he says, "why should the reader listen to his opinion?"

Occasionally an unknown writer will send in a lighthearted piece that Gagen can use to balance a "heavy" page, or a personal essay on a subject—dealing with teenagers, for example—with which he believes many readers will identify. He tries always to think of the page as a whole, to make sure that its parts complement one another. This morning's op-ed page, for example, included two columns about television coverage of the U.S. Senate, which began two days ago. Bob Healy, an associate editor who was Steve Kurkjian's predecessor as Washington bureau chief, wrote about his early days covering the Senate, when it was considered "a place for giants." He told tales of the giants, including one in which Senate majority leader Lyndon Johnson summoned Healy when Healy returned from a trip with John Kennedy. After a few minutes of small talk, Johnson lunged out of his chair, grabbed Healy, and said, "You don't think that skinny little guy is going to be president, do you?"

Healy's column contended that television will change the Senate forever; viewers will realize "that there never were any giants in the first place." Just below it, Gagen ran a column by McGrory, who maintained that television won't change the Senate at all. "The Senate is always transfixed by its own image," she wrote, "and being televised deepens its self-absorption." The final word on the subject came from staff cartoonist Paul Szep, whose drawing ran at the top of the editorial page. It showed a woman in a bathrobe, toothbrush in hand, shaking her husband, who had fallen asleep in front of the television. "Wake up, dear," she said. "The Senate coverage is over."

Gagen already has a pretty good idea what he wants to do with tomorrow's op-ed page. He's planning a three-part package on terrorism's effects on European travel: a cartoon by syndicated cartoonist Pat Oliphant, plus columns by Goodman and Ronald Israel, a Newton resident who recently went to Europe and West Africa against the advice of family and friends. In addition, Gagen has a funny piece about spies by Buchwald, and Turner and Nyhan have columns due. Nyhan is writing about candidate Royall Switzler's admission that he lied about his military record, and staff cartoonist Dan Wasserman plans to expound on the same subject.

Wasserman, in fact, is drawing right now, sitting quietly amid the editorial writers as the meeting bounces from topic to topic. How will tax reform affect the Columbia Point housing development across the street? What's really going on at Westfield State College? A front-page story today reported that the college paid a student a $10,000 settlement after he charged that a college official had sexually assaulted him. The matter never went to court, and reporters haven't yet discovered who authorized the payment. A lot more dirt will come out on that one, the editorial writers agree. "It doesn't give me great confidence in the Board of Regents," Nolan says.

From there the talk turns to traffic, the Supreme Court, foreign affairs, and politics at all levels. Nolan wants to write about the significance of an Alan Cranston–Ed Zschau Senate race in California. McLaughlin points out that tomorrow marks the fifth anniversary of the day that the Centers for Disease Control noted the outbreak of a mysterious illness. The illness turned out to be AIDS, and McLaughlin thinks that the anniversary provides a good occasion to castigate the Reagan administration for not doing enough to fight the disease.

Although Nolan won't choose tomorrow's editorials until later this afternoon, the AIDS piece sounds timely. It's a contentious issue, just the type he wants the page to address. If the editorial makes people angry, so be it. "Everybody's in favor of sunshine and against Dutch elm disease," he says, "but that doesn't mean we should restrict ourselves to those topics."

Interesting as he now finds the job, Nolan resisted taking over the editorial page for a long time. He covered the White House, Congress, and the State Department during his years as a Washington reporter, and he was hooked on the action. "How can I write editorials?" he asked when the offers came. "I never read them." When he gave Taylor that answer one day in 1981, the publisher surprised him. "That's exactly why you're the right man for the job," he told Nolan. "You'll bring a fresh approach."

Those words, plus a promise of autonomy, were enough to start Nolan packing for Boston. As editor of the editorial page, he would answer only to Taylor. Until then, the paper's editor had been in charge of both the news and editorial departments—a setup that created a potential for manipulation, though none had been alleged. "I suppose a different person than [Tom] Winship could have been ordering news stories with one hand, and editorials to support them with the other," says Jack Driscoll—who, as Nolan once did, says he doesn't read the editorials. ("What I mean," Driscoll explains, "is that the paper's editorial position is irrelevant to me.")

Driscoll says that under the old editorial department setup, "there could have been abuses, and maybe there were some problems, but they were never intentional." Since the change, the department has remained so thoroughly removed from the sometimes fractious newsroom interactions that some staff people have taken to calling it Switzerland.

After twenty years of squelching his opinions as a reporter, Nolan found the transition to editorial writing more difficult than he'd expected. He wasn't one of those reporters who insist that their opinion-forming generators have rusted shut from disuse ("People who tell you they don't have opinions are lying," he says), but neither was he the type whose long-dormant judgments burst forth at the flick of a switch.

"This job has a news sense to it," he says. "We try to stay on top of things. Still, the change took me a while. I'd say, 'Gee, I feel very strongly about this subject; maybe I shouldn't write about it.' Then I'd say, 'Ha! No, now I *should* write about it.' "

For the last five years, Nolan and his editorial troops have mustered daily to battle the great enemy: wishywashiness. Ideology is negotiable, he tells the writers; clarity is not. When someone proposes that the paper address a particular subject, Nolan's response is always the same: "What should we *say* about it?" (When someone proposes an editorial he doesn't consider worthwhile, his response is more low key. "No rush," he says, and the writer gets the message.) He aims for editorials that represent both sides fairly, but that very clearly choose one.

"I never want to see people scratching their heads and saying, 'What's the *Globe* mean here?' " he says. "That's when we've failed. And it happens. We're trying to reduce that."

• • •

Wow. This is Dick Lehr's first visit to the Washington bureau's new offices, and he's impressed. The décor might be considered ordinary at a high-powered law firm, but by newsroom standards it's practically palatial. Lehr, a general assignment reporter, flew in from Boston this morning to work on a project on political asylum. He took a cab to Pennsylvania Avenue and walked through a modern ground-floor shopping complex to reach a center core of mirrored elevators. Whisked to the third floor, he stepped off onto a quiet expanse of pink and gray carpeting and walked down the silent beige-walled hall, past the offices of various news organizations and columnists.

Inside Suite 3800, Lehr noticed the brass coat tree, the framed pastel flower print from the Museum of Fine Arts, the quiet conference room, and, most impressive of all, the individual offices for each writer (okay, so the front wall is a just a partition; the writers still have storage space and privacy undreamed of in Boston). In the waiting area was a much more characteristic sight: Someone had taped a color picture of President Reagan's face over the switchplate, and the switch protruded through the president's nose.

Steve Kurkjian calls Washington the pinnacle of bureaus. It's the place to which most political reporters, and quite a few on other beats, aspire, and the *Globe* offers only nine chances to get there. John Robinson, who arrived from Boston less than a year ago, describes the current Washington crew as "a few seasoned reporters and all these puppies." All nine members of the bureau have considerable reporting experience, but five of them haven't been in "the District" long.

Robinson did not follow the traditional City Hall/State House route to Washington. In Boston he was at various times a business editor, a crime reporter, an editorial writer and, most unorthodox of all, a society reporter ("wonderful time, great parties"). His present assignment, covering the New England congressional delegation, is his first try at politics. He respects the *Globe* management for ignoring the usual protocols and sending him to Washington. The demands of government coverage are so varied, he says, that the paper shouldn't limit itself to one kind of person. Nevertheless, he realizes that the bureau's new makeup could pose dangers for the *Globe*. "We're green," Robinson says. "We could fail, and we could fail big." Kurkjian, who took over in January as bureau chief, isn't worried.

Each Washington reporter has tales to tell about getting to know his beat. Their impressions of the governmental treadmill vary widely, but woven through all the stories are two common threads: a sort of awe-in-spite-of-itself at hobnobbing with important people, and a pronounced frustration that the *Globe* is not a more visible force in Washington. "People don't get the *Globe* in the morning down here, and this is a news-hungry town," Kurkjian says. "Our reporters have broken great stories that would be page one in every paper in the country, but if the wires don't pick them up, nobody here ever knows." The *Globe* carries a lot of clout among the New England congressional delegation, however, and Kurkjian likes to point out that syndicated columnist David Broder once called the *Globe*'s Washington bureau "pound for pound" the best in the city.

Both the awe and the frustration of Washington work were evident on one recent day when reporter Adam Pertman roamed his usual beat, the Capitol. As the press corps filed into House Speaker Tip O'Neill's office for the morning briefing, a New York reporter good-naturedly teased Pertman about writing for "a second-rate New England newspaper." No, he joked back, "it's a first-rate New England newspaper; it's a second-rate *national* newspaper." Later, as Pertman walked through the halls near the Senate, Robert Dole passed by and greeted him. "It really is a kick when the majority leader knows your name," Pertman said afterward. "I mean, who the hell am I?"

John Robinson got much the same kick when he arrived in Washington and called to request meetings with the congressmen and senators from New England. They all responded, and soon he found himself drinking beer with

Senator Edward Kennedy and eating breakfast with some of the others. "All of a sudden these guys I see in the newspaper are sitting there telling me inside stuff—or at least what seemed to me like inside stuff," he recalls. "I've got to admit it was exciting."

At first Robinson was surprised at how easy it was to plug in to the network of Washington happenings. Having met the congressmen helped, and he kept bumping into college friends who were working as lobbyists and press secretaries. Then he realized that he had peeled back only the outermost layer. Beneath it lay a tight web, intricately woven. "It's there for the exercise of power, not for reporters," he says, "and it's where the real action takes place." He decided that Washington is the opposite of the way he sees Boston, where a nearly impenetrable exterior conceals a warm interior.

The most extreme stories of acclimation to Washington come from Susan Trausch, who moved to the bureau in 1982 to "do features and float around." After seven years of writing business stories and a humor column for the *Globe* in Boston, it didn't take her long to form an opinion of Washington. In its shortest version, that opinion goes like this: "This town is nuts, absolutely mad." The longer version involves words like *warped* and *weird* and *sick*. What she saw in Washington seemed alternately so infuriating and so ridiculous that she took time off to mold her observations into a book called *It Came from the Swamp: Your Federal Government at Work*. One reviewer said the book was particularly good at describing "the earnest, goodhearted lightweights who snooze in most of the chairs in all three branches of our government."

When Trausch talks about the absurdity of official Washington, she often mentions the displays of craziness that take place on the steps of the Capitol. In the book she describes what she saw there one spring day in 1985:

> The prime minister of Turkey was being ushered in to address a joint session of Congress as anti-Turkish demonstrators marched with signs; as a high school band from Illinois played "God Bless America"; as students and teachers posed with their representatives; as a religious

fanatic shouted that somebody, presumably his congress-
man, was killing God; and as a marketing team from
American Cyanamid stood holding huge color photographs of cockroaches to promote a new insecticide while
Rep. Silvio Conte jumped up and down in an extermina-
tor suit shouting, "Squash one for the Gipper!" because
the product was being manufactured in his district.

In person, Trausch's stories center on the chill she felt
when she arrived in Washington. "I never expected the wall of
resistance I encountered here," she says. She remembers, for
example, wanting to do a feature about the people who sit all
day addressing the White House Christmas cards. "I called up
all hot about the idea, and what I got was a bucket of cold
water over the phone. Some automaton told me, 'But there's
no press release on that.' " She remembers closed-door hearings where the sign on the door said "Do Not Enter," but
insiders—the only ones who could find the room because of
the building's strange numbering system—knew they could
go in. "I think they close the door to make people interested,"
she says. "If they held hearings outside on the Mall, everyone
would realize how boring they are."

Trausch spent fifteen months as a beat reporter, a member of the pack, on Capitol Hill. "It was just death as a
writer," she says. "The president burps, and everybody reacts." Pertman, who has the job now, says that the Hill is "a
great place to work, with a really terrific bunch of people."
For him the bad times come when there's too much to cover,
or on those rare days when so little is happening that he paces
around the Capitol, compulsively checking each place where
he might have missed a story and crashing into other nervous
reporters pacing the same circuit.

Trausch sees her mission now as writing stories that go
beyond "The State Department said today . . ." The other
Washington writers are trying to do that, too, but Trausch
insists that she will write a news story only if someone chains
her to her terminal. "I just try to come at things like a normal
person—like somebody who just got off the bus from Dubuque," she says.

Dubuque is a popular metaphor in the bureau. Robinson sees his job as trying to balance national news with news important to New England. "I don't want to get too parochial," he says, "but at the same time if I didn't pay attention to the parochial, I'd lose readers. They might as well be reading the *Dubuque Times*." In his eight months in Washington, Robinson has come up against a paradox faced by hundreds of political writers before him: Politics is exciting, but capturing that excitement in a news story is difficult. "There's a certain way to write political stories, and it undermines the vigor," he says. "I want to present the information to readers as if they were here. The people down here are spending our money, making decisions that affect our lives."

Part of the problem, according to White House correspondent Walter Robinson (known as Robby, and no relation to John), is that the daily routine is so time-consuming, and so numbing, that it can sap a writer's energy for tackling more enterprising projects. Robinson enjoyed covering City Hall and the State House in Boston, and, like Pertman, he found covering Capitol Hill a lot of fun. He's less enthusiastic about the White House.

"This job is the most prestigious, but it's probably the least desired because it's so restrictive," he says. "The Reagan administration spoon-feeds us in small, unnourishing doses a couple times a day. The trick is to get behind the veil." That was easier to do during Reagan's first term, Robinson says, when power struggles among James Baker, Michael Deaver, and Ed Meese left cracks through which information could seep. Now, in the second term, many of those cracks have been sealed. If the administration wants to leak something, it turns to the *Times* or the *Post* or the networks. "The rest of us just have to hustle," Robinson says.

On the bright side, institutions in Washington go out of their way to make routine assignments easier for reporters. When the White House reporters show up at Andrews Air Force Base to follow the president on a speech-making trip, advance copies of the speech are waiting for them. Most of the reporters sit with portable computers in their laps and write their stories on the plane as they fly to the president's

79

destination. Within twenty minutes after Reagan delivers the speech, the reporters are given an "as said" copy. They check it to make sure the quotes they chose haven't changed, add some color from the scene, and they're done. "Some days you feel like a stenographer," Robinson says.

Following the president has its grim side, which Robinson labels "the body-watch mentality." Reporters accompany the president everywhere, even to appearances that promise to be boring. Something unexpectedly interesting might happen, but more to the point is the possibility that something terrible might happen. Robinson notes that the television networks send out two crews with Reagan, so that one camera is always trained on him. Just in case.

Covering the White House can be frustrating. Although everyone claims to recognize that the *Globe* can't do everything the bigger papers do, Robinson can't shake the feeling (encouraged by some of the editors, he thinks) that he ought to be trying to match the *Times* and the *Post* and the wires. The big guns in Dorchester say the Washington people shouldn't feel guilty if the paper has to run a wire story out of Washington. Kurkjian agrees, but in the next breath he says, "Just because the *Globe* pays good money for the wire doesn't mean we like them to use it."

All in all, in Robinson's view, the job of White House correspondent is overrated. Even so, he's happy in Washington. "I love covering politics and government," he says. "I can't think of any better life." Working on the Ronald Pelton story for the last two weeks has been especially interesting, both because the information is so intriguing and because Robinson himself was an intelligence officer in the Army. But he has not, not even for a moment, enjoyed dealing with the government over the secrecy issue.

Of the three *Globe* writers who have been meeting with the National Security Agency, Robinson has felt the most frustrated by the sessions. He understands the need for caution—revealing certain intelligence data, he knows, could cost an agent his life—and he says he went to the first meeting with high hopes. But this morning, as he and Fred Kaplan sit reviewing the situation and waiting for Kurkjian to call from

Boston, the phrase "entirely unproductive" keeps coming to mind.

The government had said it would help reporters decide which information about Pelton's alleged spying was safe to print, and Kurkjian maintains that he got some answers on that score through "telepathy." Robinson, however, believes that the government people were no help at all. They wouldn't specify which information would be harmful and why; they just kept insisting that nothing should be printed. Though the officials were unfailingly polite, Robinson felt an implicit threat every time they brought up the 1950 law restricting what the media may publish about communications intelligence. The height of absurdity, in his opinion, came when one of the government officials suggested that if the *Globe* printed anything about the intelligence operations Pelton was charged with compromising, the paper could damage the chances for a new superpower summit and arms reduction agreement.

Robinson says he was truly disappointed that the government officials wouldn't deal with the issue on merits. The more he thinks about it, the more he thinks they weren't worried about national security so much as protecting their own image. He can certainly see why they wouldn't want to spread the word that "we're bumping around Soviet harbors in subs in a risky operation with an uncertain payoff."

Kaplan wasn't wild about the government's attitude, either, but he's more understated about expressing his feelings. "They didn't really come through on their promise," he says. "They didn't discuss how to minimize the damage. They just said over and over, 'Don't print.' " At first, he says, he felt a sort of thrill to be dealing with such sensitive information and such important people. But the thrill was quickly "overwhelmed by skepticism and disgust with myself" at having to clear the story in advance.

Defense is an uncommon beat, and Kaplan took an uncommon route to the *Globe*. He wrote his first freelance story on defense in 1976, shortly before he began graduate studies in political science at MIT. In 1978 he became a defense policy aide to Representative Les Aspin. He stayed until 1980

81

when, at age twenty-six, he signed a contract to write a book on defense called *The Wizards of Armageddon*. In November 1981, while he was working on the book, a *Globe* editor who remembered his earlier stories called and asked Kaplan if he would write occasionally on defense for the Sunday paper. With his money supply dwindling, Kaplan said yes. The book came out in 1983, Kaplan kept writing for the *Globe*, and in July 1984 he joined the Washington bureau—without ever having worked in Boston or, in fact, ever having worked for a newspaper. He remembers it as a double trauma: That summer he not only turned thirty but also started working full-time again.

Kaplan did most of the reporting on the Pelton story, and Robinson did most of the writing. Both are deliberately vague about where the information came from. Kaplan describes his part this way: "You look around, you call people, you have chance meetings with people who know a little about one part of it, you get glimmerings second- and third-hand." As always, he got caught up in the excitement of intensely pursuing, and then finding, information so few people knew. He's modest, however, even about that. "We're certainly not the only people in town to get this information," he says. "I just hope we print more of it."

Because Kaplan has a doctor's appointment this afternoon, he and Robinson are talking about the Pelton story now, trying to anticipate any new issues Boston or the NSA might raise. They reassure each other for the thousandth time that the meetings with the government were unavoidable; no newspaper would have just forged ahead.

Dick Lehr, the reporter visiting from Boston, talks with them long enough to know there's a big story in the works. Then he gets busy settling in, making some calls before he heads out on the interviews he's scheduled for his own story. As another reporter walks in, Lehr looks up, and they both laugh. It's Peter Mancusi, who sits not far from Lehr in Boston, arriving to work on a Sunday story on the Supreme Court. Neither knew that the other was coming to Washington.

●   ●   ●

A terrible thing happened to Paul Szep last week. He and some other cartoonists were invited to the White House, and during lunch Szep realized that no matter how hard he tried, he couldn't dislike Ronald Reagan. He felt the way Joan Rivers must have felt when Elizabeth Taylor lost weight: What's there to make fun of now?

"These are not great times for cartoonists," Szep muses as he sits, sketching absent-mindedly, in one of the two barber's chairs in his office. He is wearing striped pants with cuffs, and his hair tumbles in tight curls over the collar of his purple polo shirt. "You can't draw Reagan as a mean-zo, and [Massachusetts Governor Michael] Dukakis and [Boston Mayor Raymond] Flynn are both trying to do a good job every day. But for a cartoonist, the ideal is not to like these people."

He brightens as he remembers better days. Richard Nixon was a picnic, "the quintessential cartoon character." Ed King, Dukakis's predecessor as governor, was fun to lampoon, and Jimmy Carter was good because he was "kind of a squirrely guy." Of course, none of their characteristics were as extreme as Szep portrayed them, but cartoonists have a license to embellish. They also have, in Szep's opinion, a license to go after errant politicians and institutions on the reader's behalf. A reader who's furious about his taxes might feel helpless in the face of the IRS, but at least he can get a vicarious thrill from a cartoon that portrays the agency as a bunch of bumblers.

Szep was the *Globe*'s first staff cartoonist, an Ontario College of Art graduate hired in the late '60s with one year of newspaper experience. For years he did five cartoons a week, then four, winning two Pulitzer Prizes in the process. Now he draws three cartoons a week for the paper and one for a television show. (Like many newspapers, the *Globe* has forged an uneasy alliance with television. In addition to Szep, columnist Mike Barnicle and sportswriter Will McDonough appear regularly on local magazine shows, and *Globe* political reporters make occasional appearances on public television's news analysis shows, which Tom Oliphant labels "locker room talk.") On the days Szep doesn't draw, the paper usually runs a cartoon from Dan Wasserman, who works at the *Globe* but also draws for other newspapers through the Los Angeles Times Syndicate. Sometimes the *Globe* also runs cartoons by other syndicated cartoonists whose work comes in the mail.

Like an editorial writer, a cartoonist must have a clear point of view. The cartoonist's point, however, must be easily conveyed in pictures and must remain clear even when reduced to a five- by six-inch block. Aside from reading six newspapers a day, Szep isn't sure what he does that makes cartoons happen. "If I could define it, it would be easier," he says. For as long as he can remember, he has thought in pictures, not words. Other people remember witty lines and good quotes; he remembers metaphors and analogies that form pictures in his mind. As soon as he heard about the Hands Across America fund-raising event for hunger, for example, he started picturing a different kind of chain. That idea became a cartoon a few days ago, when he drew a chain of weapons encircling the globe and called it Arms Across the World.

Szep is continually surprised that he receives fan mail. People usually write to a newspaper only when they're angry, but he gets complimentary letters, too. On the other hand, a solitary picket still marches in front of the *Globe* every Saturday, protesting a cartoon Szep did a few years ago that involved a leprechaun and the Irish Republican Army. Though he doesn't set out to upset people, he's glad for evidence that readers are paying attention.

Now Szep is sitting in the barber's chair, brainstorming. Because Wasserman is doing tomorrow's cartoon, Szep is free to think about Friday. He's not feeling particularly outraged about anything, and he's not ready to fall on back on what he calls a "*New Yorker*-type cartoon"—a timeless drawing about some social issue. With any luck, he'll be able to forget politics and have fun with a cartoon of Celtics star Larry Bird.

· · ·

If this were a writing day, Ellen Goodman would be checking her watch to see if she could meet her self-imposed quota:

84

twenty-five typewritten lines before lunch. But it's Wednesday, the plateau between her two writing days, and her column for tomorrow is done. She's out of the office, proudly watching her daughter's high school graduation, but in a way she's still working. A columnist is always working, she says; anything she sees or hears could point her down the trail of another seventy-five-line thought.

When people talk about the *Globe's* best writers, Ellen Goodman's name always turns up near the top of the list. Jack Driscoll, whose office looks out on a highway billboard of Goodman's face ("Ellen Goodman writes with style, with substance, without peer, for the *Globe*," the billboard reads), says the paper had always had some good writers, but in the 1960s it hired a cast of stars, led by Goodman. She was twenty-six then, a reporter from Detroit. In 1971, four years after she arrived, she ventured into column writing once a week. By 1974 she was a full-time columnist, and two years later her column was syndicated across the country.

Goodman believes that her column found an audience because she challenged the assumption that people carefully separate their public and private lives. "I really do think we all get up in the morning and worry about our weight and nuclear war and what's in the freezer and Nicaragua," she says. Seeing the continuity among those thoughts enabled her to write about both politics and issues of home and family. As a result, some editors weren't quite sure what to do with her; about a quarter of the papers that run Goodman's column put it somewhere other than the op-ed page. But for the papers that saw it as editorial material, the column brought subjects to the page that hadn't been there before. Although Goodman is proud of that accomplishment, she doesn't consider it hers alone. "If I hadn't done it, somebody else would have," she says. "It was coming."

In a largely impersonal world and a largely impersonal newspaper, a columnist is personal. Readers don't read columns; they read columnists. They want to know what that particular columnist thinks, and how he or she reached that conclusion. For this reason, Goodman says, a columnist is always putting herself on the line. "Everybody has an opinion on what I'm writing about, but that doesn't mean they've thought out all the implications," she says. "I have to get the information together. Maybe my first reaction to something is 'yuck' or 'weird.' My job is to figure out *why* yuck, *why* weird, and to do it within constraints of time and space."

Her basic text is the newspaper, the one common ground most of her readers share. From that starting point she may take off in any direction, linking a news item to something she overheard in the supermarket, something that happened to her, something she read. Her windowless, unadorned office is filled with articles ripped and clipped from magazines and newspapers, none of which she can find when she needs them. She believes her readers expect her to write about certain subjects, chiefly so-called "women's issues." Aside from that expectation, however, she feels free to write about whatever interests her.

People often tell her, "You wrote just what I was thinking." What they really mean, Goodman believes, is "You wrote just what I was thinking *about*." If a column works, it clarifies the thought process, both for the readers and for herself. If it works, people who disagree with her conclusion should still be able to see that she understands their thinking. In twelve years of column writing, her thinking has had to change along with the issues. To illustrate, she describes the stages through which one fictitious member of the women's movement has passed. Stage 1: My husband won't let me work. Stage 2: I'm working, but he won't help with the housework. Stage 3: He won't do 50 percent of the housework. Stage 4: He can't get parental leave to take a turn with our child.

In tomorrow's column, Goodman's focus is more political. She's written about the response to Americans' terrorism-induced fears of traveling abroad. It seems to her that while British hotels and airlines are trying to lure American visitors through advertising, Britons in general—and to some degree, Europeans in general—are trying to make Americans feel guilty for fearing terrorism. Editorial writers abroad are calling Americans wimps and chickens. Goodman understands the feeling; no one likes to hear that other people are afraid to visit the place where he lives. But she resents the implication that taking a non-European vacation is somehow disloyal. "As tourists from the United States," she wrote yesterday, "we are not required to stand tall for America beside the Eiffel Tower, nor do we have to make a political statement out of a plane ticket."

Not until the last quarter of the column did she acknowledge that she is planning a trip to France in the fall. Including this tidbit without stressing it is typical of her style. Though she believes people identify with columnists—"Hey, Ellen Goodman can't get a plumber to make house calls, either"— she has no illusions that readers want to hear every detail of her life. Thus, while she sometimes uses her daughter's experiences in a column to illustrate a point about young people, she rarely refers to her daughter by name or gives other information about her. "I use my experience only if it connects with other people's," she says. "Whose personal life is that interesting?"

. . .

The newsroom has burrowed into the day's routine. Jack Driscoll, Tom Mulvoy, and the two deputy managing editors, Helen Donovan and Al Larkin, are filling one another in on how tomorrow's paper is shaping up. David Mehegan, back from his interview about raccoons, is busily phoning real estate agents, searching for house hunters who have been forced to look far from Boston. Steve Marantz is in Attleboro interviewing the owner of the Roger Williams Mint, which, he noticed in a wire story yesterday, is making the new New York City subway tokens.

Ray Richard is trying to get permission to talk with some maximum-security prison inmates who are scheduled to receive degrees Saturday from Boston University. Business reporter Charles Radin, who spent the morning wallowing in financial statements at the state division of insurance, is listening as Paul Volcker and other world financial leaders brief reporters on the morning session at the International Monetary Conference. Volcker is making Radin nervous; he seems to be implying something without quite saying it, and Radin's not sure what.

Larry Tye is jogging along the ocean, trying not to think about tooth implants. Farther north, Ellen Bartlett is glaring at the ocean. She was supposed to be doing interviews on Petit Manan Island, twenty miles off Bar Harbor, Maine, but the weather has grounded her. The story sounds like a good one: The U.S. Fish and Wildlife Service is poisoning gulls on the island in order to help another bird species, the tern. Bartlett, one of four reporters who cover northern New England from a bureau in Concord, New Hampshire, calls her editor to ask about alternate assignments.

David Chandler has spent the morning calling the members of the presidential commission investigating the space shuttle *Challenger* explosion. Their report, scheduled for release Monday, has been extensively leaked already, but he wants direct information. The families of the shuttle crew are in Washington today to be briefed on the report. Chandler's editor, Nils Bruzelius, suggests that he call the families after the briefing to see what they'll say about the report. Chandler gets their numbers from another reporter who covered the recovery of the shuttle's crew cabin. But when he calls the presidential commission's office, he is read a statement saying that the families have agreed not to answer questions about the report. The statement asks the press to respect the families' privacy.

Chandler tells Bruzelius, who confers with other editors and returns with a verdict: Try reaching the families when they return from Washington, but don't ask them specifics about the report. Just see what kind of reactions they have to the briefing. Chandler isn't sure what he thinks of that idea— not that he really has a choice—but he's soon distracted from it. Bruzelius and Royal Ford, the national editor, have decided that he should fly to Washington tomorrow and stay until the *Challenger* report is released Monday. That way he can coordinate the story better with Walter Robinson and Fred Kaplan, who have been working on it down there.

Chandler makes reservations to fly out of Boston tomorrow morning. Then, just as he's starting to worry about the families again, a story moving on the wire reshapes his afternoon. Datelined Huntsville, Alabama, the story begins: "William Lucas, director of the NASA facility that supervises the rockets blamed for the explosion of the space shuttle Challenger, said today he will retire effective next month in the latest of a string of personnel changes stemming from the accident." As soon as he reads it, Chandler is on the phone, calling NASA spokesmen and commission members for comment. At least he can be sure of one byline tomorrow.

• • •

Two days at the Crossroads squatter camp—two days awash in rain and mud, surrounded by burned-out buildings and burned-out lives—have left Phillip Van Niekerk feeling drained. Two groups had fought for control of the camp, long a symbol of resistance for black South Africans, and the more politically radical group had lost. But as always in South Africa, there is more to the story than that. Opponents of the government say it encouraged the violence because it wanted to move the people of Crossroads to a camp farther from Cape Town; the law severely limits blacks' movements in and near cities. For years the Crossroads squatters were united in their opposition to this government plan. Then, the critics contend, one of the camp's leaders allied himself with the government, and in the last week he and his followers have helped drive 30,000 people from the fringes of Crossroads. In return, these critics maintain, the group remaining at the camp was promised tarred roads, schools, clinics, and other improvements.

Van Niekerk, a South African who writes part-time for the *Globe*, came to Cape Town from Johannesburg to see for himself. He found that most of the squatters who were driven from Crossroads by fires and fighting had refused to go to the official resettlement camp. The camp, Khayelitsha, is thirty miles from Cape Town, ten miles farther than Crossroads. Instead, they took shelter in emergency tents in the nearest township. Storms moved in to compound their misery, and some people spent entire nights standing, trying to light fires between downpours. They told him that the police had done nothing as they were beaten and forced from their homes.

89

"I think there is no God for the black people," one woman who had fled Crossroads told Van Niekerk yesterday. "Otherwise, why would He make us suffer like this?"

Van Niekerk wrote a story for this morning's paper, and today he returned to the camps, trying to understand. Now, as he arrives exhausted at his room in Cape Town, the telephone is ringing. It's a journalist friend, calling from Parliament to tell him that the government had just banned all meetings to commemorate the June 1976 Soweto uprisings. Countrywide protest meetings and a general strike have already been planned to mark the anniversary of the uprisings, in which hundreds of blacks died. The government's existing ban on outdoor meetings is regularly defied, but this ban extends to indoor meetings as well.

Calling around, Van Niekerk learns that a newly formed coalition of civil rights groups is holding a news conference to protest the ban. Before he leaves, he phones Kathy Tolbert, the foreign editor, in Boston. It's nearly noon there, approaching 7:00 P.M. in Cape Town. She agrees that the story is important and tells him to go ahead. He has seven hours until the *Globe*'s deadline, but he knows he'll never stay awake that long. He'll go to the news conference, get as many comments as he can from other people, and sketch the story out before he dictates to Boston. It should be an easy story to write; the news is clear.

"Easy" is a relative term in South Africa, which Van Niekerk in his formal, understated way calls "quite a hostile environment for reporters." The government's restrictions on the press are so sweeping that much of what happens cannot technically be reported. Each time a reporter writes a story, he is deciding whether to break the law. It's not something Van Niekerk likes to talk about, but he does say that he's never gotten into trouble over anything he's written for the *Globe*.

During the Soweto uprisings ten years ago, he was a college student. Eventually he wound up at the *Rand Daily Mail* as a political reporter, and when the *Mail* closed last year, a friend told him that the *Globe* might be looking for a correspondent. Now, despite the restrictions and the frustrations, he finds the job exciting. Maybe *exciting* isn't quite the right word, he says, but "professionally, this is a fascinating place to be." So much is happening, and it's so important that the world know about it. Getting around the rules is a daily challenge.

Still, no story is really easy here. This is his country, and he's torn by what he sees it becoming. "Of course I have emotions about what's happening," he says. "It's impossible not to have feelings, but the first lesson one learns is to separate those feelings from the job." When people ask him why he stays in South Africa, Van Niekerk has a simple response. "I'm South African," he says. "To leave would be extremely difficult."

Noon

Do marshmallows grow on trees, or are they made of plastic?

—a caller to the *Globe* switchboard

Hockey Fan has a problem. She wants to make a Paddington Bear for her new grandchild, but she can't find a pattern. Does anybody out there know where she can buy one?

Irene Keegan is typing Hockey Fan's plea into the computer. In a few days it will appear in Confidential Chat, the 102-year-old forum in which *Globe* readers, shielded by pen names, share their secrets. Between fifty and one hundred "Chatters" write in each day, seeking or offering recipes, patterns, and advice on personal problems. In this morning's column, Undercover Me wanted to know what to do about the spidery veins in her legs; she's tired of hiding them under jeans all summer. Cape Cod Gal proposed a detailed seven-point plan for The Chaos Kid, who had written that her messy home was impossible to clean. Nothing is impossible, Cape Cod Gal assured the Kid: "All you need is a little self-discipline and plastic garbage bags."

Keegan and Marjorie McManus maintain the confidential files that list the real names and addresses of 100,000 Chatters. Only they know the true identity of Cape Cod Gal and The Chaos Kid—and Prefix and Maniac Baby and Sir Galahad, who writes in Elizabethan prose. Only they know the real name of Cheating Heart, who was swamped with letters when he begged for advice on how to untangle himself from an extramarital affair. A few writers told him to forget the untangling and enjoy a good thing while he had it. One letter that said the opposite—and asked such questions as "Did you really think I didn't know what was going on?"—was signed "Your Wife."

A newspaper talks to its readers, and Confidential Chat is one of many ways that readers talk back to the *Globe*. Each week about 400 people also write letters to the editor, and sixty more call or write ombudsman Bob Kierstead, the reader representative. Readers call the sports department to ask about scores and trivia, call Living to ask what color stockings to wear with a denim skirt, call the switchboard to ask how to rid their homes of mice. They call the library to find out when a particular story ran, call circulation to ask why they found their paper in the bushes, call Ask the *Globe* to complain about consumer fraud anywhere in the country. They call the city desk to suggest new stories or criticize existing ones. Just a few minutes ago, Dave Morrow picked up the phone to hear someone shilling "the biggest story in the entire world." And there's one person who calls every day, without fail, to warn that the *Globe* is going to be indicted for something. Some days it's libel, others fraud.

All the departments listen to the readers' calls, keep notes, and sometimes profit from them. "It's hard if someone is rude or mean, but we manage to be polite on the phone," says Faith Freedman, a college student who works as an editorial assistant in the newsroom. "We just try to keep them calm, ourselves calm, and everyone happy."

For Keegan and McManus at Confidential Chat, reader contact is their only business. Many writers simply want their letters forwarded to a particular Chatter, rather than published in the paper, and McManus complies; in fact, she sends each Chatter a copy of every letter that arrives with his pen name on it (except for the rare ones that are nasty or upsetting). She also records the new pen names that come in each day, changing some slightly so no two are alike. At last count, Rambo, Rambo 2, and Rambo 3 numbered among the Chatters. Finally, McManus types the recipes received in answer to published requests. They run in a special Chat section in the Wednesday food pages.

Keegan, meanwhile, answers the phone and combs the files for recipes and patterns to fill Chatters' requests. If none of the thousands of recipes and patterns on file fits the bill, the request is printed in the paper. She calls people whose letters need more information or who didn't give a pen name, and she types into the system the letters that Ralph Hubley chooses.

Hubley, a layout editor in the Living department, spends one day each week, plus a little time on other days, doing the Chat. With a practiced eye he flips through letters from lonely prison inmates, letters from people looking for birdhouse designs, letters signed with pen names that have been passed down through the generations. Not much happens in the world that doesn't wind up in Confidential Chat. The subjects have changed a little over the years—questions on AIDS are creeping in, and more women now ponder career-related problems—but marriage and children are still the language Chatters share.

Like the op-ed page, the Chat column aims for balance. Tomorrow, for example, Hubley has chosen four pattern requests (from Four No Trump, Capeway Woodstock, and Rural Running Red, in addition to Hockey Fan), a letter from a fourth-grader who knows the name of a story Jewel's Mom was looking for, and a lyrical piece on fighting loneliness ("Focus on some little simple thing which brings you pleasure") written by Timing to a Chatter named Pink Daisy. To top things off, he's running a long letter to Stranger in Paradise from Frogs Have Wings, who draws liberally from the Bible ("Judge not, lest ye be judged") while condemning the practice of living together without marriage. In between biblical references, Frogs lays it on the line: "I know of at least one woman who's a mental and emotional wreck thanks to the cretin she lives with."

• • •

"Why was Odie pink?" the small voice on the telephone asks Donna Bains. Luckily, she knows the answer.

Odie the dog is a character in the comic strip Garfield. Usually he's yellow in the Sunday comics, but three days ago he turned up pink in many newspapers, much to the consternation of children across the country. Bains, an executive secretary in the newsroom, explains to the boy that someone must have put the wrong codes on Jim Davis's original comic strip when it was sent to Buffalo for printing, causing Odie to change color from coast to coast. The boy thinks that's pretty funny, and they chat for a while about comics.

Comics are serious business to *Globe* readers, often serious enough to send them to the phone. The switchboard once received 600 calls on a Sunday because the person who laid out the comics had forgotten to include Bloom County. The callers were outraged; they suspected that their favorite comic strip had been censored. "That shows you the state of the art," says Bob Kierstead, the ombudsman. "The world is falling apart, everyone's taxes are up, people are dying, and what do you get calls about? Bloom County."

Since becoming ombudsman in February 1982, Kierstead has enjoyed talking with readers about every imaginable subject. This year, however, even he has had his fill of the comics. In January the *Globe* lost some of its most popular comics because one syndicate—owned by Rupert Murdoch, who also owns the *Globe*'s chief competitor, the *Boston Herald*—would not renew the *Globe*'s contracts to buy them. Many readers saw the loss as an injury, and the paper's choice of new comics added the proverbial insult.

Readers reserved most of their abuse for a larger-than-normal strip called Zippy the Pinhead, a survivor of underground papers on the West Coast. Zippy features off-the-wall characters uttering off-the-wall dialogue that some readers find not only inscrutable but also offensive. Others, primarily college students, have called to applaud the *Globe*'s "courage" in giving Zippy a home.

In this morning's strip a character named Griffy tries to indoctrinate Zippy on the dangers of the neighborhood nuclear plant. Zippy, looking as dense as ever in his polka-dot dress, responds with such comments as, "Is it a place where baldness and dandruff are permanently cured?" Although today's installment was in relatively good taste, Kierstead tends to agree with the elderly woman who called one day to tell him she had just thrown away her lunch. She'd lost her appetite, she said, reading Zippy.

As Kierstead sees it, being ombudsman doesn't preclude him from having opinions, or from expressing those opinions to readers. When a reader calls to say he thought a particular column was lousy, Kierstead often surprises the caller by agreeing with him. The columnist may be a friend of his, but, as Kierstead says, "This isn't a job where friendship means a damn."

After four years as ombudsman, Kierstead has developed an informal catalogue of common reader complaints. Most common of all are complaints about the physical condition of the paper—pages that are blank or inked solid gray, folio lines cut off so that page numbers are unreadable, ink that rubs off on readers' hands. He collects the complaints, along with the sample "garbage" readers send him, and consults with the production department. Occasionally he writes a column explaining the industry's progress in developing low-rub ink and the *Globe*'s progress in instituting quality-control measures.

The rest of the calls involve content. Often, readers call claiming that the paper has made a mistake. Although many times this claim simply means that the facts do not jibe with the reader's opinion, some callers point out what sound like legitimate errors. Kierstead gives the information to managing editor Tom Mulvoy, who works with the reporter and editor involved to see whether a correction is needed.

The calls Kierstead has received this morning illustrate the range he encounters. Several people called for more information about a four-year-old boy who had become ensnared in red tape after allegedly being abused by his family. Columnist Mike Barnicle had written about the boy in Monday's paper, and the callers wanted to know what they could do to help. After consulting with the newsroom, Kierstead learned that a story updating the boy's situation had been written for today's paper but had been crowded out by other stories. He gave the callers the gist of the information and passed along an editor's promise that the story would run tomorrow.

Barnicle also prompted another call to Kierstead this morning, this one full of compliments about today's column on the much-publicized "man shortage." Barnicle began the column by alleging that a wild band of single women, crazed by statistics showing their slim chances of ever marrying after age thirty, had attacked him at the Harvard subway stop and chased him up the escalator. Between giggles over the column, the caller begged the *Globe* to keep Barnicle so she wouldn't have to read the competition, which she said would be "intellectual suicide."

Kierstead also talked this morning with a reader who thought the *Globe* was falling down on the job because it hadn't found out on its own that gubernatorial candidate Royall Switzler had lied about his military record. Why did you wait for him to hold a press conference? the caller asked. It was a good question. Four years ago, the *Globe* disclosed that the campaign literature being circulated by another Republican candidate for governor contained false statements about his past. Kierstead, however, knows of no way to explain why reporters discover some facts and not others. It's like asking why the IRS doesn't catch every tax evader.

Another reader called this morning to complain that a Sci-Tech story published Monday had undermined the dignity of the late scientist Dian Fossey by calling her a "gorilla investigator" instead of an internationally known scholar. The most substantive complaint, in Kierstead's view, came from a reader who believed that the *Globe* had been seriously overplaying the continuing story of Irving Fryar's alleged gambling. Fryar, a New England Patriots wide receiver, was the subject of an NFL investigation into charges that he gambled on games.

When the charges surfaced last week, the *Globe* ran the story on the front page. That was ridiculous placement, the caller told Kierstead. He also complained about today's story, in which the *Globe* reported that although a lie detector test had supported Fryar's contention that he had never gambled on NFL games, the test had not addressed the issue of gambling on college games. The caller labeled the story's tone "petulant" and theorized that the paper ran it as some sort of retroactive justification for the prominence it had given the gambling charges in the first place.

Kierstead agreed with the caller's first point: In his opinion, the original Fryar story didn't deserve the front page. The Sports front, maybe, but not page one. But Kierstead wasn't ready to condemn whoever made the decision. He explained to the caller that story play is a judgment call made by editors who face deadlines and a tidal wave of stories that neither Kierstead nor the readers can fully appreciate. The caller didn't seem convinced, but at least he had found someone at the paper who would listen to his views.

Kierstead then returned to writing a column for Monday's op-ed page, in which he is responding to an eighth-grade class that criticized the *Globe* for identifying some of the semi-finalists for an important state job as women and blacks. In this case, Kierstead thinks the paper did the right thing, but the column will applaud the students for their sensitivity.

It's been a good morning. He hasn't had to deal with the thing that bothers him most: carelessness in stories. Like the old-timers in the newsroom, Kierstead remembers the days when reporters faced a lot more deadline pressure than they do now. He simply cannot forgive writers who don't bother to check things out. Not long ago the paper ran a story about a woman who lived on "Morton Avenue"—which anyone familiar with Boston geography knows is really Morton *Street*. It sounds like a small error, but Kierstead knows the devastating effect small errors can have. If the paper messes up a story about tax reform or some other complicated issue, few people will recognize the mistake. But just let readers notice something like "Morton Avenue," and immediately they'll start thinking, "If these guys can't even get the small stuff right, what else are they doing wrong?"

Kierstead knows that some people—especially people in the newsroom, where he was an assistant managing editor before becoming ombudsman—think he's nothing more than a glorified public relations man. The charge doesn't bother him. He sees his true function as a listener, someone readers can call to get the attention they deserve. He doesn't always defend the paper, and he doesn't always stroke the callers. Anyway, he says, there's nothing wrong with a little p.r. "We are a manufacturer of newspapers," Kierstead says. "We are a business. Maybe it's a very special business because we have protections in the Constitution, but we have to deal with our consumers in no different manner than any other company should."

·   ·   ·

The Massachusetts State House is in an uproar. It took a few hours for the news to get around, but now no one can talk about anything else: State Representative Royall Switzler, the Republican candidate for governor, has admitted that he lied for years about his Army record. He was a sergeant, not a captain; he was not a member of the Special Forces; and he never saw action in Vietnam. Now Switzler is being mobbed by reporters and his fellow legislators everywhere he goes, and the *Globe*'s State House phones are ringing wildly with rumors of other lies.

Bruce Mohl, the *Globe* reporter who attended Switzler's news conference yesterday afternoon, is still feeling a little dazed. News conferences are part of the routine of political coverage, but rarely do they produce real news; reporters usually have a pretty good idea what will be said before the speaker opens his mouth. Yesterday, the group that gathered at a downtown hotel was more curious than usual. Switzler had been in virtual seclusion since the party drafted him at its April convention, and speculation was growing that he might not want the candidacy. Still, because yesterday was the deadline for filing signatures to qualify for the September primary, everyone figured that Switzler had called the conference to announce the start of his active campaign. The story was expected to be so routine, in fact, that only one television crew showed up, and only a few radio reporters carried tape recorders. Once Switzler started to talk, Mohl wished he had brought his.

The candidate got right to the point, saying that he wanted to bare his soul. His admissions so surprised the reporters that, for once in their lives, they were speechless. The *Globe*'s State House bureau chief, Joan Venocchi, says that the announcement left reporters "as amazed as you can ever be in the news business." A radio reporter was the first to come to his senses. He quickly asked Switzler about Vietnam, and the question brought out more specifics about the candidate's deceptions. Mohl sat there feeling the adrenaline pumping, thinking, "He's writing his own death warrant." Then came a starker thought: "Only three hours until deadline."

Mohl ran back to the State House, literally chasing a few people from whom he wanted comments. He made some calls, talked briefly with the other five reporters in the tiny bureau, and then wrote fast, trying to convey not only Switzler's statements but the condition in which they had left the Republican Party. He was pleased with the story, but he knows it left a lot of questions for him to answer today.

Meanwhile, unbeknown to him, editors on Morrissey Boulevard have been discussing whether the story may have downplayed Switzler's offenses. Mohl's lead said Switzler "allowed incorrect information about his military background to appear in political brochures," and the headline said, "Switzler says he portrayed self inaccurately." The *Herald*'s headline said, "Switzler: I Lied About My Past," and the lead referred to his announcement as a "political bombshell." Though the people at the *Globe* often view the *Herald* as sensationalistic, some of them think it told the story more clearly this time. In addition, because the *Globe* ran only five paragraphs of the story on page one, readers had to turn to page seventeen to find out what Switzler had actually lied about. No one is blaming Mohl for that.

Mohl has spent the morning talking to as many people as he could from the group that has called with tips. Switzler said the embellishment of his military record stopped in 1980, but quite a few people seem to remember his talking since then, both on the House floor and elsewhere, about being a Vietnam veteran. Trouble is, there's no local equivalent of the *Congressional Record*, so it's nearly impossible to find out who said what when. Before the legislature started tape recording its sessions last year, notes put together by a news service were the only available record. But House debates go on for so long, and Switzler has been such a prominent debater, that Mohl doesn't hold out much hope of finding anything that way. He keeps taking calls while he ponders his next move.

The State House bureau is not the perfect place for pondering. About the size of a suburban bedroom, the fourth-floor cubbyhole is home to an office assistant and six writers with their desks, computers, files, and piles of paraphernalia. If they all push their chairs back six inches, they meet in the middle. When Venocchi came to the bureau from City Hall last October, she realized that she'd have to use a phone booth in the hall if she wanted to make a personal call. Gradually she noticed that everyone else in the bureau was doing the same thing.

Bob Turner, an op-ed columnist who works out of the bureau, drives to Morrissey Boulevard to write when he can't stand the noise. Usually, though, he tries to stick it out, figuring that the cross-pollination of ideas is worth the extra time. At any rate, around the State House, the *Globe*'s quarters are considered luxurious. Reporters from all the other papers and broadcast outlets have to share a single pressroom.

Like the Washington bureau, the State House bureau sometimes feels it's getting mixed signals about whether it should try to cover everything, or choose its targets and dig deep. Unlike the Washington reporters, however, the people at the State House don't have to worry about clout. They've got it. Because no one else has as many reporters as the *Globe* does covering state government, no one else has as much access—which is not to say that the paper doesn't occasionally get scooped. Venocchi, who in a previous job was accustomed to "lurking outside doors and using body blocks" to get people to talk, learned about clout as soon as she arrived at the State House to become bureau chief. Her first day on the job, the governor, House speaker, and Senate president all called and invited her to come and get acquainted.

Her growing familiarity with the beat has bred in Venocchi a healthy respect for the reporters she supervises, as well as a continuing affection for political coverage. It has also fueled her conviction that politics is "a man's world—no, a boy's world, very *little* boys." State House staffers must constantly stroke and cajole the tremendous egos in state government, and reporters are expected to join in. Between the game playing and the incessant assault of potential stories, writing often seems like the easiest part of the job.

It's hard to formulate a master plan for State House coverage, Venocchi says, because events tend to sweep reporters along. Today Mohl, who came to the bureau from the Business section four months ago, is the one being pushed by the giant broom. Although most Republicans are rallying around Switzler, touting his voluntary admission as proof of his candor, the Democrats are tearing him apart. Switzler has been known as a House gadfly, always making accusations about other lawmakers. Now some of the people he's accused are taking great delight in his discomfort. Mohl is on the phone listening to yet another rumor when he hears that Switzler has emerged from the House. He races down the hall to find the candidate at the center of a mob of reporters, patiently answering anything they ask. Switzler is still being very cooperative with the media, but Mohl knows that his cooperation is likely to melt away as quickly as the party's support for his candidacy.

Mohl hasn't gotten everything he wants by the time the impromptu news conference breaks up, but he's confident that Switzler will talk to him on the phone later. He returns to the bureau and within minutes has in his hands a piece of paper that begins to shape his story for tomorrow. It's a copy of a July 1985 interview in which Switzler told a suburban weekly that he had been a Green Beret in Vietnam and an adviser to a South Vietnamese battalion, and that he had seen "activity" against the Viet Cong.

Unless Switzler says the newspaper misquoted him, the story means that his misrepresentations didn't stop in 1980, as he claimed yesterday. The reporter who wrote the 1985 story now works for a Democratic political consultant at the State House. Mohl will have to mention in his story that the consultant was the one who released the '85 interview, but if it's accurate, the partisanship won't reduce its importance.

Somewhere beneath the flurry of activity, Mohl is still feeling a little sorry for Switzler. It took courage to stand up and admit he'd lied; there's no evidence that Switzler had been found out and was trying to beat someone to the punch. In addition, Mohl had previously interviewed Switzler's wife, and he admires her for standing by him. As Mohl ran out of the news conference yesterday, part of his brain realized with regret that the Switzlers would be going through hell, especially once the reporters got into their feeding frenzy. The thought didn't keep him from doing his job, but it did give him pause.

Nevertheless, the man lied, Mohl told himself last night, and no one can shield him from the consequences. At 6:00 he stopped writing and ran out to the State House lawn, where he knew that at least one television crew would be interviewing Switzler for its newscast. Another reporter had had the same idea, and when the cameras turned away, he asked Switzler about his past statements that he had "seen action in Vietnam."

"Yes, I saw it on television," Switzler replied. After that, Mohl didn't feel so bad.

•   •   •

Bob Turner considers his job the best of its kind outside Washington, and better than only a few jobs there. Now that his column for tomorrow is finished, the job is looking better all the time.

Turner writes an op-ed column on local politics that runs Tuesdays, Thursdays, and every other Sunday. Although he's convinced that news stories have more impact than columns, he can't think of a better place than Boston to do what he does. Massachusetts, he likes to point out, is one of the few large states whose capital is also the biggest, most interesting city. Then there's Boston's history, and its residents' long tradition of embracing politics as part of their lives. And who could fail to be captivated by the contrasts? Here's Massachusetts, this liberal, lopsidedly Democratic state, supporting capital punishment and a tax cap that forces all kinds of cuts in services. He wouldn't exactly call state politics intelligent, but it's certainly intellectually active. Massachusetts seems to him a place where new ideas can find fertile ground.

None of those superlatives, however, means that writing a political column is easy. Every Monday and Wednesday morning Turner stands in the shower and asks himself: What do I need to finish this one? And then: Can I get it by noon? If the answer is no, he has to switch subjects and find one where he can wing it. And that's just the beginning. Not only is he physically surrounded by other writers in the cramped bureau, he's psychologically surrounded by special interests who want to put their own spin on his columns. He listens to them all and fights to keep his mind his own. Sometimes he has to go to great lengths to do it.

Recently, for example, a very aggressive lobbyist tried to persuade Turner to write a column supporting the lobbyist's position on a particular bill. Turner happened to agree with the position, but he had no intention of writing a column on demand—especially a demand made by someone who wanted the column to appear *before* the hearing on the bill. The more the lobbyist pushed him, the more Turner resolved not to do it. When he wrote about that issue, he said, it was going to be his own piece, not some command performance that one side or the other could photocopy and hand out at a hearing. If he did that, he'd be a campaigner, not a columnist.

Turner has no illusions that his columns make things happen. If he did, the illusions would have been destroyed by the recent referendum that upheld the death penalty. Turner had written extensively against capital punishment, but as far as he could tell, his columns didn't affect the outcome at all. Nor should they have, according to his theory. "My role is putting some argument into the mix," he says. "As long as I've expressed my view in the best possible way, I've done my job."

Lobbyists aren't the only ones who have trouble accepting that view. Turner says that when Michael Dukakis, with whom the *Globe* has generally had a good relationship, regained the governor's office in 1982, he seemed to think that the paper would help him institute his agenda. Sophisticated as he is about politics, the governor seemed surprised when Turner didn't agree that they were in this thing together.

For tomorrow, Turner has written about a local issue from a national perspective: what's happening in Washington with the Massachusetts proposals to rebuild the horrendous highway morass leading to Logan Airport. That section of the interstate is known as one of the most congested and dangerous in the country. He met his noon deadline for the column, and now he's planning to head to Morrissey Boulevard to spend the afternoon working on a Sunday magazine piece about celebrities in politics. Turner's wife, Otile McManus, is also writing for the Sunday magazine these days, a break from her usual job as an editorial writer. Tonight, if Turner's head cold doesn't get worse, he'll accompany her to a dinner held by the Historic Neighborhoods Foundation, where Mc-Manus will present an award to the *Globe*'s architecture critic, Robert Campbell. She is a past recipient of the award.

Thinking about tomorrow's column as he contributes to the bureau brainstorming on the Switzler story, Turner knows just what his editors will say. The column contains more reporting than analysis and more analysis than opinion, someone is sure to tell him. That mix, he knows from hearing it a hundred times, does not make for the best columns. Although he acknowledges the wisdom of this argument, Turner doesn't want to stop thinking like a reporter. He believes that hard facts lend his columns credibility. "If I didn't think I had some different information to report," he says, "I'd feel superfluous."

•   •   •

Lunchtime is rarely fun time in the newsroom. Often it means a tuna sandwich and a cup of black coffee in front of the terminal, trying mightily—on pain of death or, worse, electronic malfunction—not to let the crumbs fall into the keyboard. The luckier ones, the ones for whom deadline still looks like a reachable goal, wander in groups up to the cafeteria or out onto its patio, munching salads and eggplant Parmesan between futile efforts to talk about something other than work.

Ross Gelbspan and Fletcher Roberts aren't even trying. Gelbspan wants to know how Roberts is doing as editor of the medical reporters and other specialists, a job he started when a slew of newsroom changes took effect March 1. After a morning in which Gelbspan's reporting duties have included

105

listening to a local official who was upset about something he wrote, finishing a story on minority hiring, and trying to arrange for a stringer to go to Islamabad, Pakistan, he's ready to talk about editing. Until two and a half years ago, Gelbspan had Roberts' job.

Not far from the cafeteria, in the corporate dining room, publisher Bill Taylor and five of the company's top executives have begun a two-hour strategic planning session. As they talk about the June directors' meeting and the September long-range-planning meeting, Taylor becomes increasingly convinced that very soon he should take his aching head and his reading material and go home to bed.

Around town, newsroom people are having lunch with sources. Executive editor Jack Driscoll is eating with a real estate agent who formerly worked undercover for the FBI, investigating political corruption in Boston. Although he's not as good a source as he used to be, Driscoll doesn't like to cut people off when their usefulness has ended. This man is good company, and he gets around enough that he might hear something.

Business reporter Charles Radin is finding the closing lunch of the International Monetary Conference more useful than he'd expected. He's still worried about understanding what Paul Volcker has just said about the decline of the dollar, not to mention understanding the insurance company financial statements he spent the morning reading, but the seating arrangement has provided him with a good distraction. The woman next to him works for one of the area's largest banks, trying to persuade wealthy people to put their money there. How banks are catering to that segment of society is a live topic these days; maybe there's another story in it. Even if there isn't, Radin gets a kick out of the chocolate bird's nests delivered to the table for dessert.

Other *Globe* people also have official luncheon engagements. Harry King, assistant editor of the Living section, is at a Boston Advertising Club lunch, listening to guest speaker Andy Rooney. Bill Davis, editor of Sunday's Travel section, is attending a luncheon presentation by the German airline Lufthansa, which is promoting Frankfurt as the gateway to Europe. Chatting with a travel agent at his table, Davis stumbles onto a potentially more interesting story: TWA is introducing a promotional youth fare, which is big news in a city with as many college students as Boston. He'll have to confirm it when he gets back to the office.

Editorial page editor Marty Nolan is spending his lunch in Chinatown, meeting with community leaders who oppose a city building project that they fear will change Chinatown's character forever. Listening to their arguments, Nolan thinks, as he often does, of the function of the editorial page as described half a century ago by humorist Finley Peter Dunne: to comfort the afflicted and afflict the comfortable.

For some people, lunch will have to wait. Louisa Williams, assistant editor of the Sunday magazine, is busy assuring the subject of an upcoming profile that the magazine is not in the business of printing gossip. Steve Marantz, having finished his interview at the Roger Williams Mint, has driven back to the *Globe* and fallen asleep in his car. He thinks he has a good story, and maybe a quick nap will make him forget that he was up half the night with his three-month-old son.

Dave Morrow is calling City Hall reporter Michael Frisby to give him the go-ahead on a trip to Puerto Rico to cover the U.S. Conference of Mayors. Morrow hasn't been able to think of a way to go along. Ray Richard, meanwhile, has just gotten permission to visit the state prison at Norfolk, about forty miles southwest of Boston, to interview some of the five inmates who are getting college degrees. The prison tells him that the photographer must unload all film from her cameras so that the cameras can be searched. Richard passes along the warning, and he and the photographer leave in separate cars. He'll be staying longer than she will.

Jim Franklin doesn't want to go to lunch until he really gets rolling on his Paulist Center story. The story started with telephone tips, mostly anonymous, that the archdiocese had cracked down on the Paulist Fathers for allowing women to speak at Mass and prayer services. Last weekend Franklin attended a Mass at the center, which is technically a Catholic chapel, and he tried to attend a meeting at which priests and other members of the Paulist community talked about the problem. The director of the center asked Franklin to leave the meeting and told him he wanted no stories published about the dispute. Since then, Franklin has been trying to convince everyone involved that a story is necessary. He doesn't need their permission to do the story, but he does need their comments to put in it.

Two days ago the center's director agreed to meet with Franklin. He was friendlier this time, but he still didn't want a story. Franklin told him that the number of calls he'd received showed that the dispute was already public, and he felt obligated to write about it. The issue of women's role in the church is important to Boston's Catholics, he said. What Franklin didn't say, but they both understood, was that he would be writing a story with or without the director's cooperation, and it would be a much more credible story if the director spoke to him. Eventually the director gave Franklin a few comments on the record. Yesterday Franklin interviewed the bishop who had warned the Paulist fathers that if their "liturgical abuses" did not stop, they could lose their right to function as priests.

This morning Franklin had an appointment that he hoped would galvanize his story: an interview with a woman who has been active at the Paulist Center. Unfortunately, she was so upset by the discipline applied by the archdiocese that she hesitated to say anything for fear of making the situation worse. So now Franklin faces a classic reporter's dilemma. The information he's collected isn't bad, but it's not all he'd hoped for. Should he spend more time looking, probably to no avail, for the person who will make his story soar, or should he stick with what he's got and do the best he can before deadline? He shakes off his frustration and settles down to write.

Like several other people in the newsroom, Franklin is feeling too much stress to attend the noontime stress seminar the medical department is holding. Two floors below him, eighty people have gathered in an auditorium to hear Don Seckler, a psychologist who runs the *Globe*'s employee assistance program, advise them to "learn to reset their stress meters." Stress, he tells them, is the body's physical and psychological response to challenges from outside. It's what made primitive man able to fight back when a lion attacked suddenly. "Today your boss is the lion, and you're always waiting for him to attack."

A lot of people don't want to break the stress cycle, Seckler says, because they believe that they're controlling their problems by worrying about them. They're not, or course. Medical researchers have developed a wide variety of theories on dealing with stress, and Seckler has been exploring one theory each week in this series of four sessions for employees. Today he introduces a researcher from a local hospital, who leads the group in meditation. Quiet descends as the participants try to hoist themselves to some higher, worry-free plane.

Later, Seckler says he doesn't think working at a newspaper is any more stressful than most other jobs. In many ways, he says, he's glad that stress is such a widely accepted concept; it's useful for a psychologist. "People wouldn't want to talk to me about something called a neurosis or psychosis," he says. "But ask about stress, and anyone is good for an hour."

•   •   •

Back at the School Department, Peggy Hernandez is still working the building. Since leaving the office of the source who told her about the pregnancy-prevention proposal, she's talked with her editor, who agreed that she should pursue the story. Then she did some more cruising.

On the fifth floor she stopped to chat with the department's official spokesman, a former "Globie" who likes to tell war stories. As usual, Hernandez volunteered little about what she was working on, for fear he might inadvertently tell other reporters. As long as she was on the fifth floor, she figured it couldn't hurt to stop by the general counsel's office and ask one more time about the bus drivers' contract. No news.

Three floors up, she waited twenty minutes to see another school official, who, like Hernandez, is from California. After they'd talked about West Coast school districts for a while, she asked him for a copy of the pregnancy-prevention

109

memo. He said he'd give it to her later if the superintendent approved. Then she asked about the story she'd originally planned to work on today, the one about Boston teachers' getting overwhelmingly positive job evaluations despite the system's problems. The official told her that the rumor was correct: The evaluations were positive, and the superintendent, Laval Wilson, was upset. But don't quote me, he said. Technically, a person who wants to keep a remark off the record must say so *before* he tells it to a reporter. But since Hernandez was just chatting with this man, not formally interviewing him, and since they know each other fairly well, she didn't push the point. She was still sure she could get the information elsewhere.

She returned to the fifth floor, where deputy superintendent Joseph McDonough happened to have a free minute. He confirmed, on the record, the basics about the job reviews, and he said he'd give her his memo on the subject if Wilson approved. Now, as Hernandez leaves McDonough's office, she happens to spot Wilson at the end of the hall, heading for a meeting. She grabs the superintendent before he reaches the door and asks him for a copy of McDonough's memo. He says no, but he gives her enough explanation so that she thinks she can write the story.

With her stomach demanding lunch, Hernandez makes one last stop. She asks the assistant to the School Committee president to let her know when he gets the pregnancy-prevention memo. He says he will. Then, after picking up some food, she goes back to City Hall to eat, return phone calls, and start writing the evaluation story. Somewhere along the line she's learned that the *Herald* has the story, too, thus reducing its already minor excitement value. She hopes one of her other stories comes through.

• • •

Pam Cox and George Smith listen carefully as Dave Morrow outlines their first assignment as *Globe* reporters. Their mission on this, the first day of their summer internship, is to talk to residents of three city housing projects where police protection might be reduced. Using a federal grant, the Boston Housing Authority has been paying the police department to have officers patrol the projects, an arrangement called "team police" because the officers are under the joint direction of the police department and the housing authority. But federal budget cuts mean that the housing authority may not be able to pay for the patrols after October.

"Mike Frisby will do the overall story on the situation," Morrow tells the two interns. "You guys do the people angle. What do people think of the team police? What do they think the projects would be like without them? Talk to the residents, talk to the cops." He'll need about fifty typewritten lines, he says.

Morrow gives the interns the name of a woman who directs the tenants' organization at one of the projects, Orchard Park, and recommends that they call her. Then, after helping them arrange for a photographer and a company car, he returns to his desk on the other side of the newsroom. They're on their own.

Smith prays that Cox will drive. Cox is from Dorchester and goes to Suffolk University in Boston, and she knows her way around. Smith arrived from Ohio three days ago, on his twenty-first birthday, and he's in no hurry to begin solo navigation of these crazed environs. He did go to school in Andover, Massachusetts, for a while, but that was before he started college at Oberlin. It seems like a lifetime ago. He's a New Yorker, and he's a long way from being an expert on Boston.

Even amid his first-day jitters, Smith couldn't help noticing that Morrow sent a white intern to a project in Irish South Boston, and he's sending Smith and Cox, both of whom are black, to Roxbury and Dorchester. Though he knows that's a wise plan from a safety standpoint, Smith wishes it didn't have to be that way. Not long ago, out in Ohio, he went to cover a basketball game for a local paper and realized he was the only black person in the stands. During the game, a few people threw things at him—pennies, candy, wads of paper. He didn't like it, but he wasn't scared. In fact, he hopes that sometime this summer he'll get an assignment in South Boston, so he can compare the experience. Mostly what he wants, though, is what Morrow has already given him, a

111

chance to do newswriting. Then he can compare it with the sportswriting he's already done and see which direction his career ought to take.

Cox, too, is excited about the assignment, but she's less intimidated; she grew familiar with reporters' routines during a recent stint as an office assistant in the *Globe*'s State House bureau. This will be her first byline, though, and she's eager to get started. As she and Smith pick up their notebooks to go, Morrow swings by to remind them to be careful. A reporter Cox knows stops and offers the same advice. She suggests that Cox hand over her diamond engagement ring and her pearls for safekeeping. Feeling a little guilty, Cox does. It's not just for safety, she tells herself. The jewelry could set up a real barrier between me and the people I'll be interviewing.

Back at the city desk, Morrow peers over the shoulder of Marvin Pave as Pave adds to Today's Look, a list the editors keep in the computer to remind them what stories need covering and who's been assigned to cover them.

"We could use an intern on this one," Pave tells Morrow, typing another assignment onto the list. "I think there's one left." For two blinks of the cursor, the remark hangs in the air. Then they both start laughing. "Sounds like a bowling alley," Pave says. "Just knock 'em down one by one."

1:00 P.M.

The only trick I know is to be as persistent as hell.
—Walter Robinson, White House correspondent

Maybe bicycle messengers would be a good one. The proliferation of French bakeries? And look over there—school kids
taking a tour of City Hall.

Brad Pokorny is trolling for stories (a ride in an armored
car?). He's walking around downtown, trying to find a good
subject for City Life, a feature that's supposed to convey the
color and flavor of Boston and its people. (Who are all those
tourists at Quincy Market? Why did they choose to come to
Boston?) The story doesn't need to contain news (the secrets
of hotel doormen?), just to illuminate one of the quirky corners that make the city so unmistakably itself (a sporting
goods store in the middle of the financial district?).

Trolling on foot is a luxury Pokorny's schedule has allowed him only five or six times in as many years at the
Globe. Trolling by phone is a daily routine, for him and most
other reporters. This morning he was lucky; the calls came to
him.

The day started with a pleasant surprise. As he picked up
the paper in one hand and a blueberry square in the other, he
saw that his story on proposed condominiums in nearby Revere had made the front page. He couldn't know the entire
combination of circumstances that had put it there, but he
was glad he had chosen to stress the universality of the condo
conflict. Conflict is one of the main measures of whether a
story is news, the others being impact, timeliness, novelty,
and the interests of readers. Pokorny saw the controversy in
Revere as typical of what's happening all around Boston,
where a booming economy and a burgeoning demand for

housing have developers snatching up every available piece of land. He stressed that angle in the story, and it not only made page one but also got good play: two photos, a main head and a drop head (a smaller, second headline), and a box around the whole thing.

After a few more satisfied looks at the paper, Pokorny picked up a pile of early-morning phone messages. Not recognizing some of the callers' names, he thought they might have called about the condo story. He was right. The first caller turned out to be a man who had been a fellow student in a Soviet foreign policy class Pokorny took at Harvard last fall. The man had read the Revere story and wanted to tell Pokorny that his neighborhood, Allston-Brighton, was embroiled in a dispute over condos as well. Someone wanted to build twin twenty-four-story towers in a parking lot behind a car dealership, and the neighborhood had organized to oppose the plan. As the man talked, Pokorny took notes, typing into his terminal as fast as he could. The results were nearly indecipherable to anyone but the typist. The notes read in part:

> we're at the poitn wher it is o dense out here thatht bueisns distict is bout to be gerryamnded intoe th back bay becuae of popuation densiey. so to tell us we need 400 untis of housing is craxzines. mroe that theya t they wnat ot build this tower right smakc int eh middle of a n indsutl zone. the ae nothign but factoesi or parkign lots aroudn it. I don't want to live in a neigh borhood that has a 24 stoy towr lomming over it.

The man mentioned that the *Globe* had written about his neighborhood not long ago. Pokorny made a mental note to look into that; with so many potential stories to choose from, the paper shouldn't cover the same areas over and over. The caller also provided phone numbers of the neighborhood groups that were fighting the condos, as well as some information about the developer. Pokorny thanked him and hung up, intending to untangle his notes before the gibberish started to look like gibberish. But the phone rang again; another caller wanted to talk about the condo story.

This man, who didn't want his name in the paper, said he had heard that the Federal Emergency Management Agency (FEMA) was worried about the Revere proposal Pokorny had written about. Rumor has it, the caller said, that a big wave could seriously damage the sixteen-story waterfront building. ("It just blue printe for ceirtn disatr," Pokorny's notes quoted the man.) Pokorny took the caller's name and number, though he promised not to print them. The FEMA angle might be worth pursuing if he wrote again about the Revere condos, but he didn't feel the need to jump on it right away. The caller had no actual knowledge of the federal agency; he was just passing along what he'd heard. The idea would keep while Pokorny ransacked his desk for City Life possibilities.

Reporters hoard story ideas. They scribble them in the margins of notebooks and on the backs of press releases, type them into computerized files with cryptic names, scrawl them on scraps of paper that migrate to the bottoms of pockets or purses until they grow rag-soft from wrinkling, the penciled abbreviations rubbed to a gray smudge. The lists remind the reporters of the quick one-day feature they can do the next time they're stuck, the newsier idea that needs a phone call or two before it's solid enough to propose, the "I'll get to it someday" promises made to editors whose suggestions failed to inspire. (With any luck, the editor will forget the idea or propose it to some more desperate soul before it rises to the top of the list.) Then there are the wish lists of big projects—requiring time or money or plane tickets, or all three—that the reporter dreams of tackling someday, when the topic is current and his stock in trade is soaring from some fresh success.

This man, who didn't want his name in the paper, said he had heard that the Federal Emergency Management Agency (FEMA) was worried about the Revere proposal Pokorny had simply, meaning. Pokorny dug out several lists of story ideas, some old and some older, and added a few new thoughts, keeping one eye trained in the direction of his editor, Barbara Meltz. Every time he was off the phone she was on it, or in a meeting or talking with another reporter. Finally, just before noon, he saw her walking across the newsroom. He followed her back to her desk, where they sat for half an hour discussing story ideas. Together they assigned top ranking to two possibilities: from Meltz's list, spending a day at a dog-training class; and from Pokorny's, visiting a hair-styling salon in the financial district to find out what customers talk about in the chair.

Pokorny returned to his desk, left a message for a man who runs a dog-training class in Cambridge, and suddenly realized that he had encountered that rarest of newsroom rarities, a free afternoon. The City Life story wasn't due tomorrow, all seemed quiet on the news stories he'd been following, and—probably because it was Intern Day—no one had corralled him to perform some small immediate task. He was free, and he was determined to resist the urge to feel guilty. He decided to go downtown and do what news people are supposed to do but rarely can: observe the world and think about how the newspaper should reflect it.

So here he stands outside the Hotel Meridien, talking with the doorman and watching hundreds of potential stories pass by (the Senior Shuttle? street vendors selling jewelry?). He mentally expands the doorman idea to include all the behind-the-scenes activity at a hotel, then rejects the whole thing as too ambitious for a City Life piece. Anyway, he can't spend the entire afternoon just walking around and chatting; it's time he did some real interviews. He asks the doorman to recomend a hair-styling salon where financial types go. Armed with a few suggestions, he starts walking.

He glances into an old-fashioned barbershop that looks great but isn't what he had in mind (maybe a story on old-time barbershops?). The next place, a modern chain salon, seems perfect. After Pokorny talks with the receptionist and a stylist, the manager eagerly shares his own views about the clientele. "Down here people are dictated to about how they should dress and look by the old bureaucracy," the manager tells him. "So we try to give them something that's more in tune with their lifestyle." Then he calls his corporate headquarters to get permission for Pokorny to talk to customers.

116

The customers don't have much to say. The place is convenient, they work better when they look better—the usual stuff. The manager tells Pokorny that when the salon opened, 95 percent of the customers were women. Today, nearly half are men. One male customer says he'd like to try a punk look but doesn't think it would go over well at the office.

One of the stylists is particularly forthcoming about his clients. "There is so much stress in these people, it's incredible," he says. "It's always a rush—'Get me in and get me out.'" While he snips, the stylist says, his clients talk about their jobs, the ups and downs of their lives, their forays into real estate. "We try to keep away from politics and religion," he says.

"Ever get any stock tips?" Pokorny asks.

"I wish," the stylist replies. "Believe me, I try to weasel a few, but they keep their mouths shut."

•   •   •

Reporters are totally dependent on other people for their stories, and today Judy Foreman can't find anyone she needs. A log of her frustration would look like this:

Beginning at 10:00, she made half a dozen calls to Boston University, looking for a heart doctor to comment on a study in the *New England Journal of Medicine*. The study, which is embargoed until tomorrow, involved giving an enzyme called streptokinase to heart attack victims. The enzyme is supposed to gobble up blood clots, restoring blood flow to the heart. When Foreman couldn't find the doctor she needed, she tried going through the B.U. press office, but that road also led nowhere.

Next she tried calling another heart specialist, this one at Brigham and Women's Hospital. In Boston, luckily, there's no shortage of doctors, though not all of them like to talk to reporters. Attempts to reach this particular doctor turned out to entail a lot of back and forth with the p.r. people, with no results.

After she'd played telephone tag on streptokinase for a while, her editor, Fletcher Roberts, pointed out the front-page story in the *Herald* about former U.S. Senator Paul Tsongas of Massachusetts. Tsongas had left the Senate in 1984 after learning that he had cancer of the lymph nodes; yesterday he said he was 95 percent cured. Even more interesting, he said he planned to undergo a month-long bone marrow removal-and-replacement program that could cure him completely. The story isn't really news; Tsongas has mentioned the possibility of a marrow transplant before. Now, however, it sounds definite. In addition, there's an element of catch-up to the story: If *Globe* readers happened to see the front page of the competition this morning, they might wonder why the *Globe* doesn't have the same information. Usually, because the *Globe* is the biggest paper around, other papers and broadcast outlets feed on its stories. "Every television guy running around the State House is carrying a *Globe*," one of the State House reporters says. But sometimes the *Globe* does the chasing.

Abandoning streptokinase, at least temporarily, Foreman called the hospital where Tsongas plans to have the transplant, but the press people either couldn't or wouldn't talk. She tried to reach Tsongas at his home, his Boston office, and his Washington office. No luck. She tried to reach his wife and several doctors who had treated him. Nothing.

Meanwhile, the story had reminded her of something else she'd been meaning to look into. The American Association for the Advancement of Science was supposed to have a paper available this week on genetic diseases treatable with marrow transplants. She called the association's Washington office and was told that the paper was embargoed until Friday.

More calls to the Dana-Farber Cancer Institute, where Tsongas planned to have the transplant. Nothing.

Having left messages everywhere she could think of, Foreman switched to a fourth story. She called a man who'd been active in the fight against AIDS and asked about a new study of people who seem to have survived the disease. Not much information yet.

Dana-Farber again. No help.

Brigham and Women's again. This time she asked not only for the heart specialist, who still wasn't there, but also for a bone marrow specialist who might be able to explain in general terms the procedure Tsongas would undergo. He wasn't there either.

A new thought: try Tsongas's administrative assistant. Good idea, but he's out of town.

One more try at Brigham and Women's. Nothing.

Now that morning has turned to afternoon, she wins a minor victory. The first doctor she called, the one at B.U., calls back, and she asks him about streptokinase. Considering everything that's come up since, she probably won't even be doing the story now, but at least she's finally connected with someone.

Hanging up, she gets a belated message that Tsongas's doctor had tried to call her. The message says he was leaving the office and would be unavailable the rest of the day.

At this point she has three choices: find a padded cell and scream, switch professions immediately, or jog her troubles away. She joins the group changing into running clothes.

. . .

The morning after Richard Baker designed his first page for the *Globe*, he watched as one of his fellow subway riders glanced at it, then dropped the paper on the floor. More riders entered and exited, trampling and ripping the paper to filthy shreds. "Pick that up!" he wanted to shout. "Don't you know how hard I worked?"

That was last year; now Baker is resigned to the fate of his efforts. "I'm not creating art," he says. "I'm working with stories to convey them visually."

Baker, who designs the Living page, is one of ten full-time and seven part-time designers in the editorial design department. (Separate departments do promotion design and advertising design.) Ronn Campisi, Baker's boss, says his department's role is to create pictures from ideas. Those "pictures" comprise all the type, photos, and illustrations on the page, and the way those elements relate. The pictures communicate to readers the newspaper's intent.

"Before you think about what you're reading, you respond visually to something," Campisi says. "There's a whole visual vocabulary that people instantly understand." Creating

119

instant understanding is anything but an instant process. The designers read all the stories that will go on the page and experiment endlessly with headline styles and sizes, column widths and photo arrangements in an effort to convey just the right mood. When they're finished, they step back and try to look at the page as if they knew nothing about it. What visual message is it delivering? The process is similar to the one undertaken by reporters, who learn as much as possible about a subject in a limited time, then try to write for a reader who knows only what they knew before they started.

Campisi is part of a team that has embarked on a redesign of the entire *Globe*. As far as he's concerned, the effort is long overdue. Although the paper has won design awards, he sees it as a patchwork of approaches that all too clearly show their motley origins. There's no visual stylebook to refer to, no standards that clearly tie each section to the others. He believes that the sections should have a family resemblance with built-in differences—much the way different models of cars from the same manufacturer resemble one another but have features uniquely their own.

Though the paper's design isn't consistent enough for Campisi, he acknowledges that it has improved considerably since the design department started with two people eight years ago. In those days, few "word people" would admit that photos, never mind the overall look of a page, were important. Today, however, most writers and editors realize how dramatically visual impact can improve readership of a story. In fact, now the newsroom often wants more miracles than the designers can perform.

Several people in the department are skilled at composing maps and charts to help explain stories. In addition, Campisi maintains a list of 300 freelance illustrators, most of them in New York and each with a highly defined style. He or one of the other designers simply picks the illustrator whose style best fits the project at hand. Today, for example, designer Holly Nixholm is working on the Living page for the Sunday paper, using a collage of 1950s paraphernalia—cars, furniture, clothing, Hula Hoops, and, in the corner, Ronald Reagan climbing a ladder—created by a freelance artist who

120

specializes in photo collages. By using many freelancers instead of keeping a few illustrators on staff, the paper can tap a limitless range of styles. Usually the department gives the freelancers at least a few days' lead time to work on an illustration, but occasionally someone must, as Richard Baker puts it, "promise our first-born" in order to get a local artist to take a deadline assignment.

One of the department's newest services is computer-generated graphics. Using an Apple Macintosh and a high-quality printer, the designers can create graphs and charts of almost anything. For a story about housing costs, for example, they might draw the outline of a house, complete with smoke curling from the chimney, and repeat the outline in different heights to create a bar graph showing rising costs over the years. The computer gives them infinite freedom to enlarge and shrink the type and the various visual elements (tall, skinny houses; short, fat houses; houses with steep or gently sloping roofs) to fit a particular space or a particular emphasis.

The technology is still new enough that the few papers using it for design work are considered test sites by other papers thinking of investing in the hardware. This afternoon, in fact, the editor and photo editor of the *Worcester Telegram* have scheduled a visit to see what the Apple can do. Campisi likes to tell visitors that the computer not only allows its users to work faster and produce more informative graphics, but it also forces both designers and writers to make specific choices about the information they want to communicate. "You can use a computer to produce wonderful things," he says. "But if you don't start with a good idea, you can use a computer to produce incredibly ugly garbage."

Even with the computer, most design work still involves good old-fashioned mental gymnastics of the type Baker has been performing today. In a relaxed-looking outfit that includes a single earring, black high-top sneakers, and a string tie anchored by a silver and turquoise ram's head, he has spent the last few hours reading over the Living stories for tomorrow and trying to envision a page that includes them all. He's made a few rough thumbnail sketches, and now, in

121

the partitioned-off space that serves as his office, he is arranging elements on a full-sized board (heavy paper) called a broadsheet. He works on a drawing table, right below a black-and-white photo of Joan Crawford's face with a real cigarette pushed between her lips—and, by way of literary allusion, a tiny wire coat hanger dangling from the bottom.

Baker hasn't had much trouble figuring out what to do with three of the four Living stories for tomorrow. He wants to tuck the review of the latest Spenser mystery into a bottom corner and play the review of John Williams's new "Liberty Fanfare" in a strip down the top left, where it will be prominent but won't outweigh the main package, the bowling banquet story and photos. Although the review will have an accompanying photo of Williams, neither story nor photo will be ready in time for the first edition. He'll have to design the page so that if the editors choose a plug story that doesn't have a photo, the block of type won't be too overpowering. And then there's the hole at the bottom left, where he plans to put the story and photo of the athletic shoes with the dual lacing system.

He's a little puzzled by what to do with the bowling banquet story, part of Nathan Cobb's American Pop series. After reading it several times, he still chuckles at the lead:

> See the men sporting spiffy pastel jackets, the women sashaying past in dreamy coiffures created this very afternoon. See the hully-gully earnestly danced, long-neck beer bottles energetically opened, mounds of roast beef efficiently doled out. See the four-piece band segueing neatly into "New York, New York," the glitzy mirror ball rotating slowly overhead, the coveted Championship Jackets being presented. Why, everyone's having a heckuva time here at the annual bowling banquet. Can I get you a little something from the bar?

Baker could do a great page using his favorite photo, a bowler holding aloft a large trophy, but he's not sure that would be appropriate. The story is more about the overall mood of the banquets than about the awarding of prizes or any other specific activity. But what the heck; it's worth a try.

Using photocopies of the pictures for tryout purposes, he carefully cuts around the edges of the man holding the funny shoes. Because the man's feet—wearing his company's shoes and prominently labeled socks, of course—are up on a table in the foreground, Baker cuts around the outline of the table, too. In photos of a single person or object, removing the background—called silhouetting—can make the image look more striking against the white page. It's not a good tactic to use all the time (some people in the photo department, in fact, think the designers use it too much), and it doesn't work on complicated photos, but today Baker thinks he'll try it on the photo of the bowler as well. If he doesn't like the way it looks, he can always make another copy and start over.

Because the Living page is supposed to be fun and accessible, it's okay if the art—photos, drawings, whatever—sometimes seems to overwhelm the type. By contrast, the Monday Sci-Tech page and the Sunday book review pages, which cultivate a more highbrow image, usually contain more type and smaller, more serious-looking art. It's all part of conveying the mood.

The pace picks up as one vision of the page begins to dominate the others in Baker's mind. A standard newspaper layout involves six columns, each two and one-eighth inches wide, but he pictures this page divided into four wider columns. He starts slapping down elements, using nonsense type of the right point size wherever he wants a headline to go. It will be up to the copy editors to write real headlines that fit the space.

First the bowling story, with the bowler's hand thrusting up and almost off the page on the upper right. He draws in enough type to "balance" the photo, then checks to see whether the arrangement leaves room for the shoe man's picture and story on the bottom left. Any spot at the bottom of a page is usually considered inferior to the top left, which is second in prominence only to the top right. But Baker hopes that by packaging the shoe story on the bottom to run more than half the width of the page, and putting the John Williams review in a single column at the top left, the shoes will still appear to be the second most dominant element.

Okay. If he puts the shoe man's picture flush against the bottom left corner, it will run five and a half inches high and seven and three-quarters inches wide. The man is facing right, so he'll lead into the page nicely. If he were facing left, the photo would have to go on the other side; the direction of movement in a photo should draw the reader's eye into the page, not off the edge. Much as they're sometimes tempted, designers and layout people do not flop negatives to make a photo face the way they want. Even if they could get away with it visually (if the photo had no lettering that would read backward, no wedding ring that would show up on the wrong hand), they wouldn't be portraying the scene as it actually was. Besides, someone who happened to notice that a photo subject's hair was parted on the wrong side would be sure to wonder what else the newspaper was doing to distort the truth.

The man in the photo is sitting, and the L shape created by his body will allow Baker to run the type down to shoulder level, to the right of the photo, in the area where he's cut out the background. He X's in two columns of type two and a half inches wide and two inches high, about the minimum depth he'd want to go. An old saw decrees that the depth of a column of type should be no shorter than the width of a dollar bill, but he's willing to go a little narrower this time. Most days he has a free hand to decide how much of a story will run on the Living front and how much will have to jump inside. Occasionally, however, an editor will overrule him, or lack of inside space will force him to drop or shrink a photo in order to run more type on the front.

If he lays in one deck (or line) of 36-point type for the head, the whole package—shoe story, photo, headline, and cutline—will be a little over seven inches tall, or about a third of the page's vertical size. That leaves him plenty of room to run the Spenser review in a single three and one-quarter-inch column to the right of the shoe story, flanked by quarter-inch rules (screened, which will make them light gray instead of solid black) to set it off. With a 24-point headline and a photo of the author, he'll still have room for more than three inches of type. So much for the bottom of the page.

Actually, Baker is doing his measurements not in inches but in picas, the standard measure in typesetting. A pica is about one-sixth of an inch, and each pica is made up of twelve smaller units called points. In a 36-point headline, in other words, the uppercase letters are half an inch tall (thirty-six points is half of seventy-two, the total number of points in an inch). The story on the upper left of the Living page—the plug for now, the John Williams premiere later—is in a single column three and a half inches, or thirty-eight picas, wide, with two decks of 36-point head.

Above and below this story, Baker draws in quarter-inch, or 18-point, rules extending the width of the column. In the composing room, where the page will eventually be put together, the pasteup people will create the rule by laying down adhesive-backed black tape of the size the designer has indicated—anything from "hairline" width up to an inch or two. To create a box like the one Baker wants around the bowling story, the pasteup people put rules on all four sides—usually 1-point or 2-point—and connect them at the corners. The work requires a steady hand and a sharp knife.

Drawing the last few elements on the broadsheet, Baker suddenly says, "My mother in Jamaica doesn't understand what I do." (Actually, Jamaica isn't responsible for her lack of understanding. Nearly everyone in the building has lamented at some point that no one "outside" understands his or her job.) Then he steps back, surveys the design, and decides that the page looks pretty good. Even as he makes the judgment, he imagines the Living editor telling him that American Pop is about banquets, not bowlers winning prizes.

As it turns out, that's exactly what happens. Before the afternoon is over, Baker will redesign the page using a photo of bowlers at a banquet table. It's a less interesting photo visually, but it more accurately represents the story.

The author of the bowling banquet story, meanwhile, hasn't entirely relinquished control. Nathan Cobb closed up American Pop this morning in time for his editor to make a

125

printout for Baker to read, but Cobb is still wondering whether he got the tone right. Tone isn't like spelling; you can't program a computer to check it. It's the undefinable "sound" a story creates, and different readers may interpret it differently. Neither Cobb nor anyone he knows makes a habit of going to bowling banquets, but he doesn't want readers of the story to think he's condescending to people who do.

The point of American Pop, after all, is to cover things the paper might not cover otherwise, not even in feature stories. The idea originated about eighteen months ago, when Cobb was beginning to get the sinking feeling that, having written 500 Living pieces, he was spinning his wheels. Cindy Smith, who was then the Living editor, suggested that he try writing about popular culture—not television, movies, and music, which were being amply covered, but things like hot rod shows and Tupperware parties. It sounded like a refreshing change, and Cobb has been writing American Pop pieces, as well as other feature stories, ever since. Some of the activities he's chronicled are not in what snobs might consider "good taste," but they involve millions of Americans. In Cobb's words, "They're us."

The idea for the bowling banquets piece came from a conversation with current Living editor Mike Larkin. In its entirety, the conversation went like this:

Larkin, walking by Cobb's desk: "Bowling banquets?"

Cobb: "Hmmm, bowling banquets."

That was enough to get Cobb on the telephone, arranging to attend six banquets in the next two weeks. He aimed for both geographical and human diversity—men's leagues, women's leagues, mixed leagues, and bowlers of various ages. Some of what he found he could have predicted, chiefly the innumerable platters of warmed-over roast beef. (One organizer told him he'd switched to Chinese food one year, and the bowlers had rebelled.) But there were plenty of surprises: the giant-sized disc jockey who billed himself as the Golden Hippo, for example, or the league that included three nuns, two deaf people, and a bowler with a wooden leg.

Although the research was enjoyable, the writing was difficult. "Writing never, ever comes easy to me," Cobb says.

First he tried writing the story as a series of vignettes from various banquets. It started getting too long, though, without seeming to say much of anything. Realizing he didn't have the kind of anecdotes that could stand alone, he closed that version on his screen. He didn't "spike" (kill) it, just in case some of the phrases or ideas could be resurrected in another context. He started over, sketching a general bowling-banquet scene in the beginning, then connecting the specific activities he'd found at various places. He wanted the story to have a voice—a style and point of view that were his alone—but he didn't want it to take sides. Striking that balance proved tricky. If he hit it right, some people who read the story would go away thinking that bowling banquets were horribly boring, and others would think that they were great fun.

Now, looking over the finished product, he's fairly happy with the tone and happier still with the content. One of the first things he noticed while making the rounds of banquets was that they seemed to follow a pattern. To his surprise, the participants not only confirmed his observation but said that the sameness was part of the attraction. "They really don't change much from year to year," one man who'd been to hundreds of bowling banquets told Cobb, looking not the least bit bored. "The format is set. It stays the same."

So, after hitting some of the highlights of the banquets— the dancing, the music, the shearling-lined championship jackets—and mentioning that some leagues now eschew trophies in favor of cash or booze, Cobb returned to the theme of sameness. "As long as there are bowling leagues," he wrote, "there will be bowling banquets." He listed some of the eternal characteristics (Horse's Ass awards, teams that call themselves the Pinbusters), then ended with a look forward to next year's banquets: "probably same time, most likely same place, definitely same thing."

• • •

Belatedly, someone calls the city desk to report that a group of witches has been picketing the state film bureau, protesting plans to film John Updike's novel *The Witches of Eastwick* somewhere on the South Shore. A town in Rhode Island has already refused to become Eastwick for the movie, saying it didn't want to be associated with the bisexuality and other exotica that helped make the book a bestseller.

Small crisis: A knot of editors forms near the city editor's desk, briefly debating exactly where in Boston the film bureau is. The question turns out to be moot. Although the photographer gets downtown quickly, the witches have dispersed. An intern is assigned to try to reach them, and Warner Bros., by phone. Someone remembers the name of the self-proclaimed "official witch of Salem," who is always in the forefront of any gathering of witches. With any luck she'll know about the protest, and maybe the AP will send a picture.

. . .

After a fifteen-minute nap in his car, Steve Marantz is ready to start writing about the local mint that's making $5.75 million worth of New York City subway tokens. He's feeling optimistic about the story. Although the Roger Williams Mint in Attleboro is the largest private mint in the country, it has gotten almost no publicity. The owner says that he purposely maintains a low profile, in part because some of the companies for which the mint makes coins and medals like to act as if they made them themselves. Marantz isn't sure why the owner agreed to talk to him—and, in fact, the man didn't say as much as Marantz might have hoped—but he thinks the mint will make an interesting story. One shot the photographer took, of the owner scooping tokens from a giant cart, looked particularly promising. A good photo will increase the story's chances of getting good play.

Speaking of good play, he needs to let his editor, Barbara Meltz, know what he's up to. He tells her about the mint building, about the secrecy, about the owner's saying "I feel like Midas" as hundreds of tokens cascaded through his fingers. Sounds good, Meltz agrees; maybe it will make page one. Marantz is skeptical.

Talk of the front page starts them dissecting a story he did last week about a resort development in western Massachusetts. The story required a lot of work, and both Marantz and Meltz pictured it as front-page material. Last Sunday, however, the story ran at the bottom of the front page of the New England section, an addition to the Metro/Region section that's published only on Sundays. Frustrated at what he considered a low-visibility display, Marantz has developed a theory that he outlines for Meltz now: The story's anecdotal lead was all wrong for page one, where the editors wanted something punchy and information-filled. Meltz protests that a good subject, written well, should be able to make the front page whether or not it fits someone's preconceived pattern. Then she adds a dose of realism. People have been writing an awful lot of anecdotal leads lately, she says, and at least one top editor is getting tired of them. Marantz might be wise to try a punchy news lead next time he thinks he has a shot at page one.

Marantz heads upstairs to make a salad in the cafeteria, brings it back to his desk, and picks up the phone. Before he ventures to label Roger Williams the largest private mint in the country, he wants to check with some people in the industry. Calling the subject of a story the "biggest" or "oldest" or any other superlative is almost guaranteed to produce calls from somebody bigger or older, just as saying a person is the "only" one doing XYZ invariably brings out of the woodwork dozens of other people who have been doing XYZ for years. Better to be sure.

He makes the calls and is sitting glaring at his recalcitrant lead when Meltz stops by with a tip: A group in suburban Westwood claims it was snubbed by the Statue of Liberty celebration committee. She wants the story for Friday, so Marantz calls the contact and sets up an interview for tomorrow. He'll do it right after his morning interview with the state police on the black market for illegal steroids in bodybuilding gyms.

• • •

Steve Marantz and Brad Pokorny aren't the only reporters bouncing ideas off Barbara Meltz today. Peter Sleeper, fresh from a morning of leads that haven't borne fruit, is thinking it's about time to give his editor a progress report. So far, three potential stories have taken up his day.

Story I: Tried to follow an earlier story about the district attorney investigating the way the Framingham planning board approves development proposals. Sleeper has been waging a telephone campaign to sway a good source who's reluctant to talk. The man keeps promising to call back but never does. Finally, after Sleeper called him again this morning, the man agreed to meet him tomorrow, although he said he was doing it only because "I want to tell you 'no' in person." Despite that comment, his agreement is a good sign. Once a person goes so far as to meet with a reporter, he usually ends up saying something the reporter can use.

Story II: Drove to Wellesley to interview a fuel oil dealer about "dirty tricks" being used by one of his competitors. It had taken Sleeper days to get this man to agree to talk, and even then he wouldn't reveal his competitor's name. Sleeper has heard other rumors on the subject as well. The story sounds good, but it will need a lot more work.

Story III: Fended off calls from people in the small central Massachusetts town of New Braintree, where the state plans to build a medium-security prison. Since Sleeper wrote last year about the local furor over putting a 1,000-bed prison in a town of 600, the story has been taken over by the State House bureau because the governor has gotten involved. Sleeper tries to explain this to the New Braintree residents who call, but they're intent on convincing him that someone is taking kickbacks. He passes the tip along.

At this point, Sleeper tells Meltz where the first two stories stand. She's interested in both of them and, to his amazement, doesn't push to have them done for tomorrow. The Framingham story, they agree, probably won't make the front page or even the Metro front, but it's important to show suburban readers—not to mention the suburban papers, which cover their towns more exhaustively than the *Globe* ever could—that the paper can stick with a developing story. The two of them like the oil dealers story for a different reason: It's about the "little guy," not the big corporations and government panels that can eat up all the news space if reporters aren't vigilant.

•   •   •

A dozen striking students huddle in the cold kitchen of the Valentin Letelier School in Santiago, Chile, plotting their next move. Pam Constable huddles with them. Like other

130

groups around the city, these students have been protesting the government's plan to turn over administration of their high school to local mayors, a move they see as one more sign of repression by the regime of President Augusto Pinochet. Constable wants to hear for herself what's motivating them.

The students are articulate about their goals. "The regime is waging a psychological war to stop political dissent and privatize the economy," one seventeen-year-old tells her. "Schools are an important channel in that war. We must fight this without fear, or the repression will grow."

Constable has returned to the students' story after a morning of interviewing union officials, trying to grasp the mood of the country. A strike or some other form of nationwide protest seems imminent, and these are the people who would know about it. First she spoke with the president of the truck owners' union, who had been a fierce opponent of Salvador Allende in 1973 and later joined the opposition to Pinochet. In his office, freezing cold like most buildings in Santiago in winter, he told her that more and more people were feeling tricked and betrayed by Pinochet's regime. "We are not extremists," he said. "We are not Communists. What we want is a return to democracy."

Next she interviewed a long-time postal service driver who is head of the white-collar union federation. The longer Pinochet stays, he told her, the harder it will be to restore real democracy. "We are the next Cuba, the next Nicaragua," he said. A clerk, dressed shabbily but carrying himself with great dignity, served them tea. She and the union president spoke admiringly of the way Chilean compassion and culture have persevered in the face of adversity.

An appointment at noon brought her to the office of one of the most influential men in Chile, a much-arrested and -lionized official of the copper workers' union. He told her that his weeks in prison had merely strengthened his resolve to fight Pinochet. "Sometimes I think Chile is too democratic," he said. "We debate everything with nice words and long discussions, and nothing happens. Well, sooner or later people will grow tired of it, and then . . ." As he spoke, she jotted down not only his words but also notes about his rough

131

clothing and down-to-earth attitude. The pictures on the wall showed him shaking hands with the pope at the Vatican.

Days like this, when she rushes from interview to interview, keep Constable on the happy side of the line every foreign correspondent must tread: the border between freedom and loneliness. The line always looks thinnest on her first day in a country, when she awakens early in a strange hotel room, excited to begin exploring. Then it hits her: She has no routine to follow. She doesn't know what she'll be doing all day, and there's no one to ask. All she knows is that at the end of the day—or, if she's lucky, the end of the next day—she'll have to write. In her words, she is "literally, physically, completely on my own."

She can call her editor, 5,000 miles away. Sometimes that takes the edge off the loneliness. But her editor can't, as she might if Constable's beat were New England, provide her with names or phone numbers of people to contact for stories. She's got to find those herself. Usually, if she has time to prepare for a trip, she starts making a list of sources before she leaves Boston. She calls State Department specialists, regional experts at Boston's many universities, and other journalists who have covered the area, compiling names of the people to whom access is easiest. When she arrives, she sees those people first and asks each of them to recommend others.

If she's sent to a country suddenly, because of a coup or a natural disaster, it's easier to know where to look. "In that case, events overtake you," she says. "You do what everyone else is doing. When there's a lack of big breaking news, that's when you're on your own." Part of the solution is to remember why she's in this particular country. If nothing of international importance is happening, she's probably there to chase down a trend that's significant to the region. Sometimes, however, she goes to a country simply because she hasn't been there in a while. On those mornings, when she awakens to a void where structure ought to be, only one thing works. She reads all the morning papers, finds a quote from someone who sounds interesting, and calls that person. "I just read about you," she says. "May I come over and talk?" Almost invariably, the conversation breaks the loneliness barrier and starts her functioning like a reporter again.

Today she's barely been alone for a second. She came directly to this high school from her morning of union interviews, and now she's going back out to the streets, where, if the pattern set in the last two days holds, the police will soon appear to break up the groups of demonstrating students. Most of the high schools outside Santiago have already been "municipalized," or turned over to mayors appointed by the government. Government officials say the change is necessary to cut spending so that Chile can renegotiate its huge foreign debt. Run by the mayors, they say, the schools will be more efficient and will have a more "personal" atmosphere.

The students and teachers, however, fear that their academic independence will be threatened, and that the mayors will try to make the schools profitable at the expense of quality. So they have been fighting. Today Pinochet's wife issued a statement putting forth the theory to which the government has subscribed all along: The students are not protesting on their own but are being manipulated by "hidden instigators" who want to use the issue for political gain.

Out on the streets, the students, in their blue uniform blazers or white smocks, gather in doorways carrying books, talking of their fears for the future. "This government has taken away our right to work, to eat, to have decent homes, and now it's taking away our right to education," one student tells Constable. He is guarding the entrance to a 170-year-old high school from which twelve Chilean presidents have graduated.

In other groups she meets teachers who tell her they are not worried by Pinochet's order that students denounce anyone who propagates anti-government views. It is a teacher's duty to inculcate democratic values, says one man who has been teaching for forty years. "If the government believes it can keep students from involvement in social and political issues," he tells her, "I say they don't know the history of Chile."

As the military police rumble onto the downtown boulevards, a dangerous ballet begins. The students drop their books and run out into the streets, shouting slogans at the police. The police chase them with sticks and water cannon trucks. The students run away laughing, then regroup and taunt the police again. As Constable watches from the side-lines, faces peer out from store windows. Each time the police trucks pass too close, the shopkeepers matter-of-factly pull down their metal curtains, sealing themselves off until the tensions retreat below the surface again.

2:00 P.M.

When you work for the biggest newspaper in New England, everyone wants to knock you off.
—Ollie Rodman, display advertising manager

So far so good, George Smith congratulates himself as he and Pam Cox walk back to the company car they've parked at the Mission Hill housing project. It wasn't easy approaching strangers on the street to get reactions to the possibility of cutbacks in police protection, but they did it—not just here, but at two other projects as well. Their first assignment as *Globe* summer interns seems to be going pretty well.

Pulling up to the first project, Orchard Park, would have been even more intimidating if they hadn't had an appointment to see Sarah Flint, who heads the tenants' group there. She was angry about the proposal and had a lot to say, including one quote they're sure will find its way into the story: "Orchard Park has been used as a dumping ground for the city's problems." The tenants have a good relationship with the team police, Flint told them; the regular city police don't seem to come through very often.

They appreciated Flint's outspokenness all the more when they started trying to interview other residents of Orchard Park and Bromley-Heath. Many of them hadn't heard that the housing authority might no longer be able to afford the team police. Of the people who seemed to know what Cox and Smith were talking about, few wanted to say anything. One woman started giving them her opinion, then "flipped out" (Cox's words) when the photographer who had accompanied the two interns took her picture. Although the photographer assured the woman that the photo would not be published if she didn't want it to be, the promises didn't seem to calm her. "I want your name and number," the woman told the photographer. "If my picture is in the paper, I'm coming after you."

Things got a little better after that. Smith and Cox talked to one of the cops at Bromley Heath, and to a store owner and a couple of twenty-year-olds who were hanging out. Here in the last place, Mission Hill, they found a man who had lived in the project twenty-three years and had dealt with both city and housing authority police.

Neither Cox nor Smith is too sure how the writing process should work on a story that will carry a joint byline. As they reach the car, Cox is proposing possible divisions of labor as Smith searches his pockets for the keys. Actually, he's been patting his pockets for the last twenty yards, not wanting to believe what an immediate flash of insight has told him: The keys are not there. Here he is on his first assignment as a *Globe* reporter, an internship hundreds of college students would kill for, and he has locked the keys in the car.

• • •

All day Marilyn Won has been dividing her attention into smaller and smaller parcels—at first simply tiny, then microscopic, then subatomic. So many advertisers needed so many kinds of service that she felt like Gulliver, tugged in a thousand simultaneous directions by polite but insistent Lilliputians. It's almost a relief now to focus her energy exclusively on one project, and a big one at that: trying to persuade a new downtown shopping mall to take out a full-page ad in the *Globe*.

The marketing director of Lafayette Place looks interested and asks all the right questions as Won and her supervisor, Eamon Galvin, show her the prototype they've developed. The layout would not only advertise the whole mall but would also provide space for twenty individual stores to display goods. The stores' leases, Won knows, require them to participate in cooperative advertising. She feels a surge of satisfaction as the marketing director agrees that the ad would reflect the mall's upbeat ambience.

In the short history of Lafayette Place, which opened last year, *upbeat* would not leap to mind as the word to describe relations between the *Globe* and the hotel/shopping complex. Even today, as they all smile and nod in harmony, no one in the room has forgotten the architectural review that ran in the paper last September. Critic Bob Campbell got right to the point: He called Lafayette Place "the biggest architectural bomb to hit Boston in years" and, later in the piece, "the worst possible lesson about how to build in a city." Campbell was unimpressed by the mall's doughnut-shaped interior and outraged by the dark exterior, which he likened to "an enormous grim cliff of damp cardboard." He ended his review this way: "Lafayette Place is further evidence of the need for Boston to establish some kind of process to prevent buildings like this from happening."

Needless to say, the developers of the complex did not feel that the *Globe* had put out the welcome mat. The review was greeted almost as unenthusiastically in the newspaper's advertising department, where dismay was tinged with *déjà vu*. The *Globe* had also run a negative review of Copley Place, the last shopping complex to open downtown, and the advertising people had had to grin and bear it. They know better than to say anything to the people on the news side.

After the Copley Place review appeared, display advertising manager Ollie Rodman recalls, "I got some phone calls and I went up there and I got nailed by a couple of people. You live with that. It's separation of church and state. They [writers] do their thing, which is healthy, and we sell our ads."

Despite this philosophical attitude, honed during twenty-six years at the *Globe*, Rodman sometimes jokes that his survival depends on lying about his occupation at cocktail parties. "I never say I work for the *Globe*, or someone will start knocking me over the head for some stupid editorial," he says. Then, after a stage-whispered "only kidding," he acts the part of a cowering party guest. In a pleading voice: "Hey, I don't write for the *Globe*, I don't write for the *Globe*, leave me alone, give me a break, it's Saturday night."

Usually, however, Rodman evinces an almost religious zeal when he talks about selling ads. His salespeople are a breed apart, he says, an ambitious crew out "spreading the word" about the *Globe*. The work they do, the tools they use, the fruits of their labors are by turns "super" and "excellent" and "neat." Rodman sees potential advertisers around every corner in Boston, the sixth-largest advertising market in the nation, but competition from other media grows fiercer by the minute. The advertisers must be coddled, wooed, convinced that there's no better return for their money.

The importance of advertising to a newspaper can't be overstated. Together, sales of classified and display ads brought the *Globe* $280 million in 1985. That money paid for 4.1 million inches of advertising at an average rate of $67 an inch. Circulation, the only other significant source of revenue, brought in $68 million. Generally, the newspaper's revenue comes 80 percent from advertising, 20 percent from circulation.

Advertising people rarely use the word *ad;* in this era of specialization, it's too general to be informative. They talk instead of "retail" and "general," "national" and "co-op." These building blocks form a pyramid, split neatly into halves for display and classified ads, with advertising director Jack Reid at the top. Marilyn Won and Eamon Galvin, who work for Rodman, toil on the display side of the pyramid.

The two main divisions of display advertising, general (also known as national) and retail, represent the difference between a particular brand of, say, soup and the stores that sell it. The soup manufacturer pays the national rate to buy an ad promoting his product; the store pays the lower retail rate to advertise that brand of soup, along with other things the store sells. The retail and general division each have a senior manager who reports to Rodman.

Retail ads are ads for stores or chains of stores. Twenty-one salespeople patrol geographically divided territories selling retail ads for the *Globe*. Each of the four retail divisions—Boston, south, west, and north—has a sales manager; Galvin is Won's sales manager in the Boston division.

The general division also has four subdivisions, set apart by subject rather than geography. There's travel, which includes airlines and hotels; amusements, including theaters and restaurants; financial, which comprises banks and stockbrokers; and a large fourth category that includes food, liquor, tobacco, cars, and appliances. The *Globe*'s general division employs seventeen salespeople and four managers.

Retails ads have always constituted the bulk of newspaper advertising. Most stores can neither afford nor benefit from advertising in a national publication; they need a local medium for their message. In recent years, however, more corporations have begun advertising in newspapers. That trend, along with increased competition in such fields as long-distance phone service and health maintenance organizations, has helped general advertising carve out a larger niche.

Because national advertisers have headquarters all over the country, the *Globe* taps the general ad market not only with its own salespeople but also with salespeople employed by a company called Million Market Newspapers. For example, several chains with Boston stores—including Nieman-Marcus, Radio Shack, and Color Tile—have their headquarters in Dallas/Fort Worth. The advertising people at these chains deal both with a particular salesperson at the *Globe* and with a particular rep who works in Dallas for Million Market. The Boston and Dallas reps are in constant communication. Million Market also sells ads for other large papers, including the *Detroit News*, the *Milwaukee Journal*, and the *Baltimore Sun*. Together, the papers can afford representation in far more cities than they could alone.

In recent years, too, newspapers have started going after the millions of unclaimed dollars lurking in an area called co-op advertising. The co-op system works this way: A store places an order for so many pairs of blue jeans. Depending on the size of the order, the manufacturer of the jeans then makes available to the store a certain amount of money to advertise his product. Most larger stores know that co-op money is available and know how to use it. Many smaller stores, however, do not.

The *Globe* has one sales manager who spends all his time on co-op ads. He deals with manufacturers, finding out which local stores sell their product and are eligible for co-op money. Then he goes to the stores, advising them on how they can collect more co-op dollars. Sometimes the manufacturer will provide a camera-ready ad layout called a "slick." A small store might be content just to drop its name and logo into the blank space on the slick and call it an ad. A larger store would probably want to develop its own layout.

There's no requirement, of course, that local stores spend their co-op money—or any other advertising money— at the *Globe*. They can advertise instead on television or radio, in other city papers, in local magazines or in national magazines that offer zoned editions, in one of the twenty-six suburban dailies or dozens of weeklies and shoppers. They can sign up with a direct-mail company and send out circulars that reach every household in a particular area. When they advertise in a newspaper, they reach only the people who read the paper.

"The competition is deadly," Rodman says. "Years ago, a salesperson could go in and talk about the weather and come back with an ad. Today you can't do that."

The tougher the competition, the more tools the salespeople must develop. They still sell most of their ads in the main news sections of the paper, but more and more they try to help advertisers target a particular audience. Maybe the advertiser could best reach potential customers through Sci-Tech on Monday, Business Extra on Tuesday, the food pages on Wednesday, Calendar on Thursday, Sports Plus on Friday. Maybe he'd do best with a pre-print, a circular sent to the *Globe* already printed, then inserted into the paper. Maybe what he really needs is Sunday's Travel section, or even a particular Sunday Travel section, like the annual winter section that features Caribbean cruises. Maybe he'd be perfect for the fall fashion roto (short for "rotogravure," the printing process used for most newspapers' Sunday magazines) or the Your Home roto. Or maybe he'd like to start a steady relationship with the *Globe* Sunday magazine—which, the advertising managers are happy to tell you, ranks first in the nation in retail advertising, and second only to the *New York Times* Sunday magazine in general advertising.

With a universe of media to choose from, however, modern advertisers can't rely on a salesperson's assurances. They need proof—cold, hard numbers—that their ad dollars are going to buy them the right kind of customers. That's where surveys come in. Want to know how many people who live within a thirty-mile radius of Boston City Hall and have incomes over $40,000 read the *Globe?* Research can tell you. Want to know how many of them also read other newspapers, listen to a particular radio station, or watch a particular channel on television? Research has that, too. You can find out how many *Globe* readers shop downtown, how many go to particular suburban malls. Where they buy their cars. Where they eat. How many have kids in college.

The endless permutations and combinations of these nuggets of information form the basis for sales presentations. The salespeople choose the statistics that pertain to a would-be client and, sometimes armed with colorful graphics, set out to win him over. Meanwhile, every other publication and broadcast outlet is making the rounds with its own set of figures, carefully tailored to emphasize its strengths and minimize its weaknesses.

Sophisticated demographics help, but the ad rep's strongest sales tool is the same today as it's always been: his or her own aggressiveness. It takes a certain kind of person to thrive on the unending routine: making the rounds of non-advertisers, providing ninety kinds of service to established advertisers, checking ad proofs for accuracy and placement, keeping up with the latest research and the paper's special promotions, trying to win the incentives the department offers for selling particular kinds of ads.

Won, for example, did a dozen different things today before she and Galvin met at Lafayette Place to make their presentation. After waking early, worried about the debut of her Guide to Art Galleries, she arrived at work before 9:00 and immediately checked the gallery guide layout. The guide, which will occupy half a page in tomorrow's Calendar section, includes eleven art gallery ads. It also includes two "plugs" or "house ads," which are ads for the *Globe* itself. Small plugs are sometimes used to fill space when an advertiser pulls out or a story comes up short; larger house ads, up to a full page, are used to promote a special section, such as the one Sports is doing on the Celtics, or a program, such as

141

the annual book fair. In tomorrow's gallery guide, a half-inch plug giving the phone number for home delivery will even out two columns of ads, and a slightly larger plug will announce the date of the next gallery guide and provide Won's phone number for prospective advertisers. The guide also has a "header" or "lid," a logo including type and a drawing that extends over the four columns and ties the package of ads together.

The layout looked fine, so Won "released" the ads, freeing the composing room to process the page when the editorial copy, a restaurant review, was typeset and ready. Though she'd been able to put the finishing touches on the gallery guide in less than fifteen minutes, she knew that it would remain in her thoughts all day. It was her idea, her project, and its success or failure was her responsibility. She tried to put the guide out of her mind as she checked the paper, not for news but for ads. She was especially worried about one clothing store ad, for which she had had to order major corrections the night before. She was in luck; the corrections had been made and the ad looked perfect in the paper.

At that point, the people who put together TV Week, the television listings booklet in the Sunday *Globe*, called to issue an ultimatum. A local optician, an account Won is handling for another salesperson, had not paid his bill, and the TV book had to be finished by noon. Either the company paid, or its ad would be dropped. Won sighed as she dialed the optician; he had promised her a check three times already. As she'd expected, he was angry when she reminded him of the deadline. She tried to be reassuring, telling him the paper really wanted his ad but couldn't release it unless he could guarantee receipt of a check by noon. The man said he couldn't do that. He told her to forget the ad.

After making two calls to kill the ad, Won stayed on the phone from 9:30 until noon, pitching next week's Celtics championship section to her regular accounts. It's a great opportunity, she told them, to cash in on the huge readership and the wild Boston pride that are bound to result from yet another Celtics victory. Though the paper had done similar special sections in the past, it had never before sold advertising in them. (The Sports department, for its part, wishes no ads had been sold in this one, either; the ads will lock the section into a layout that may not be the best editorially.)

By 10:00, an ad agency she'd called at 9:00 had called back to reserve some ads for next week and an ad in the Celtics section. Just when she'd started to feel pleased, however, the man from the agency told her he'd been dissatisfied with the placement of his client's ad in Sunday's paper.

At 10:30 the optician called back to say he wanted his ad in TV Week after all, and he'd guarantee payment by noon. Won had to swallow hard and tell him she'd try her best, but it might be too late to reinstate the ad. Within ten minutes, however, she'd gotten the TV Week people to agree to put the ad back in, and the credit department to agree to release the account. Taking no chances, she arranged for a messenger to pick up the optician's check.

Then the marketing director of Lafayette Place called, asking her to bring some additional demographic information when she arrived at 2:00. Won called the research department to request the information, then walked down to the composing room to find out why the proofs for a couple of tomorrow's ads hadn't come upstairs yet. After a brief meeting with Galvin to discuss their Lafayette Place presentation, she drove downtown to talk with the owners of a jewelry store that had never before advertised in the *Globe*.

New business is the fuel that drives every salesperson. Rodman states it simply: "Our goal is to increase advertising linage for this newspaper. We don't want to go backward, we want to go forward." He says his people have been trained to spot a "Coming Soon" sign in an empty field (though empty fields are getting scarce around Boston), call the developer's number, and find out what's coming. Maybe a retail chain will be opening its first Boston-area store there, and the *Globe* can get a jump on the competition by paying a call to get acquainted.

Salespeople also keep an eye on what's happening in the marketplace. As Rodman puts it, "We love a war." When competition in a particular industry heats up, the competitors tend to pour more and more money into advertising. Recently, for example, a discount appliance store in Boston started a saturation ad campaign to acquaint readers with its merchandise and prices. Soon, not wanting to be left out, other appliance and stereo stores started advertising more often.

A war might start when car manufacturers try to outdo one another with low interest rates, or when airlines wage a battle of the fares. An airfare war is especially good for newspapers because the discount fares usually carry too many restrictions to be adequately described on radio or TV. "If you hear it on the car radio, you might remember '$99 to Denver,' " Rodman says. "But if you really want to travel, you're going to buy the paper and study that airline ad. We've got an airline war going now. It's marvelous."

Though generating new business is a salesperson's goal, the process can be excruciatingly slow. Stores, especially small stores, may require piles of statistics, gobs of reassurance, before they're ready to part with so much cash. Often a salesperson visits a potential advertiser three or four times, for an hour or more each time, and comes away without having sold a single line. True, the client may suddenly wake up two months later and decide he can't survive another day without a *Globe* ad, but that prospect is small comfort as the salesperson trudges back to her car after the third fruitless call. She'd do it all again tomorrow, though. New business is good not only for the paper but also for the salespeople, who earn extra money for signing up a new advertiser. They also get bonuses if they increase their linage a certain amount from the same period last year.

Won was fairly sure that the jewelry store owners with whom she had a noon appointment weren't ready to advertise. On the other hand, they'd requested some pretty specific information; maybe they could be convinced. Either way, she always enjoyed that moment when she broke free of the office and hit the open road—or, to be precise, the winding, traffic-clogged road. Because she lives in the South End, not far from the *Globe*, she's an expert at navigating the side streets when the expressway looks impossible.

The couple who owned the jewelry store listened carefully as Won explained basic advertising theory, correlating revenue curves with advertising curves. She told them about various ad sizes and corresponding costs, predicted the ROAI (return on advertising investment) they could expect, and laid out some common advertising patterns among jewelry stores. Though the owners didn't recoil in horror, it quickly became obvious that the rates were more than they were willing to spend. Won shifted tactics slightly, telling them about the *Globe*'s competitive CPM (cost per thousand readers reached) and the effectiveness of a consistent campaign of small ads.

To herself, she described the couple's reaction as "receptive but resistant." When she'd answered all their questions and exhausted all her approaches, she gave them some printed information and packed up to go. As always, she scheduled a follow-up meeting in a few weeks. She doubted it would work, but maybe her message would get through over time.

She had one more stop to make before going to Lafayette Place. The new regional manager of a chain of camera stores gave her some corrections for his next ad and launched into a description of the staffing problems he was having. Although the chain advertised heavily on radio and TV in other parts of the country, in Boston it was advertising only in the *Globe*. Headquarters is pleased with the results, he told her.

Won liked this guy. He was new to his job but seemed to understand both the market and the function of advertising. Come to think of it, she liked nearly everyone she'd met selling ads, even the people who wouldn't buy them. Her accounts range from the classiest jewelry stores to the dingiest pawn shops, and, though she's afraid she sounds like Pollyanna saying it, she's found someone interesting almost everywhere she's gone.

Of course, she reflected as she headed for Lafayette Place, she hadn't always been sure the job would turn out so well. When she started, she was assigned a task often given to new people: Take these dead accounts and try to reactivate them. One of the accounts was a furniture store that displayed some rather unusual merchandise.

One day, as she walked through the store with the owner, they passed a bed the likes of which Won had never seen before. The mattress was round, and above it another circular piece was attached at an angle, so that the two parts looked like an open scallop shell. Embedded in the top half of the shell was a television. Partly to make polite conversation, partly to keep herself from laughing, Won asked, "Do you sell many of those?"

"Oh, yes," the owner replied. "Prostitutes buy them. It's an expensive piece, but they figure it's a good investment because they can raise their rates."

.   .   .

From behind a bulletproof window, a guard tells Ray Richard to put his watch, wallet, and other valuables into a locker. Richard locks them in and pockets the key. Photographer Suzanne Kreiter does the same. Then they sit, waiting to talk to inmates at the Massachusetts Correctional Institute at Norfolk who have earned college degrees while in prison.

Kreiter has never been in a prison before, and she's nervous. Richard is edgy, too, but not about his surroundings. He's counting back from his 6:30 deadline: If he has to cool his heels for an hour, then interview the inmates for an hour, then spend another hour driving back and maybe a half hour answering phone messages and doing other miscellany, he'll have two hours to write. He wouldn't want to cut it much closer than that.

Richard has spent a lot of time in prisons. Not long after he arrived at the *Globe* thirty years ago, he interviewed four inmates at the state prison at Walpole. A few years earlier, at the Charlestown prison, the four inmates had led an uprising that resulted in replacement of that prison and brought about reforms in the state's penal system. The interview at Walpole marked the first time a reporter visiting a Massachusetts prison had been allowed to talk with inmates outside the visitors' room, and outside the presence of guards. For Richard, the interview led to a long string of prison stories, from coverage of bloody riots to features about prison life. In 1967 he won a public service award for writing more than sixty stories about Bridgewater State Hospital, where hundreds of men were being confined without hearings.

Today's story will be much easier; he knows that's why it took him only a few hours to get permission for the interviews. A publicist at Boston University, which offers the courses the inmates took, alerted the *Globe* to the story and made the necessary arrangements with the Norfolk prison. Richard knows that B.U. wants positive publicity as much as the prison does. Everybody wants good press, and sometimes it seems that everybody has a press agent whose sole purpose in life is to deluge newspapers with calls and letters. But in this case Richard agreed with the p.r. person. Inmates who earn college degrees will make a good, upbeat story. If the inmates had graduated a few weeks ago, at the height of the college commencement season in Boston, no amount of prodding by B.U. could have gotten them a story. There just wouldn't have been time. But things are quieter now, and the story offers ready-made what reporters usually have to search for: the human element that attracts readers.

Richard has been in the business long enough to see the demands of newswriting change. Once it was enough to write, "The city council voted last night to raise taxes," then detail what happened at the meeting. These days, however, most people get the outline of events from television or radio. They look to the newspaper to tell them *why* things happen and, more important, what impact the day's events will have on their lives. A story on a tax vote now, for example, would explain right away how much an average city resident's taxes would rise, maybe using real people as examples. The search for the human element applies to every other kind of story a newspaper covers, including the endless graduations every spring. It's not enough to write about the blistering heat or pouring rain, then list the speakers and quote their clichés about the future. Reporters search instead for the interesting graduate or the telling detail that will make the story come alive.

Richard usually likes to do background research before he goes out on an interview, but today he hasn't had time.

147

Although B.U. has given him the names of five inmates who are scheduled to receive degrees Saturday, he doesn't know which ones he'll be talking to this afternoon. He does know something, however, about the inmate mystique. He's learned that some inmates avoid interviews, fearing that calling attention to themselves will make it more difficult to find a job when they get out. Many don't want their pictures taken, lest a reader decide that the person pictured looks like someone who committed another crime years ago. And some inmates resent all reporters because of the publicity the media gave their crime and subsequent trial.

On the flip side, many inmates crave contact with the outside world. Richard figures that the inmates who are about to become college graduates will welcome the chance to show that they've made something of themselves. The key, though, will be getting them to relax while they're talking to him. He doesn't want the terse answers a criminal would give in a police interrogation, which is the only kind of questioning to which most inmates are accustomed. He needs quotes with feeling, real insights into what's made these people study so hard to reach a goal.

Richard and Kreiter have been waiting nearly an hour, without explanation, by the time a guard comes to escort them inside. After several unsuccessful attempts to get through the metal detector, Richard has to take off his wedding and college rings, then his belt, then his shoes. On the other side, the two of them pass through a series of locks. Two doors lock them into a box, then another opens to let them out, then two more lock them in again. As they inch along toward the interview, Richard feels like a ship navigating a canal.

•   •   •

In the classified advertising department, the tyranny of the white lights is in full swing. The night crew has come in at 2:00 to join the day crew, which arrived at 8:30 A.M., and most of the 113 desks and telephones in the room are occupied. By the time the last call is answered at 9:30 tonight, the salespeople will have typed as many as 8,000 classified ads into their computer terminals.

The *Globe*'s classified advertising has boomed with the local economy. Classifieds, which are much smaller and cheaper than display ads, now bring in almost as much as their more visible cousins: 46 percent of the paper's total advertising revenue, and 42 percent of the linage. On the display side, retail ads account for 39 percent of the linage and 29 percent of the money; national ads for 20 percent and 25 percent, respectively.

The boom can be measured not only in dollars but also in blinks of white light. Positioned on the supporting pillars around the classified ad department are bulbs that blink on whenever calls are waiting to be answered. The lights may signal one unanswered call or one hundred; only the managers, who have access to the computer that monitors the phone lines, know for sure. The salespeople, for their part, do whatever they can to make the lights go out. If no calls are coming in on their private lines, they push the "voluntary" button that connects them with the main ordering number. They have no idea what sort of ad request will be waiting at the other end. Sometimes dozens of salespeople are on voluntary calls, typing away, and still the white lights blink and blink.

Advertising people like to point out that the dominant paper in any city is usually the one with the strongest classified base. When people move to a new area, they buy the paper with the best classifieds to help them find a job, a house, an apartment. Once they've found those things and put down roots, most people keep reading the same paper they bought that first day.

The people who service these classified shoppers are known as "inside" or "outside" salespeople—not "ad takers," they'd like you to know. The inside people sell ads by phone, the outside people by visiting accounts much the way display salespeople do. "Anybody can be an order taker," says Jean Bazzinotti, the telephone ad manager. "These people are professionals. They're selling."

Salespeople must pass typing, spelling, and grammar tests. They must familiarize themselves not only with *Globe* policies but also with state laws in such areas as equal opportunity in jobs and housing. Above all, they must sell, helping customers find the best way to deliver their message. Unlike car salesmen, classified salespeople often sell by showing the customer how to spend less money. A few dropped words, a few strategically placed abbreviations can make an ad a line shorter and a line less expensive.

For a room in which more than one hundred people set their biological clocks to the rhythm of the telephone, the classified ad department projects a surprising air of serenity. The phones "ring" with a subdued electronic noise; the voices answer directly into headsets that seem to swallow the sound. Viewed from chair level, the rows and columns of salespeople working at their stations form a high-tech quilt pattern: partition, forehead, headset, partition, forehead, headset. The directions to a particular person's station would read like crossword-puzzle instructions: three partitions across, two foreheads down.

Salespeople call one another by their first names, but they assume a new identity the moment they press the telephone button. Their clients know them by their business names—simple names like Carol Hill and Scott Simon that are easier to remember and, according to the classified managers, project a more professional image. The business names also provide a modicum of protection, as one supervisor found when a disgruntled customer wrote her a threatening letter after a salesperson inadvertently mentioned the supervisor's real name.

Along with writers and editors, telephone salespeople are among a newspaper's biggest beneficiaries of the computer revolution. The job can still be tedious—it's difficult, for example, to summon much enthusiasm when an employment agency is dictating an electronics ad that begins "VAX, VMS, MVA, Unix"—but now a computer performs many of the rote tasks. The computer "knows" right away which callers are bad credit risks. It totes up the cost of an ad in seconds, never growing impatient or sloppy when it must figure and refigure the changes.

Salespeople take ads on the IAS, the Integrated Advertising System that in 1985 merged the computerized ordering and processing systems for all display and classified ads at the *Globe*. The key that unlocks the IAS is the customer's phone number. If he doesn't have one, or if the computer matches his number with a record of unpaid bills, the customer will have to pay for his ad in advance. If he proposes that someone else pay—"Bill this to my father in Florida," for example—the salesperson will check with the other source of payment before hitting the button that sends the ad to the typesetter.

Once the customer has been found to be a good credit risk (or at least, not a known bad one), the salesperson hits the "new ad" key, calling up a screenful of blank spaces already coded with the proper margins, type sizes, and indentations. Although salespeople are trained to take every possible kind of ad so that they can deal with the "voluntaries," on their private lines they specialize. They may do primarily real estate or automotive or business ads, three self-explanatory categories, or they may specialize in an area that covers a greater range. The Market Basket category includes, among other things, yard sales, sporting goods, yachts, and death notices. (The classified department takes the paid death notices, while the newsroom writes obituaries of people who were well known locally.) Help Wanted includes not only job ads but also ads for camps, schools, dogs and cats, poultry and pigeons, livestock and lost bankbooks.

Within a salesperson's area of specialization, many of the accounts are regulars, real estate or employment agencies or auctioneers who call every week and know just how they want their ads to read. A caller running an ad for the first time, however, might need help. Should he list his car by the make or the year? Does the color matter? How about the wire wheels? Should he mention the price and risk scaring off potential buyers, or leave it out and have to take a lot of useless calls? How many days should the ad run? The salespeople make suggestions and hit the H & J (hyphenate and justify) button and then the Quote key, telling the computer to count the lines and figure the cost. If the price sounds too high for the customer, the salesperson can try eliminating a few words (so much for the wire wheels) and computing again. Whenever they can, salespeople like to sell ads that will run more than one day; the ads work better, and the seller gets a bonus.

When Julie Green, the assistant telephone manager, first started working at the *Globe*, classified ad takers, as they were called then, typed the ads on typewriters and dropped the typed sheets onto a conveyor belt. The women at the other end of the belt checked the spelling and sent the ads to the men who set the type. Today, there are no "checkers." Since the department was computerized in 1980, the ads have gone into the paper exactly the way the salespeople type them. The computer organizes them alphabetically or numerically within each category and spits them out, typeset, the morning before they are to run in the paper—except for the huge Sunday Help Wanted section, which is printed Friday. The process of running the long streamers of ads from the computer through the typesetter and out is called, unceremoniously, "classified dump."

The classified department has no peak hours—unlike the ombudsman's office, which people tend to call in the morning, while their anger at the paper is fresh—but it does have seasons. This being early June, the big categories are real estate and autos. Spring gets people thinking about new cars, and the end of school puts families in a rush to move and get resettled before September. Help-wanted ads are always heavy because the local unemployment rate is low, but most of them don't come in until Thursday, when the deadline for the Sunday section is 4:30. A salesperson might take sixty job ads on a Thursday, and maybe one hundred real estate ads, which tend to be shorter, on a Friday, the deadline for the Sunday real estate section.

Although managers avoid the word *quota*, they do require a certain level of productivity from salespeople. The computer can report not only how many lines of advertising each person has sold, compared with his own record or with other people's, but more arcane information such as the average amount of time a salesperson spent on a call. The pressure for productivity, combined with the ceaseless ring of the telephones, creates an atmosphere of both camaraderie and stress. "Fast-paced like a tank" is the way classified manager

Frank Limoncelli describes his department. "Just be in it, not under it."

•   •   •

Jack Driscoll ambles through the newsroom on his way to the Wednesday meeting. Every afternoon at 2:30, the editors meet to discuss the next day's paper. On Wednesdays they expand the meeting to a larger room and a larger agenda: what the paper will be doing not just tomorrow, but in the near future. Each editor must come prepared with one new story idea for any section of the paper.

At some newspapers, an appearance by the top editor in the middle of the newsroom would be greeted with fear, or at least awed reverence. Driscoll is greeted with smiles and jokes. The reporters and editors respect his judgments and his ability to determine their futures, but no one seems intimidated by him. It's hard to be intimidated by someone who looks like Tip O'Neill with a smaller nose, acts like everybody's next-door neighbor, and sprinkles his conversation with disclaimers like, "As far as I know—but then, I don't know much." An editor a few steps down the organizational chart says Driscoll is so accessible that people often bother him with problems that really shouldn't require the executive editor's attention.

Ask Driscoll if being the top editor at one of the nation's top newspapers makes him a powerful man, and he reddens and laughs. "I don't like that word terribly much," he says. "It has the connotation of someone exerting his own will. My way of operating is trying to build a consensus for decision making and direction of the paper, and being a catalyst for change." Some people find it strange, Driscoll says, that when he attends the daily news meetings, he speaks very little. There's nothing strange about it, in his opinion. He's there to see what's going on and to contribute ideas if they're needed, not to get in the way of the people who run the day-to-day operations. "I'm not looking for power, and I don't think I need to have it to do what I have to do," he says.

Today, as he passes through the newsroom, he's greeted by reporter David Mehegan, who is leaning back in his chair with his hands behind his head, the picture of relaxation. "What do you think of my story so far?" Mehegan asks.

153

Driscoll bends down to look at the screen of Mehegan's terminal. Except for the blinking cursor, it's blank.

Driscoll is still chuckling when he arrives at the mezzanine-level conference room, and when the meeting starts he tells everyone the joke. Then, cued by glances from managing editor Tom Mulvoy, the editors begin their rapid-fire recitations of the stories they're offering for tomorrow. Driscoll and Mulvoy take notes.

"Interferon was approved by the FDA," says business editor Lincoln Millstein. The anti-cancer drug was developed by a company in Cambridge. "We'll do the impact on business. Fed chairman Volcker's in town speaking to bankers. Radin's there. A study says Lawrence, Lowell, and Nashua are among the fastest-growing cities for jobs. We've got a wire story but we'll staff it." In other words, Millstein plans to have a staff reporter rewrite the wire service story to spotlight, and include more information on, the local cities that came out at the top of the national survey.

As Millstein slows down, assistant sports editor Don Skwar gears up. He's feeling much too frazzled to take the time for this meeting, but because sports editor Vince Doria is out of the office briefly, Skwar didn't have a choice. "Sox at Fenway," he says. "Many off-day Celts stories. Ryan's doing the impending championship. Montville's unsure. Thomsen's got the Houston guards. Madden's doing Walton; it was nine years ago tomorrow that he won with Portland. Shaughnessy's got a baseball column, McDonough's got the Bruins, Borges is in Dallas for the Fryar press conference."

"A lot," national editor Royal Ford begins, answering Mulvoy's unspoken question, "What have you got?"

"First there's underwater secrets [the Pelton story]; it's almost ready. Also, Pollard [another accused spy] and his wife pleaded guilty, and we've got the closings in the Pelton trial. John Robinson's doing job training for people on welfare. The Mass. program has worked so well that bills were introduced in Washington today to start similar programs in all the states. And tax reform is on the Senate floor. Tommy says there's opposition, and not from the expected spots. On the shuttle, Bill Lucas, who ran the space flight center, is out, and four or five bodies are flying around at Morton Thiokol. The families of the seven astronauts were briefed on the Rogers Commission report today. Nobody thinks they'll talk, but we need to make a run at it."

Foreign editor Kathy Tolbert picks up the thread. "The South African government has banned all meetings, including church services. There was some kind of rampage at the Golden Temple. The Soviets have expanded the danger zone around Chernobyl. A soccer riot in Mexico."

Mulvoy breaks in. "We need to do more on the World Cup games," he says. "We're getting scolded quite a bit in calls and letters."

"We're just too tight today," replies Skwar, who knows that the remark was directed at the Sports department. "Maybe we could get Phil Bennett." Bennett is the reporter newly stationed in Mexico City. As a few people nod over this proposal, Ben Taylor starts running down the local list.

"Judge in Attleboro is deciding the BRI case, the autistic kids. The archdiocese may call for the ouster of the Paulist fathers. That's possibly a pretty good story. Feature from Steve Marantz on a private mint that's makin the New York subway tokens. We're trying for follows on Westfield and Switzler. Problem with Westfield is that Curwood's got back trouble. He's trying to write in bed."

"What about the State House? The attorney general's office?" Driscoll asks. He wants to be sure the paper explores all avenues on the Westfield story, which involved a state college's paying a student $10,000 after the student charged that a school official had sexually assaulted him. The story is still developing; reporters are trying to find out who authorized the payment and why. "What right did the college have to take that $10,000?" Driscoll asks.

Taylor nods and writes something down as Dick Powers gives a quick list of available photos: "Pickets, construction traffic, tokens, Sox, and Pops."

"Picks at Edison?" Taylor asks. He doesn't think the electric company strike has been covered well enough. "It seems to be falling between Metro and Business," he says.

"Bruce Butterfield's doing a piece on what's going on in labor in Massachusetts these days," Millstein says. "Maybe he could get it in there. There seems to be a trend toward management seeking concessions on work rules rather than economic issues."

The two deputy managing editors, Helen Donovan and Al Larkin, shake their heads as Mulvoy silently solicits their contributions. Since they have no reporters under their direct supervision, they have no stories to offer for tomorrow. Then, with one last piece of advice on the Switzler story—"Do a library check; cross-reference Vietnam"—Driscoll shifts the meeting from everyday routine to the Wednesday special: proposing story ideas.

"This one's from Dave Greenway and Kathy and Royal," Driscoll says. "A liberation theology project." The idea touches off a series of comments around the room:

"Perfect for Jim Franklin."

"Yeah, get Franklin to do it."

"By September or October, maybe."

"When is the pope coming?"

"Not till '87."

"When Phil Bennett was in Peru, he interviewed the father of liberation theology."

"So we can schedule it for next week?" Driscoll says to general laughter.

The laughter continues as Tolbert mentions the idea she proposed last week: Whatever happened to the "sensitive man" of the 1970s?

"We're going to do it," Ande Zellman, editor of the Sunday magazine, says at the same moment that Ford pipes up, "I've been sensitive ever since."

This week, Tolbert's idea is to write about foreigners who operate opposition political organizations while living in the United States. The group bats that one around awhile, then listens to the next person in line, Gerry O'Neil, head of the Spotlight investigative team.

"We've been getting calls the last few weeks on the shifting nature of Forest Hills," he says. "Looks like the next yuppified area. It would be nice to do it in advance of all the townhouses landing there."

"A real estate piece?" someone asks.

"Who owns the land?"

"Maybe a Neighborhoods piece."

"Bet there's a good bar there where you could get a real sense of the place."

Helen Donovan moves on to the next idea. "This one's from Greenway," she says. "He knows a guy who had a farm on Nantucket and recently sold half the farm for $5 million. He's still living there as a caretaker."

"Only in America," someone says.

"Only on Nantucket," another voice answers.

"My idea is SALT," Donovan says. "And discernible shift in the White House between the Weinberger and Shultz factions?"

Taylor says that London reporter Steve Erlanger, who's been in Boston today, told him that if both sides wanted, they could strike a deal on arms control in three weeks.

Arts editor John Koch proposes a story about come-ons the military uses in recruiting. Do the kids who enlist get what they were promised?

"Fred Kaplan will love it," Ford says.

"Do you get to drive a tank?" Millstein asks. "I'll do it."

"They do a monthly recruiting magazine for high schools," Larkin says. "It's all full of promises."

"Wait a minute, the Army doesn't deceive people," says Victor Lewis, the assistant foreign editor. "They tell a kid, 'You can do such-and-such if you pass a test,' and then the kid doesn't pass and he says he's been gypped."

By this time the meeting has lasted more than an hour, and people are beginning to sneak glances at their watches. The more time they spend in this room, the more they'll pay with deadline problems later. They run through the rest of the ideas quickly.

Mulvoy: "The aging of airline carrier fleets."

Zellman: "The 'best swelter' list. What do people really read at the beach—*War and Peace* or trash?"

Skwar: "I've got nothing that doesn't have Larry Bird's name on it."

Millstein: "A day in the life of Boston business. Six to ten reporters could start at 12:01 and follow all different kinds of people working—a ship captain, a truck driver, a computer worker, a money manager. The idea is when we finish, we'll have learned why we have the strongest economy in the U.S."

"Raccoons," says Lucy Bartholomay of the editorial design department. The editors who were in the morning meeting break out laughing. "We've got them in the attic, and the pest control people say they basically own our house," Bartholomay says.

With grimaces of sympathy, others around the table contribute their own raccoon sightings.

"I've heard somebody's designed special traps," someone says.

"Then it's a business story," Millstein jokes.

"Or the At Home section," someone says. "At Home with Raccoons."

"Actually," Taylor says, "this subject came up this morning and we thought it had pretty much been done. But we can do it again; it's a hardy perennial."

"What's the disadvantage to having them in your attic?" Larkin asks Bartholomay.

She looks chagrined. "Well," she begins, "the other day we found a big stain on the ceiling."

"The problem," Koch proclaims in a mock-serious tone, "is that they don't flush."

On that note, the meeting breaks up. Dick Powers walks back to the photo department wondering how he can persuade a photographer to take the time find a raccoon in the wild. The answer comes quickly: money. He'll offer a $100 bonus to the photographer who finds and photographs a raccoon. A sudden thought stops him on the stairs. What's he going to do if nineteen staff photographers come in with raccoon pictures?

As the sun rises, a few reporters start work in the newsroom. Most of the building is empty.

Out on the road, photographer Tom Landers checks with the photo department by radio to get his next assignment.

Executive editor Jack Driscoll takes his second look at the morning paper as soon as he arrives at his office.

While reporters work to convey the day's events in words, cartoonist Paul Szep portrays the news in pictures.

In the classified advertising department, salespeople are busy taking ads and typing them into their computer terminals.

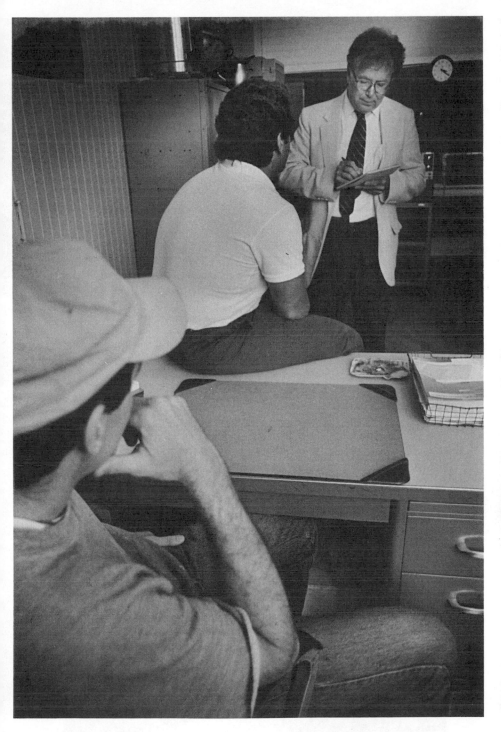

Reporters spend most of the day out on assignment. Here, Ray Richard interviews inmates who have earned college degrees while in prison.

Back in the newsroom, no reporter can write without the
necessities: telephone, notebook, computer terminal, and
coffee.

Two editors look over a story as the writer (right) reacts.

Late in the day, editors from each department gather around the conference table to describe the stories they're offering for the next day's paper.

The newsroom that was nearly empty this morning pulses with activity as the reporters' deadline approaches.

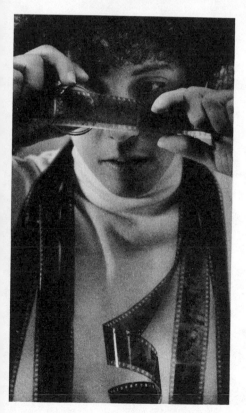

Having developed her film, a photographer examines the negatives to determine which ones are best.

An editor dummies the front page, drawing lines to show where each story and photo will go.

Using the dummy drawn in the newsroom, pasteup artists in the composing room assemble photos and strips of type on the page.

A laser transfers the page image onto a piece of acetate called a laser mask. The mask is used to produce an aluminum plate of the page for the presses.

Rolls of paper travel from the warehouse to the pressroom.

The aluminum plate that will print the front page is attached to the press cylinder with other pages.

When the first finished papers roll off, the pressmen check to make sure the pages are in order and properly inked.

A steady stream of trucks arrives to take away the 514,000 papers that will be printed tonight. As the paper hits the street, the cycle is beginning again.

3:00 P.M.

*I hope I never reach the point where a dying kid is
just another story.*
—Colin Nickerson, Africa correspondent

The pilot, a white mercenary who said he hailed originally from Rhodesia, had filed a false flight plan back at
the airport in central Namibia, naming an agricultural
project near the northern border as his destination. Now,
as the Okavango River hove into view, he brought the
twin-engine Piper into a sharp dive—vanishing from the
radar screens of whoever might be watching—then hur-
tled across the muddy, crocodile-infested waters into
Angola.

The small aircraft skimmed over the savannah at
treetop level, setting herds of wildebeest into a stampede,
terrifying elephants. It took more than an hour to reach
the landing strip hacked out of the southern African
bush. A trio of men toting automatic weapons emerged
from the shade of an acacia thicket. "Welcome to free
Angola," one said.

The man the rebels were welcoming was Colin Nickerson, the
reporter who wrote those words a month ago. Angola was the
last stop on a trip that had taken him through four countries
and four war zones. Not once in three months of travel did he
encounter another journalist. Today he's back in the *Globe*
newsroom, arranging visas for his next trip and reflecting on
the ironies of his life.

"I hate war," Nickerson says fervently. "I hate being close
to it, and not only because I might be killed. I hate seeing
what it does to people." Therein lies the greatest irony: The
thing he hates turns out to be the thing he writes about best.
The longer he covers Africa, the more war dominates his life.

159

Struggling to find a workable attitude toward war, he has run head-on into further ironies. Unless he somehow steels himself against the starvation and death he must witness, he can't do his job. But if he builds his defenses too high, if he pulls back too far, he can't convey what he sees to readers who have never faced it. The more bearable war becomes, the worse he feels about himself.

"I'm most afraid of getting inured to it," he says. "I can't let suffering become commonplace."

Although Nickerson has officially been the *Globe*'s Africa correspondent only since January, he has made five swings through the continent in the last three years. He covers Africa the way Pam Constable covers South America: traveling to two or three countries, then coming home to regroup. Because Nickerson must go farther, he stays longer. The *Globe* does not maintain a bureau in either Africa or South America. That's fine with Constable; though it would be comforting to have a place on the continent she could call her own, she welcomes the chance to jet home regularly. Nickerson, however, thinks that the *Globe* is making a mistake trying to cover Africa without an established base of operations. Still, he's always glad to come home—and by "home," neither he nor Constable means Boston. To Constable, the closest thing to home is North Carolina; to Nickerson, it's Vermont.

Ten years ago, Nickerson was working seventy hours a week for the princely sum of $65, writing for a small weekly paper in northern Vermont. He moved on to a daily, then to the *Globe* bureau in New Hampshire, then to Boston. All the while he was hoping to go overseas someday, preferably to Asia. While he was still "upcountry" (the nickname for the northern New England bureau), the *Globe* sent him to do a story on Cape Verde, a West African nation with strong ties to Massachusetts. In the heyday of Massachusetts whaling, the whaling boats had often picked up extra crewmen in Cape Verde on their way around Africa. Many of those sailors settled permanently near Boston, where their descendants live today.

Nickerson thoroughly enjoyed this first trip to Africa, though he realizes now that it was far from typical. For one thing, everyone in Cape Verde seemed to have heard not only of Boston but also of the *Globe*. In some houses, Nickerson saw pages of the *Globe* tacked to the walls; the Cape Verdians in Massachusetts used the newspaper as packing material when they sent gifts to their relatives in Africa.

Later, when he began returning regularly to Africa, he was thrilled to find anyone outside a big city who had heard of Massachusetts, never mind Boston. In the bush, in fact, some people confused the United States with England. They were familiar with the countries that had colonized Africa, but the United States simply made no difference in their daily lives. As for journalists from the United States, few Africans, except for South Africans, had ever encountered one. The ones who had, tended to divide them into three categories: *New York Times*, television, and "American journalist."

From his berth in the third category, Nickerson deals daily with the ultimate irony: His job is to cover Africa, but, by his own admission, that's impossible. "You can't cover a continent," he says. "You can't even really cover one small country. All you can do is look for themes, events, places where something's happening."

His recent trip to Angola demonstrated the way he chooses his subjects. In April the United States began sending $15 million in "covert" aid to the insurgent group UNITA, led by Jonas Savimbi. UNITA had fought Portuguese colonial rule and now fights the Soviet-sponsored government that took power after Angola gained independence in 1975. Many Americans had never heard of Savimbi before he turned up in Washington, widely touted as a hero. "Who is this guy?" Nickerson wondered along with the rest of the country. "There are so many rebel groups in the world; why are we helping this one?" He began making arrangements to find out.

Deciding to cover a rebel group is not like deciding to cover a game at Fenway Park. No subway goes to the rebels' door. No press agents roll out the red carpet and issue the necessary passes. UNITA maintained an office in Lisbon, Portugal, but Nickerson knew that hooking up with the rebels in the bush would be a matter of planning and luck.

161

He'd learned about back-door entrances two years earlier, when he and photographer Stan Grossfeld tried to get into Ethiopia to document the famine there.

"When we wanted to go to Ethiopia, the government told Colin and me basically, 'You may not enter,' " Grossfeld recalls. "Did that make us want to go home? No, it made us want to go there more. Here you've got this Marxist government using food as a political tool. So you find another way." Nickerson and Grossfeld took a gamble and flew to the Sudan, hoping that from there they could sneak into Ethiopia with a group of rebels fighting the Ethiopian government. The gamble paid off, but their march with the rebels proved long and harrowing. Once they reached Ethiopia, the suffering of the people so horrified them that they wondered why they'd wanted so badly to come.

Typically, Nickerson speaks of Ethiopia briefly and quietly. "I still have terrible dreams about the things we saw there," he says. Just as typically, Grossfeld vents his emotions in long bursts of words. One burst goes like this:

"I felt like a whore the whole time we were there. The stuff I *didn't* take pictures of was so much worse—a kid with pieces of his face eaten away. I'd think, why am I recording this misery? The textbook answer is I'll show this stuff because it's important that people know it. But in reality I just wanted to go home and hug my girlfriend and go to bed with the covers over my head. It bothered my inner soul too much. I kept wondering, how could anyone be racist if they saw what I saw? These people love their kids. They're just like us, only they have more courage. I thought, if I can get across that love and determination, maybe people will do something. And they did."

When Grossfeld and Nickerson returned to Boston talking about Ethiopia, the *Globe* canceled its Christmas party and donated the money the party would have cost. With individual contributions added, the company sent $60,000 to the famine relief efforts. That made Grossfeld and Nickerson feel a little better, but they still had trouble dealing with the plenty they'd always taken for granted. To this day Grossfeld can't walk past the food stands of Quincy Market, Boston's

mall-ing of the historic area around Faneuil Hall, without launching into a mental tirade on the piggishness of
Americans.

He's glad that Americans in general, and *Globe* employees in particular, responded so generously when images of the
famine dominated their newspapers and television screens.
But nothing that's happened since Ethiopia—not the dona-
tions, not the Pulitzer Prize he won for his photos—can
change the helplessness Grossfeld felt as his camera framed,
again and again, the silent tableaus of starvation. "When I
was there," he says, "I just had to do it, and try to keep the
tears from getting in the viewfinder so I couldn't focus."

Nickerson, too, will never forget. In some ways, Ethiopia prepared him for what he would see as he covered the rest
of Africa. Grossfeld, for his part, swore off suffering after
documenting another round, this time in the Mideast. "Now
I'm trying to avoid war and sadness," he says. "It screws me
up for God knows how long. Send some other kid."

In Africa, that "kid" is Nickerson. Because he's not much
of a photographer—which probably hurts readership of his
stories, he says, since the photo agencies don't have many
stock photos of the areas he covers—he paints his pictures
with words. Subjects for the pictures are everywhere. Everything in Africa is so unusual, so foreign to Americans' understanding, that the pictures cry out to be painted.

Picture this: Having hitched a ride with relief workers,
Nickerson arrives in a remote village in Mozambique. The
village elders line up to greet him. Just then, the village comes
under heavy mortar attack. Nickerson wants to run for cover,
but the elders hold their ground, one by one extending their
formal welcome as the shells whiz by. "Maybe we should
wait," Nickerson suggests through a translator. "It is nothing," the elders reply.

Or picture this: He sits for days in a hotel in Namibia—
"In Africa, *hotel* can mean a room with a dirt floor, no
plumbing, and scorpions running around"—waiting to be
contacted by someone who can take him to UNITA's base
deep in the Angolan bush. When finally he meets the white
mercenary pilot and they are skimming the treetops in the

middle of nowhere, plunging toward the crocodile-infested river, he thinks about the implications of a crash. The pilot has filed a false flight plan. If they go down, no one will even know where to look.

Or this: In central Angola he sees the young casualties of the civil war. Children lie in agony on the dirt floor of a makeshift medical center. Some of them are missing limbs. All of them are starving. Nickerson cannot bring himself to take notes. Later he writes about the scene in his journal. Elsewhere in rebel-controlled territory, he interviews a Cuban prisoner of war who lives, unguarded, in a thatch hut. "I do not try to escape because there is nowhere to go," the prisoner tells Nickerson. "All around here there is only bush. I would be eaten by lions or hyenas."

Or, finally, this: After spending two weeks with the UN-ITA rebels, Nickerson wants to get the government side of the story. At one village he visits to conduct interviews, he plans to stay for an hour or two. Instead, he's trapped for several days because the village is being shelled—by the very rebels he just left.

The ironies are everywhere. Nickerson says that no one can truly cover Africa without getting out of the cities and into the villages, where 80 percent of the people live. But outside the cities there's no transportation, and often no roads. There's certainly no one who speaks English—but then again, Africa has so many languages that people in villages just a few miles apart may not be able to talk to one another. It would be nice if one language could get him around the continent, the way Pam Constable's Spanish opens doors in most of South America, but so far he's made do with English and French, and help from translators. "Language makes covering Africa more difficult but also easier," Nickerson says. "There are literally thousands of languages. Nobody understands anybody else; everyone's as lost as I am."

Africa presents other problems as practical as language. When he's not covering breaking news, Nickerson sometimes delays writing until he returns to Boston. Waiting goes against the journalistic grain, but it's easier than trying to find a telephone in Africa. Big cities usually have decent phone service—though he remembers waiting two days for a phone line when he was trying to dictate from Khartoum, Sudan—but there's no use looking for telephones in the villages. There's no use looking for water faucets, either. On the way to Ethiopia, he and Grossfeld drank from the same camel holes as their rebel guides, and in other countries he has seen village women walk miles every day for a single jug of water.

Transportation, communication, sustenance—these considerable problems pale when compared with the big one: physical danger. Nickerson mentions it reluctantly. "The moments of real danger are really quite brief—a matter of minutes," he says. "But they're terrifying." Often he travels with missionaries or relief workers, and if they hear shelling ahead, they stop. "You try to be sensible," he says. "That's one difference between reporters and photographers: Photographers feel they have to run *toward* the trouble." Even photographers, however, don't behave like the "foreign correspondents" in movies. Now that he's living the life, the film image makes him laugh. "One doesn't go skipping through war zones," he says.

When Nickerson talks about his job, he doesn't stress the danger or the disease (dysentery and malaria are occupational hazards), or the heat and humidity that make the Congo region "like walking through a super-heated shower." For him the attraction is the people, the daily opportunity to puzzle out a different culture and pass his new-found insights along to hundreds of thousands of readers. "It's fascinating work," he says. "How could I ever be bored?"

Despite the hardships of their daily lives, he has found Africans unimaginably generous. "The government officials are paranoid and suspicious; they don't want to talk," Nickerson says. "But the ordinary people are the most gracious and polite people you can imagine. They have nothing, but they'll always welcome you. They're embarrassed to have so little. In Sudan they would say, 'Let us bring you bread,' but I would know they had none for themselves."

Even his growing respect for the people comes with irony attached. The more affection he feels, the angrier he gets about the effects of war. "Angola should be a rich nation," he says. "People shouldn't be suffering. But they are, because you can't solve political problems with rocket fire."

Sometimes Nickerson sees Africa as a reporter's Eden. Story ideas dangle from every tree like ripe fruit, bursting with the juice of novelty. Nothing that happens seems ordinary; everything is worth writing about. Best of all, the stories are his for the picking; rarely does another reporter enter the garden. But every Eden has its serpent, and this one assumes the form of a question: Does anyone at home care? On good days he stares the serpent down and vows to *make* them care, to write so well that he must be read. On bad days, like many foreign correspondents, he fears that the answer to the serpent's question is no.

"Americans are terrible about foreign news, just oblivious," Nickerson says, looking back at Africa from deepest Dorchester. "We're the most insular people on earth."

• • •

On a slant-topped wooden table in the composing room, under the watchful eye of Mary Jane Wilkinson, the *Globe*'s latest lure for the business-minded is taking shape. It's a new weekly section called Money, and Wilkinson, an assistant business editor, is supervising creation of the mockup. The real thing will debut in next Thursday's paper.

Business has been the fastest-growing department in the *Globe* newsroom for the last five or six years, and the new section reflects both that growth and the increased reader interest that prompted it. "Business is *the* interesting and exciting place to be in journalism in the '80s," says business editor Lincoln Millstein. He speaks with the zeal of a recent convert. Although he came to the paper three years ago as assistant business editor, he has just rejoined the thirty-person business staff after a year spent as city editor, directing the local news reporters.

"In the '60s and '70s it was Vietnam and Watergate and going after public officials," he says. "But the '80s are a time when American journalists are learning to cover business and economics." The key word, he says, is *learning*. Business coverage hones to a painful sharpness two of the key questions that face every journalist: Who are my readers? And how do I get the information I need?

Most reporters, as they lock gazes with their computer screens, picture a person for whom they are writing. It may be an actual person, a spouse or parent or friend who's a particularly critical media consumer; or it may be a composite creation, a reader of a certain age with a particular intelligence level and particular interests. For the most part, however, this generic reader is no longer "Joe Six-Pack" or "the Kansas City milkman," two specters who haunted newsrooms of the past.

When an editor directed a reporter to write for the Kansas City milkman, he was telling the reporter to tailor his prose for an ordinary soul who didn't know much about much of anything. Today, most journalists would view that approach as condescension. They don't see themselves as saviors, reaching down to enlighten and educate the unwashed masses. Instead, they are simply representatives of the general public. They go places, attend meetings, investigate subjects that most people don't have time for, then deliver their reports via the newspaper.

As foreign correspondents wonder about reader interest in faraway lands, so business reporters have traditionally wondered whether many readers care about business. The advent of "yuppies," along with other demographic and economic shifts, has helped answer that question. More and more often these days, business news is front-page news. Millstein, in fact, believes that the question "Does anyone out there care about business?" may not have been valid in the first place. "As a business writer, you're always trying to make something you suspect may be intrinsically boring, interesting to the readers," he says. "But I think we've overstated that. I think business seems more boring to most news people than it does to everybody else."

The diversity of New England in general, and Boston in particular, complicates the quest to define "everyone else." "You write a business story and you're always worried whether the townies in a [local] pub will be interested," Millstein says. "And if they are, does that mean you're not making the story sufficiently deep for the manager of the Magellan Fund at Fidelity?"

Trying to meet the needs of this diverse audience, business writers operate on a simple theory: A good story will always be read. In the Business section, as in all other sections of the newspaper, a good story is often a story about people. For example, in yesterday's Business Extra, an expanded business section that runs every Tuesday, all three front-page stories were about people. The lead story profiled A. Alan Friedberg, whose company runs every movie theater in Boston except those showing X-rated or martial arts films. The "news peg," the reason the story was timely (the peg is also known as the "hook," on which the story hangs), was that Friedberg had just sealed his dominance by buying an art movie house, the last theater in the city that his company, USA Cinemas, didn't own.

The rest of the Business Extra front page also stressed people over dollars. One story, about a Harvard Business School graduate who had started a computer company, was a sidebar to a larger piece on the school's Class of 1981, which was holding its five-year reunion. This story not only highlighted the human angle but also followed a format, perfected by the *Wall Street Journal*, known as the "focus structure." Now used in all types of stories in all types of newspapers, this structure reports on an issue or institution through the eyes of one or more individuals. The theory is that a reader who isn't naturally inclined to read a story about, for example, real estate prices might read the story if it began with a particular person who's been priced out of the market. In its classic form, a focus-structure story begins with a person, provides a transition from the person to the larger issue, reports on the issue, then returns to the person at the end.

In the Harvard story, reporter Jane Meredith Adams focused on three people. She wrote this lead: "Steve Levitan acknowledges 'the siren sound of dollars.' Joseph M. Rault 3d craves life 'on the margin, on the frontier of finance.' Antonio DeLuca relishes 'getting a deal together.' " Her second paragraph provided the transition: "They are members of the

Class of 1981 at Harvard Business School and, five years out, they are rising investment bankers, part of a young, very rich breed that in recent weeks has felt the taint of greed and federal indictments." The story went on to explore investment banking and ethical questions raised about the field. It ended with quotes from the three graduates mentioned in the lead.

Though they try to stress the "people angle" as much as other reporters do, business writers need more specialized knowledge. The knowledge enables them to answer a question as important as the identity of their readers: Where do I get my information? "Most reporters grow up covering city government, police, and fire," Millstein says. "These are accessible institutions; they know they're responsible to the public. Business isn't as accessible. You learn to use certain techniques and tools to get the information."

Business reporters must know, for example, that every publicly traded company is required to file a financial statement. They must know where to get the financial statement, and how to read it when they get it. They need to be familiar enough with corporate structure to know which person within that structure might give them a particular piece of information, and what biases the person might have that could affect the accuracy of that information.

At the same time that reporters are learning to cover business, businesses are learning to deal more effectively with reporters. "If a disaster like the Bhopal leak had happened ten years earlier, Union Carbide probably would have clammed up," Millstein says. "Now, within limits, they help us. They realize it's in their own interest that we cover the story accurately. Both the press and business have grown up."

Millstein considers it his responsibility to keep the paper's top editors informed of major developments in business and the economy. When a big business story breaks, as when the Senate Finance Committee unexpectedly approved a tax-reform bill recently, he helps coordinate coverage with the national desk. This push to keep abreast of trends explains the genesis of the Money section. As more and more people look for places other than banks to put their money, more and more publications are springing up to serve them. Newspapers don't want to be left out.

That's the philosophy, but right now Mary Jane Wilkinson is concerned with the mechanics. She spent the morning working with the reporters who will be writing for the first Money section (the department has hired three new people in the section's honor), talking with the designers about how the pages will look, and sending the stories from the newsroom computer to the typesetter. Now she's watching as a pasteup person lays down the type to match the latest incarnation of the dummy.

When the first Money section runs next Thursday, its front page will spotlight two stories. At the bottom will be an interview, in question-and-answer format, with the new regional administrator of the Securities and Exchange Commission. The first question stresses the practical tone of the section: What are your main concerns for investors in Boston? Lest anyone mistake the Money section's advisory intent, the centerpiece story will hammer it home. The story, which says that certain high-income, childless couples will suffer if tax reform becomes law, begins this way:

> See Dick and Jane all grown up. Now 30, they have finished college, gotten high-paying jobs, and bought a condo in the Back Bay (with plenty of room for Spot), a BMW and lots of Cuisinart cookware. They should enjoy it all now; if the Senate tax plan becomes law, they are going to pay a lot more in taxes.

• • •

A dozen high school students stand clumped in a corner of the *Globe* Sports department. Passing staffers glance at them, walk a few steps farther, then turn to look again. It takes a minute to pinpoint what's strange: The boys, their hair carefully combed, are wearing jackets and ties, but from the waist down, some of them look as if they just stepped off a beach. Baggy Hawaiian print shorts or cut-off jeans hang below their suit jackets; battered sneakers cover their feet. They are athletes, chosen for the *Globe*'s All-Scholastic teams, and they're

170

here to have their pictures taken for the paper. The pictures won't show them below the shoulders.

The invasion of high school athletes merely adds to the increasing commotion in the department. Although many of the sportswriters are out of town—five in Houston for the NBA playoffs, one in Dallas for an NFL press conference, one in Paris for the French Open, one in New York for the Belmont Stakes—the staff of forty-six full-timers and thirty part-timers leaves plenty of bodies to fill the space. The closer the clock moves to deadline, the more people crowd into the room and start writing, and the more often the telephone rings.

Sports editor Vince Doria picks up his ringing phone for the fiftieth time today. "I'm in Parkman Hospital," reporter Ron Borges' voice tells him from Dallas.

"*What*??!!" Doria sputters.

"The guy came after me," Borges says.

For a moment, Doria almost believes him. Borges has been writing for the last week about the NFL player who's accused of gambling, and the player hasn't appreciated the stories. Could he really have attacked Borges?

"Just kidding," Borges says before Doria can panic.

Serves me right, Doria thinks as Borges fills him in on the press conference the player has just held. I'm the one who's always saying that the Sports section should be fun.

Fun is the word Doria uses most often to describe the place where he has spent most of his waking hours for the last ten years. Other people talk about the quality of the Sports section; he talks about how much the staff enjoys putting it together. Its reputation as one of the nation's best seems to him a nice compliment—but not a terribly important compliment, or even a very logical one.

"There are plenty of good sports sections out there," he says modestly. "You get a certain reputation. . . . Why ours came about, I don't know. It's a city that has a lot of good things to write about, and of course we have a lot of talented people." He claims to know no secrets for assembling a talented staff—"some good hires, some good luck," he says—but he knows exactly what effect that staff has: "Good people

171

generate the idea of having fun with writing. Then when new writers come in, they see that good writing is appreciated."

New writers rarely come in; the turnover rate in the Sports department isn't worth calculating, especially compared with the rate in other departments and other papers in the nothing-is-permanent world of journalism. On the rare occasions when he does interview prospective sportswriters or editors, Doria's most important consideration is how they'll fit in with the rest of the staff. "It's very subjective, hard to define, but I look for someone who's cut from whatever mold we all came from," he says. He pauses as if replaying his words, then decides that they sounded immodest. "It's not a big deal, like there's some sort of mystique that makes you a *Boston Globe* person," he adds quickly. "We've got myriad personalities, but when you're interviewing, you can tell you'll enjoy working with some people more than others." Those people, Doria says, are above all imaginative. "They're not dogmatic, not married to ideas they'll never change."

Most sportswriters grew up following sports, and they see their jobs as the best thing short of independent wealth: making a living at something they love. "I think all of us have days when we wake up and say, 'What a deal! I'm being paid good money for what many people view as child's play,' " Doria says. Then come the other days, when the image of glamor and fun gives way to the reality of writing 160 baseball stories in six months. Every job has its routines, and sportswriters gladly choose the routine of covering games over the routine of selling used cars or insurance. Still, burnout can hit sportswriters early, and then it's Doria's problem.

Sportswriting, like sports, is a young person's world. Once upon a time, when seniority carried more weight, a sportswriter might have had to wait until he was forty to earn the right to cover a pro team. Now he may have his "own" team in his twenties. "So at twenty-five you were a *wunderkind*," Doria says. "Then suddenly you're thirty-five and no one is offering to make you president of the United States. You start saying, 'This is fine, but do I want to do it for the rest of my life?' "

172

The usual corporate incentive, upward mobility, doesn't exist for writers who want to keep writing. The insurance salesman who's bored with his routine knows that if he keeps working at it, he may become a vice president someday. The sportswriter who tires of his routine sees an endless series of seasons stretching before him, unless he wants to foresake the press box for an editor's desk. A few good writers can move from writing game stories to writing columns, allowing them to bounce from sport to sport and put their own particular spin on what's happening. But not everyone can be a columnist; someone's got to cover the games. "The funnel starts getting narrow," Doria says. "It's something newspapers are going to have to deal with."

Doria dreads having an opening on the staff, not because he'll have trouble finding a good person but because he'll be deluged by so many. In the tight circles in which top sportswriters travel, he rarely needs to advertise. Earlier this year, when baseball writer Pete Gammons decided to move to *Sports Illustrated*, it seemed like only minutes before half the baseball writers in the country were calling Doria. Was it true about Gammons? Would Doria consider them?

As it turned out, Doria filled the baseball vacancy with staff writer Dan Shaughnessy, who had been covering basketball. Change—"mixing up their menu," Doria calls it—is the one incentive he can offer in the absence of upward mobility. The second part of the baseball change was Bob Ryan's return after a break that included a stint on television. Ryan agreed to cover the Celtics, which he'd previously done for a dozen years.

The shuffle completed, Doria was free to sit back and watch the *Washington Post* forge the first link in a chain of new hires. The Post hired a baseball writer from the *Baltimore Sun*. Baltimore, in turn, hired a writer from Dallas who had talked to Doria about the Boston job. Dallas hired someone from Kansas City, and so on across the country—until at the end of the chain, Doria likes to imagine, some young kid just out of college got his first sportswriting job at a little local paper.

Jeff Horrigan, sitting a few desks away from Doria this afternoon, wishes he'd been that kid. Tomorrow is the last day of classes before Horrigan graduates from Northeastern University, and he's spending it working rather than celebrating. His after-school career at the *Globe* is coming to an end, too ("Graduating seniors are kindly asked to leave by July 1," he says), and he has no idea where he goes from here. So far, the resumés he's sent to 104 newspapers have yielded nothing.

Horrigan has been in the office since noon, typing biographies of the students on the All-Scholastic golf and lacrosse teams. In a few minutes he'll leave for Weymouth to cover a high school lacrosse championship. He'll sit in the stands to keep statistics on the game and compile a scoring summary, then mingle with the players to gather quotes. By 8:00 he'll be back in the office, calling the coaches from two other lacrosse games that no one is staffing. He'll write the three games into one story and then head home to Dedham, probably arriving eighteen hours after he left.

He's tired, but he's not complaining. Horrigan is a "co-op," the name editorial assistants are called at the *Globe* because many of them are in the cooperative education program at Northeastern. In four years, he has progressed from gofer ("Hey, kid, go for coffee") to correspondent, writing two to five bylined stories a week. He's covered mostly high school sports but on occasion has been pressed into service to help with colleges or the pros. He loves it; it's just what he wants to keep doing. But Doria was right: Newspaper sports staffs aren't expanding, so there's not a lot of hiring going on. What's to become of him? He typed an individual cover letter, tailored to a particular newspaper, to go with each of those 104 resumés, and now he eagerly awaits the mail every day. But as the Real World lurches ever closer, Horrigan's image of himself as a full-time sportswriter is starting to fade. In its place a new vision is taking shape: It's summer and he's lying on a beach somewhere, watching his money melt away.

•   •   •

Back on the news side, the content of tomorrow's paper is undergoing its usual afternoon metamorphosis. No story is too small to be immune from change. Hours after early-morning reporter Paul Feeney has gone home, for example, his brief on the Quincy robberies is still developing. The police now think the three robberies were the work of two men, not one. Feeney's original lead—"Quincy police are seeking a young gunman who went on a mini crime spree, holding up three businesses in the city"—has been changed to this: "Quincy police are seeking two men who robbed three businesses in separate incidents yesterday morning." The ten-sentence item will run in New England News Briefs, known around the newsroom as "Neenibs."

It was Marvin Pave, the city-editor-for-a-day, who assigned another reporter to check on new developments in the Quincy story, as Feeney had recommended on his way out. Pave has been keeping up with dozens of other small matters as well. "The city desk isn't the most glamorous place for assignments, but it's never dull," he says. From reading the wires, listening to the scanners, and flipping through the tip sheets written by the co-ops who answer the phones, he's found out about tires slashed at a senior citizens center, an escaped prisoner on Cape Cod, a Harvard cross-country bike trip for hunger, and a Revere man fined for tax evasion. He has reporters looking into all of those. A few other stories with potential, including one about a pit bull terrier that attacked a mailman in Lynn, will have to wait until the night reporters arrive at 4:00.

When Pave mentions the night crew, Dave Morrow, his compatriot on the city desk, realizes that it's almost 4:00 and he hasn't gone to lunch yet. He's spent the afternoon making schedules for the summer interns and co-ops and editing a Sunday story on the Suffolk County sheriff's race. He just hasn't had time for lunch, and he won't be able to go now, either, unless he combines lunch with a rescue mission. One of the new interns is stranded without a car in South Boston. Morrow decides to drive there and have a co-op follow him. After some confusion, they find the intern. The co-op drives the intern back to Morrissey Boulevard, and Morrow picks up a crabmeat sub and takes it to a park where he can eat in peace.

175

Peace sounds fine to Renee Loth, who is stuck in traffic with a surly cabdriver, trying to get back to the *Globe*. She's just finished a two-hour interview that got her started on a story for the Sunday magazine, for which she is one of five staff writers. The story, tentatively titled "The Hustle for History," is about the U.S. Customs Tower, a Boston landmark that the federal government has decided to sell as surplus property. She wants to trace the process and politics by which a historic building is developed for private use. In the next few weeks she expects to read five or six books and as many studies and proposals, and to interview at least twenty people—if she ever gets out of this cab.

Loth isn't the only person thinking about Sunday on this Wednesday afternoon. The mailroom has been tying advertising inserts into bundles for delivery to the stores that sell the Sunday paper. The stores and distributors will receive several sets of bundles during the week and put them all together late Saturday or early Sunday, when they receive the news sections of the paper.

Arts editor John Koch and his assistant, Harry King, have been editing the stories that are already finished for the Sunday Arts section and working with writers on stories still in progress. Richard Carpenter, who usually lays out the Sunday Travel section, is working instead on Living, filling in for an editor who's sick. The designers gave him the dummy for the front page of the Sunday Living section at 1:00, and he started measuring type and writing headlines and captions for it. Now he's laboring over the inside Living pages, which contain stock features like Ann Landers that would be easy to lay out if this were his regular job. Since it's not, he's struggling.

In the travel department, where Carpenter would usually be, Jerry Morris selects photos of Canada for the Sunday Travel section and brings them to the design department, then settles in to finish his Globe-Trotting column, a roundup of short travel items. He's hoping that Carpenter can do the final read for him; Morris wants to "take a slide" (leave early) because his daughter is graduating from high school.

Over in the Living department, writer Margo Miller is polishing Marquee, a column on music and the performing arts that will run in the Sunday Arts and Films section. Her first item is about the new Schwann Compact Disc Catalog, and yesterday she wrote this lead: "There will still be a 'Schwann' to thumb through in record stores. But the July issue won't be the Schwann we've always consulted when buying LPs or cassettes of classical, jazz and pop music." Looking it over today, she decides that the lead isn't specific enough about how Schwann has changed. In addition, she wonders whether she can be sure everyone knows what a compact disc is. To answer both those concerns, she slips in another paragraph after the lead. It says: "That's because the smart money thinks those little silvery CDs—laser-played compact discs—are on their way to eclipsing the big black vinyl LPs." That's better, she thinks, but wait—does "smart money thinks" make sense?

Nearby, music critic Ernie Santosuosso is grappling with his own demons. He interviewed singer Barbara Cook this morning, planning to use her as the lead item in Weekend, his Friday column chronicling musical happenings in the Boston area. But his editor decided he should write the Cook story for tomorrow instead. Now, having done that, Santosuosso is left without a strong start for Weekend.

Before he became the *Globe*'s jazz and popular-music critic, Santosuosso covered rock for fourteen years; he says he got out while he could still hear his wife calling him for dinner. Now he does interviews and concert reviews as well as reporting on arts news. His interview with Cook this morning wasn't one of the all-time greats. Because the singer is appearing in Boston next week, her press people had requested the interview and promised to call Santosuosso at home this morning to give him Cook's New York phone number. He waited two hours for the call, and then when he called Cook, she told him she'd rather do the interview tomorrow. He tried not to get angry—there had probably been a communications foul-up somewhere—as he explained why tomorrow would be too late.

Santosuosso wasn't doing the interview only because the press agents had lobbied for it. Although people with a cause or celebrity to promote may disagree, a writer's choice of subjects is his own (and, sometimes, his editor's). Public relations people can be a pain if they're too persistent or unfamiliar with newspaper routine—if they call on deadline and won't hang up gracefully, for example—but sometimes they're the only way a newspaper learns of an upcoming event. Most journalists have had the disconcerting experience of being rebuked for not being omniscient. "Why didn't you cover that? What's the matter with you people?" someone will thunder, mentioning an event about which no press releases were sent out, no announcements made.

In the best of all possible worlds, a newspaper would have enough "ears" in its community to hear about everything that happens. In this world, newspapers miss a lot. Readers who favor conspiracy theories often see evil motives, political and otherwise, lurking behind the lapses. Writers and editors, as they kick themselves for missing something, can usually fit the reason into one of two categories: lack of awareness or lack of staff.

Santosuosso agreed to interview Cook because he knew that she was an interesting performer who had a following in Boston. After the initial confusion about the arrangements, she agreed to a ten-minute interview by phone. Santosuosso would have liked more time, but he was able to make do with ten minutes because he already knew enough about Cook to have developed a potential focus for the piece.

Reporters like to learn as much as possible about a person before they interview him or her. Boning up provides a number of advantages: It establishes the writer's credibility with the subject, ensures that the subject can't "snow" the writer, and avoids wasting time on questions ("Where did you go to college?") that could be answered through research. No journalist who's heard it can forget the story, perhaps apocryphal, of the cub reporter who managed to snare an interview with Vivien Leigh the night of the premiere of *Gone With the Wind*. Nervously, he began by asking, "What part did you play in the movie?" Leigh, so the story goes, walked out of the room and never came back.

Sometimes the exigencies of the news business force reporters to go into an interview knowing as little about the interviewee as that unfortunate scribe knew about Scarlett. That's when they need time and training—time to let the subject talk until a focus starts to emerge, and training to recognize the focus and run with it. Luckily, Santosuosso wasn't in that position this morning. He knew that Cook had won a Tony award in *The Music Man*, and that she'd appeared in concert at Lincoln Center last fall. Since her two engagements in Boston would be cabaret-style, at least one question was obvious: How do you modify your performance and choice of songs for a smaller setting?

Ten minutes allowed Cook to answer that question and a few others. Santosuosso typed the story on a portable terminal at home and transmitted it to the *Globe*, to give his editor a head start on reading it for tomorrow's paper. Then he left the newsroom, where he was supposed to meet the owner of a local jazz club. In keeping with the tenor of his day, however, the owner didn't show, leaving Santosuosso to ponder his afternoon dilemma: What, now that the Cook story is gone, will he use to lead Weekend? Boston has entered the early June twilight zone between the official arts seasons and the out-of-town summer festivals, and none of the items he'd planned for the column looks strong enough to go first. Searching his brain and his desk, he tells himself that if can't find something good, maybe he can rename the column "Weakend."

• • •

While some people work on the Sunday paper and others guide tomorrow's stories through their changes, Washington bureau chief Steve Kurkjian is realizing that the biggest story for tomorrow is no longer changing at all. In fact, he's beginning to feel that if he looks at the Ronald Pelton story one more time, someone will have to peel him off the ceiling. Maybe it's finally been edited enough. After all, how long can they go on worrying about what the government is going to say?

179

Much to Kurkjian's surprise, neither he nor the Washington reporters who wrote the story, Walter Robinson and Fred Kaplan, have heard from the National Security Agency or the CIA today. Maybe the government is as tired of talking about this spying business as the journalists are. Even so, Kurkjian has been on the phone off and on all day with Robinson, discussing every word and comma. Might this word increase readers' understanding of what Pelton is accused of doing? Might that one cross the line into endangering national security? Robinson agreed with some of Kurkjian's suggested changes, disagreed with others. Finally he said, "Next time something like this happens, we're *all* coming to Boston. I can't take these phones!"

The Pelton story does not, in the conventional news sense, have a lead, a one- or two-sentence beginning that sums up what it's about. Another Washington piece that's running tomorrow, Tom Oliphant's story on tax reform, carries the classic punchy news lead: "The great Senate tax reform steamroller has hit its first big bumps in the road." But Robinson found no way to put what he and Kaplan were trying to say about the Pelton case into one sentence, or two or three. The spying case is just too complicated, and the story's intent—to show as much as possible about the operations Pelton is charged with compromising—creates still more complications.

Robinson decided instead to begin with a contrast, comparing what's being said about the Pelton case at his trial in Baltimore with what's being said thirty-seven miles away, in Washington. That way, he could get in the fact that the government has threatened to prosecute reporters for publishing information that, it turns out, can be assembled "from unclassified technical manuals, pre-trial statements in open court, and even from past news reports."

Once he'd set up the comparison, Robinson was ready for his version of a "nut graf." In a straight news story, a nut graf would contain the nuts and bolts a reader needs to understand the story; in a story about divestment, for example, the nut graf might explain South Africa's apartheid system. In the Pelton story, the nut graf was more a restatement of the point made in the preceding two paragraphs:

In the two cities, the government appears to be making contradictory arguments. Prosecutors in Baltimore have asserted that Pelton sold a treasure trove of intelligence data to the Soviets that destroyed a successful intelligence program. But officials in Washington have warned that even general press speculation about the program may alert the Soviet to things they do not know.

Kurkjian agreed with Robinson's chosen approach. His only questions concerned the details: which information to include, which to leave out. But even those debates seem to have calmed now, leaving the story suspended in an unearthly quiet that's almost as disconcerting as the government's veiled threats. Why haven't they heard from the government today? After all the frustrating meetings with the National Security Agency, Kurkjian wishes he could be happy about the silence. Maybe it means that he and Robinson and Kaplan have acted responsibly. Or maybe it means that they've been too timid.

4:00 P.M.

When the writing looks easiest and flows best, that means I rewrote 437 times.
—Ellen Goodman, *Globe* and syndicated columnist

The newsroom that echoed so emptily this morning now pulses to the rhythms of humans under pressure. Nearly every desk is occupied, and nearly every occupant is bent into a pose of exaggerated concentration. The ones darting nervous glances around the room, closing stories on their screens only to open them again, then getting up to pace a circuit of reporters' desks are the assignment editors. The ones flipping through the paper, checking the lists of upcoming stories and chatting with friends as their shift begins are the copy editors. The ones attached to telephone or tape recorder headsets, staring out the window or at the ceiling, anywhere but at the relentless blinking cursor that wants to swallow their souls, are the writers.

Writing is as solitary as reporting is gregarious. All day, as they gather information, reporters labor in the public domain, jockeying for position at news conferences, exchanging ideas with sources and one another. When they return to the newsroom, they may talk with an editor or another reporter about the information they've collected, but at some point conversation ceases. As reporters face the blank screens that await their decisions, each is alone.

"Writing is hard work," a former writing coach at the *Globe* used to say. "It is time grown men and women were told this." Inside the newsroom, the statement meets with groans of recognition. Outside, it might bring giggles. The best newswriting is invisible. The reader sees the information, not the writer giving him the information. Besides, writing, unlike brain surgery or nuclear physics, is something most

182

people think they can do. Everyone writes letters, shopping lists, loan applications. How hard can it be to write stories for a living? And shouldn't people choose that living only if they find writing easy? If every word is torture, why write?

Every word isn't always torture. But every word *is* important, and the more a person realizes that importance, the harder—and the more addictive—writing becomes. Each time a writer commits himself to a word, he experiences a flash of satisfaction quickly followed by the question at the brink of the void: What is the perfect *next* word? Part of that question—What word will exactly fit my style and tone and meaning?—would haunt the writer just as acutely if he were writing fiction or poetry. But reporting adds another, more insistent, demand: What word will convey the information most accurately, and in a way that will make people want to read it?

Nowhere is that question more crucial than in the beginning, the lead. Many reporters spend as much time writing the first paragraph as they do writing the rest of the story. They know that people read newspapers in a hurry; if the writer can't grab the readers in the first sentence or two, he's lost them for good. (The headline or photo might catch them, but the writer can't count on that.) Some writers can't continue until they've crafted the perfect lead. Others tack something together hurriedly and then forge ahead, afraid that if they linger, deadline will find them still tangled in the first sentence. The story, these writers hope, will unfold in a logical progression and "tell" them what kind of lead it needs.

To force himself to settle down to the lead, each writer has developed his own form of jump-starting. Some rehearse possible leads mentally, or aloud, as they drive or ride back from an assignment. White House correspondent Walter Robinson is famous around the newsroom for retyping all his notes when he returns to his desk. By the time he's finished typing, he knows what he wants the story to say and can write it in what seems to other reporters like no time at all. One of his Washington colleagues, John Robinson, admires that system but knows it wouldn't work for him. "If I redid my notes, I'd have no energy left for the story," he says. At any rate, rewriting notes wouldn't solve his problem, which he describes this way: "I wait too long to write. Deadline is the only trigger that gets me going."

Pam Cox and George Smith don't know yet what their triggers are, and they haven't had enough experience to develop a jump-starting system. For today, their first day as summer interns, nervous energy is the only spark they need. They're happy just to be back in the newsroom. Two hours ago, as they stood in a housing project looking through the car windows at the keys they'd locked inside, Morrissey Boulevard seemed as distant as Mars. As it turned out, though, they didn't have to embarrass themselves by calling the office for help. After they had pushed and pulled at the car windows for a while, and after a passerby had tried to help them with a coathanger, along came a thirteen-year-old who knew exactly how to break into cars. So did his friends. Smith and Cox got a good laugh out of that as they thanked the kids and drove away.

Now, hunched together at a borrowed desk and terminal, they're beginning to realize the difficulty of writing a short story with a joint byline. Their editor, Dave Morrow, told them he needs only forty "twils," short for "typewritten lines," which would make the story about ten inches long in standard column width. Fine. But what should the story *say*? They know Morrow would help them choose a lead, but they want to figure it out for themselves. They remember some advice from journalism classes: If you can't decide what the focus is, turn to someone else and tell him or her what your story's about. The first thing out of your mouth will probably make a good subject for the lead. They decide to use each other as sounding boards.

"Sarah Flint was mad. She said other Orchard Park people were, too. She's the best thing we've got."

"But people in the other two projects didn't seem to care much."

"We do have that guy at Mission Hill, though. He was good."

"We can't summarize reactions in the lead because the reactions were too different."

"Maybe a range? Reactions ranged from something to something?"

"From anger at Orchard Park, to what?"

"Apathy? Indifference?"

That sounds okay, so Cox starts typing. Each time she gets stuck, Smith supplies the next phrase. Each time he can't think of anything, Cox can. They check with Morrow to make sure another story on the Neighborhoods page, where their story will run, will deal more specifically with the proposal to eliminate the team police. The less space they have to devote to the proposal, the more they can devote to the reactions. Even after Morrow assures them that City Hall reporter Mike Frisby is writing a follow to this morning's story on the proposed cuts, Smith and Cox have trouble trying to explain the complicated team police system. How can they say in just a few words that the city housing authority has been using a federal grant to pay the city police department to allow officers to patrol the projects, but now the federal grant might be cut?

They write, hit the delete button, write, delete, rewrite. In the days of typewriters, they would either have gone through reams of copy paper or have settled for a half-baked lead to avoid ripping out yet another sheet. On a computer terminal, however, revising is so easy that some reporters can't stop. They keep changing sentences, phrases, words until the moment—and often beyond the moment—they must send their story to their editor.

After much tinkering, Smith and Cox end up with this lead: "The reaction of residents at three of Boston's public housing developments to the possible elimination of team police patrols ranged from anger at the Orchard Park housing project to indifference in the Bromley-Heath and Mission Hill projects." That will do, they decide, while they plow through the rest of the story. If it's not good enough, they're sure they'll hear about it when they submit the story for editing—

or in their case, Cox says kiddingly, maybe they should call it "hatcheting." Smith isn't sure whether to laugh.

•   •   •

The best-laid plans of David Mehegan have been torpedoed by time and distance. After much searching, he found a couple from Salem, New Hampshire, who talked to him for his story on people who commute long distances to Boston because they can't afford homes in closer suburbs. The couple even agreed to have their picture taken. But they won't be home from work until at least 6:00, and there's no way a photographer can get to New Hampshire, take the picture, drive back, and develop and print it in time for tomorrow's paper. If it were a front-page photo of a breaking news story or sports event, the deadline could be stretched. But this story is a feature; it can run anytime. Mehegan's editor, Barbara Meltz, tells him she'll hold the story for Friday's paper.

Mehegan says okay, then tries to pretend the conversation never happened. "I've got to keep working on it as if it were running tomorrow," he says. "I need that sense of compression to make progress." Everyone who hears him knows exactly the game he's playing. As bitterly as reporters complain about deadlines, as sure as they often are that they could write a better story if only they had one more hour or day or week, many of them have grown so accustomed to deadlines that they can't write without the pressure. Only as the last minutes tick away does the need to finish the story seem real. One favorite newsroom yarn concerns the experienced reporter who returned from an assignment and asked his editor when the story was due. In an hour, the editor told him. "Good," the reporter replied. "I've got time for dinner."

For a while, Mehegan's strategy works. He fills out a photo assignment form, only to discover that a new form has supplanted the old one. He fills out the new one and then phones the woman from Salem to make sure that she and her husband will be home at 6:00. Then he is called down to the design department to talk about a map that will run with the story. Actually, he discussed the map with one of the design supervisors earlier in the day, but the designer to whom the project has been assigned wants to make sure she understands Mehegan's expectations.

Finally, with his third cup of coffee, he settles down to write. The words come quickly at first. He knows he wants to lead with a couple who spent four months looking for a house and finally found one sixty-five miles from the city. Although they paid $100,000 for a nine-room ranch, they consider themselves lucky. The median price of a home in the Boston area these days is $149,000, the highest in the nation.

Mehegan wants to quote the couple as soon as possible. Quotes add immediacy and credibility to a story; they let the speaker address the reader directly, without the writer standing in the way. Mehegan quotes the woman talking about the couple's long search before they saw a newspaper ad for a house in the town of Athol. "Where's Athol?" the woman asked her husband. He told her it was next to Gardner. "Where's Gardner?" she asked. That's a pretty good series of quotes, Mehegan thinks, but better still is what the woman said about the location of their new home. "If it was three hours away, we'd still think it was worth it," she said. "It's great because it's ours." Mehegan knows that readers will identify with that sentiment.

Once Mehegan has written about the couple's quest and inserted the information on median prices, the flow of words slows. As it does, the little voice inside his head grows louder. "What's the hurry?" it asks mockingly. "You don't *really* need to get it done today." He ignores the voice as long as he can. Then, when he can no longer hear the story over its taunts, he unleashes his secret weapon. He gets up, heads out the front door, and walks down to smell the beach roses on Dorchester Bay.

Although Mehegan's case might be too mild to be officially diagnosed as writer's block, Bill Miller would recognize both the symptoms and the cure. Miller, the *Globe*'s writing coach, sees blocked writers almost every day, and recently he collected their comments in an eighteen-page pamphlet. The idea for the pamphlet germinated when Living reporter Charlie Claffey wrote a story about a novelist who had been debilitated by writer's block for two decades. In the end, she told Claffey, she realized that it was self-indulgent to put the name "writer's block" on her anxiety and inability to perform. With support from other writers, she decided that the solution was simply to get on with it.

What solutions had *Globe* writers come up with? Miller wondered. He sent the question out, and it was soon obvious that he'd hit a nerve. Of the fifty-four writers who contributed to the booklet, only one, arts critic Jay Carr, said he had no problem with writer's block. Several others, however, acknowledged that the term could be a convenient crutch.

Reporter Paul Langner: "By giving it a name, the malady acquires identity and respectability. Let's rename it 'laziness,' 'lack of creativity,' 'empty mind,' or some such phrase. It doesn't matter which, as long as it sounds disreputable or seems in violation of the Protestant work ethic."

Sunday magazine writer Renee Loth: "Being 'blocked,' I think, is often just a fancy way to procrastinate."

Sunday magazine editor Ande Zellman: "Writer's block is pure and simple self-loathing. The writer feels that he or she has absolutely nothing of value to say, that it's all been said, that it will certainly be said by someone with vastly more insight, talent, good looks, and charm. Writers do difficult, ego-attached work and need more love than most people."

Whatever their definition of writer's block, everyone who answered Miller's request proposed a remedy. Many of the cures centered on physical exercise: running, swimming, walking fast outside without a coat, pacing around the newsroom. ("Take care to seem obviously idle," Langner advised. "This will draw adverse comments that, in some cases, can shame you into hitting the keys.") Also on the recommended list were hot showers, warm baths, naps, cookies, ragtime music, and rides on the subway.

Other prescriptions were more complex. Zellman's advice to editors was to wrest the story away from the writer and start rewriting it. The writer, she said, will quickly decide that he hates the editor's version, and at that point he'll realize what it is he wants to say.

Several people recommended classic journalist's tricks: Sharpen a thousand pencils. Do more reporting. Try writing on a typewriter, or a legal pad, instead of a computer. Ignore the notes and write from memory, then go back later and fill in precise quotes and facts. Start in the middle or at the end or anywhere that seems easiest. Forget perfection; lower your standards. Write as if you were writing a letter home. Actually write a letter home, or write anything, as long as you're writing.

"One of my favorite tricks is to take off my wristwatch and lay it on my keyboard," said travel writer Bill Davis. "Then I write nonstop about the subject of my story—or free-associate about anything else that comes into my head—for precisely ten minutes. Very frequently, by Minute Nine the juices are really flowing and what emerges is the lead or the theme of the piece. The important thing is to keep writing and not stop—or think about what you're doing."

Sportswriter John Powers, who won a Pulitzer for writing about nuclear proliferation when he moved temporarily to the news side, passed along some advice from Ernest Hemingway: "Write the truest sentence that you know." Arts editor John Koch proposed two cures: "One is to become an editor. Another is to try something completely different, like skydiving."

Amid all the dos was one don't, from music critic Ernie Santosuosso. "Never, never take a drink of booze," he warned, "or you'll be writing Esperanto."

•　　•　　•

Bill Miller's office is neutral territory. He does not assign stories, he does not have the power to fire, he cannot award raises or try to maneuver a protégé's prose onto the front page. He simply gives advice on writing—or, more accurately, he listens to writers and helps them see what they already know.

Miller is a writing coach, one of a breed unknown to newsrooms as recently as ten years ago. In an ideal world, his job would not exist. Editors would have plenty of time to assign and edit stories, go to meetings and take care of paperwork, and still offer writers all the support they needed. Until that paradise arrives, the *Globe* has Bill Miller.

Writers may come to Miller when they've almost finished their stories, or before they've started. They may send him a question via computer, or plop themselves down in his tiny office, across from the crookedly taped poster of the Isle of Wight, and announce, "I'm stuck." Maybe they need simple advice about style or usage, but more likely their problem is focus. They've spent days collecting all kinds of great information about a subject, and now they can't see the story for the facts.

Miller knows what's coming before the writer has finished his tale of woe. He leans forward, his steel-gray hair radiating like electrified spokes from the sides of his head. As the writer quiets, Miller's hand begins chopping the air into five vertical slices. With each chop comes a word in his British accent: "What—is—this—story—about?"

The writer settles back; this is what he came for. "It's about old people in Salem," he might say.

Again: "What—is—this—story—about?"

"It's about what it's like for a city to have so many old people."

The hand movements stop. The voice grows softer. "Is that what you've written here?"

The writer pauses, examining the printout of his rough draft. "Noooo," he says slowly, "I've written about the problems of *being* an old person in Salem. . . . Oh, I see."

Sometimes the focus is more elusive. In those cases, Miller might ask the writer to list the best and the second-best information he's collected. When that's done, the coach gives this advice: Kill off the second-best stuff. The rest is your story.

Each writer who walks into his office, Miller believes, really does know what his story is about, really does know what works and what doesn't. "They know something's wrong, or they wouldn't ask," he says. "And they know *what's* wrong; they just want someone to back them up." Miller says that no one, except for an occasional intern, comes in with a story that just isn't news and doesn't belong in the paper.

Sometimes a writer comes in because he doesn't like the advice he's gotten from his editor, but those cases are fairly easy to spot. Miller listens and makes suggestions about the story but tries to steer clear of disputes.

The need for a writing coach illustrates the difference between a reporter and a stenographer. "A person can learn to report; that's technique," Miller says. "But beyond that you become a storyteller, and that's the point at which you need more skills. You need to inform, entertain, capture the event and the readers."

Miller tries to hone those skills not only through individual conferences but also through biweekly writers' lunches on specific topics and a monthly in-house newsletter called "Glass House View." The newsletter spotlights good writing and embarrassments from the pages of the *Globe*. In the June issue, for example, Miller praised a lead Margo Miller wrote on one of her Marquee columns: "Every year, about the time rabbits have finished chewing on the crocuses and are dreaming about your first planting of lettuce, the local chapter of the Society of American Magicians gets them a little honest work at its annual convention." It panned a Washington lead in which a misplaced time element changed the meaning: "President Reagan accused Nicaragua of threatening the security of the United States and Central America yesterday and promised to give neighboring Honduras assistance in the event of an armed attack."

Miller saw two things in today's paper that he filed away for possible use in the next "Glass House View." On the positive side was the headline on a front-page story about the first day of television coverage in the U.S. Senate. Not much happened for the cameras to cover, so copy editor Bill Crawford wrote this headline: Lights, Camera, (Little) Action. On the negative side, Miller took note of this sentence in a South Africa story: "By yesterday, the three satellite camps, razed to the ground during the fighting, had been completely flattened." Not just razed, but "razed to the ground"? And *then* "completely flattened"? Strange things can happen when a writer dictates his story by phone, but an editor should have been more alert. The sentence is a study in redundancy.

191

Why are reporters like that? The question is a popular discussion topic all around the *Globe* building, and each group has its own definition of "like that."

Overheard in the advertising department: "They just don't seem to be having as much fun as we do."

Overheard in circulation: "They're always rushing around like they're so much more important than the rest of us."

Overheard everywhere: "Bet they make ten times more money than we do."

At a newspaper, as in all organizations, limited communication among departments can breed stereotypes that come to be accepted as fact—or, at least, as "factoids," the newsroom word for statements that are repeated so often that they take on an aura of truth. People in each department of the *Globe* have their own ideas about what people in other departments are like. Reporters generate more than the usual amount of speculation simply because their work is so public.

While everyone speculates, a few people at the *Globe* have done some serious thinking about what it takes to be a reporter. Managing editor Tom Mulvoy says that when he interviews would-be reporters, he looks for drive and curiosity. "It sounds arrogant," he says, "but after twenty minutes I can usually sense whether a person is curious in a journalistic way." He does not, however, look for what many people consider the typical reporter's personality: pushy, plain-spoken, and as subtle as a chartreuse suit. In fact, he says, many of the best writers are quiet and shy in conversation with strangers. "If they're nervous in the interview, that's fine," he says. "That was me twenty years ago. For a reporter, listening is time well spent."

Don Seckler, the psychologist who works part-time with *Globe* employees, has looked at the reporter's personality from another perspective. Reporters, it seems to him, are ruled by their intellects to a greater extent than people in most other professions. They draw strength from their efforts to understand the world; unlike most people, they actually enjoy being bombarded with contradictory stimuli. Sorting out meanings is the way they exercise control. Seckler hasn't developed real theories on this subject; he's just given it some casual thought. The "knowledge is power" idea has helped him understand how reporters can tolerate working in an environment where nothing—not their co-workers or bosses, not their subject matter, not the standards they must meet—is constant.

Writing coach Bill Miller says that the chief thing to remember in trying to understand reporters is their vulnerability. They're exposing themselves in print every day, putting their names out there where anyone can criticize them, not just for mistakes but for anything the reader doesn't like about the information in a story. The "shoot the messenger" response is a popular one among newspaper readers.

In some ways, Miller says, reporters are like addicts; they're addicted to learning new things every day, and to being published. "They need that jag," he says. "It's a bit of a cliché, but they need the idea that they're in print every day. They're not working on a novel that no one will see for years." The attitude that other people sometimes interpret as superficiality, Miller says, is actually the reporter's acceptance of journalism's limits. A reporter can do only so much reporting, only so much writing, before the paper comes out. Not every story will meet his standards in that time. If he's writing, for example, about a scientist's research, the reporter can't possibly grasp in a two-hour interview as much as the scientist understands from a lifetime of study.

In response, the reporter offers himself two comforts. First, he probably understands the subject as well as the average person who reads the paper needs to. And second, if this story doesn't meet his expectations, he'll have another shot at perfection tomorrow.

• • •

Ray Richard is back from the Norfolk prison, but not soon enough. The unexplained wait before he was allowed to interview two inmates has cost him a spot in tomorrow's paper. He could write the story by the 6:30 deadline if he had to, but the editors have already decided that because they have plenty of stories for tomorrow, Richard should take his time and make it good for Friday. The story will still be timely then; the inmates won't receive their college degrees until Saturday.

Although newspapers aim to put the news into print as quickly as possible, the sense of urgency doesn't always extend to feature stories—or to newsfeatures, stories that take a feature angle on an issue or person in the news (a profile of a newly elected official, for example). Editors must always think not just of tomorrow but also of the papers ahead. Will they have enough to fill the space on Saturday and Monday? Those are the traditional slow news days because the world conducts less official business on Fridays and Sundays than on ordinary weekdays. (Not much generally happens on Saturdays, either, but the Sunday paper contains more reflective and analytical pieces than live news.) Coming up short is an editor's worst nightmare. To avoid it, editors look for features or even newsier stories that can "hold," hang around a day or two without getting stale.

Holding a story grates against journalistic instinct. Editors do it only when the alternative—squashing good stories into small holes on inside pages, or cramming the paper chock-full today and risking emptiness tomorrow—seems a greater evil. Reporters agree to hold a story partly because they have no choice, and partly because they prefer good play on a slow day to burial on a busy one. The best story loses its punch if it's played so poorly that no one sees it.

Richard has been around long enough not to succumb to the flash of anger many writers feel when they hear that the "jag" of immediate publication is being taken from them. He assures his editor that the story can hold, then starts looking over his notes. If he starts writing now, it will be much easier to pick up the thread in the morning. The practice is a form of preventive medicine against procrastination. A writer who knows that he has to start a story from scratch will find many more ways to delay sitting down than a writer who knows that the work is partly done. Some reporters subscribe so strongly to this theory that they routinely "log off" their computers for the night when they're in the middle of a sentence, or even a word. That way, their first task in the morning will be an easy one, and before they know it, they'll be writing.

Though he didn't relish wasting time waiting at the prison, Richard enjoyed interviewing the inmates. One was serving time for armed robbery, the other for assault with a dangerous weapon. Both said that studying for a college degree had given their lives purpose and restored their sense of pride. Reading his notes now, Richard reassures himself that he has enough good quotes to sustain the story. "It's something that can't be taken away from me," one inmate said. "You can't take away intelligence." The other, a high-school dropout, pointed out that studying also relieved the boredom of prison life. Without his classes, he said, "I would've gone stir-crazy, literally."

•   •   •

Less than an hour into her shift, night reporter Bonnie Winston has researched and discarded one story and started another. As soon as she arrived at 4:00, Marvin Pave asked her to check on whether a large Boston Gas tank was about to be painted. Painting a gas tank normally wouldn't rate a story, but this was a special tank. Visible from the highway to everyone who enters or leaves Boston from the south, the white tank displays a design of colorful stripes painted by the artist Sister Corita. Because one part of the design resembles an old man with a beard, Bostonians long ago began referring to the painting as Ho Chi Minh. During the Vietnam war, many people objected to staring at Ho while stuck in traffic.

If Ho is going to be painted over, Pave and Winston agree, that's a story. But after several calls to Boston Gas, Winston learns that it's the other tank, a plain white one, that's going to be painted. She still thinks there might be a story in it. Boston Gas has hired non-union painters from Pennsylvania to repaint the tank, and already the gas company has received more than a hundred calls from people who believe that local union painters should have gotten the contract. Winston walks up to Pave's desk and presents her findings, but none of the editors seems too excited. So much for that story. She returns to her desk and starts making calls on another story, an update on a nurses' strike at a local hospital.

Night reporter Doris Sue Wong, meanwhile, is trying to find out about a pit bull terrier that supposedly attacked a mailman in Lynn, leaving him with cuts on his face and twelve stitches in his arm. The other carriers refused to deliver mail on that street until the dog was locked up, and now the city is considering banning ownership of the terriers. Wong has just learned that the same dog was probably responsible for a recent attack on a small child, who was bitten on the face badly enough to require twenty stitches.

While Wong and Winston settle in for the night by making calls, night editor Ellen Clegg is settling in by reading. She reads messages from the day editors about what they liked and didn't like about this morning's paper, then reads through various lists in the system to start learning about tomorrow's stories. When the top day editors leave in a few hours, after the front page has been designed, she'll be in charge. Anything that happens from then on will be her responsibility.

Clegg chats briefly with managing editor Tom Mulvoy and his two deputies, Helen Donovan and Al Larkin, to find out what kind of news day it's been. Reassured that they have a strong lineup for tomorrow, she returns to her desk to check "the book," the stack of dummies that show how much news space she and the copy editors will have to fill in tomorrow's paper. She sees that the total is seventy-nine columns—a large paper, since the news hole usually falls between fifty and eighty columns. Because tomorrow is Thursday, when advertisers make a strong push to attract readers to stores and entertainment events during the weekend, the size of the paper doesn't surprise Clegg. She routinely schedules the maximum number of copy editors on Wednesday and Saturday nights, expecting large papers on Thursday and Sunday.

Although Clegg has a "glass house," a private office on the edge of the newsroom, she spends most of her time at a desk shoved close against other editors' desks near the room's center. From there, looking toward the back of the newsroom, where steps descend to the library, she can survey the double row of local copy editors to her left, the double row of national copy editors to her right. Beyond them are the business writers and editors, and beyond them the Sunday department.

Clegg's crew of copy editors concerns itself primarily with the first two sections of the paper; copy editors in Sports, Business, and Living take care of the rest. Tomorrow, however, extra space for local and national news is scattered behind those other sections, in an area known on the desk as The Outback. The copy editors will have to schedule stories for those pages. Along with two copies of each dummy, which Clegg will give to the layout editors on the local and national desks, an editorial assistant has brought her a sheet that lists each page and how much news space is on it. She checks this list against the dummies to make sure that none of the ads was drawn the wrong size. The list is called the Chicken Sheet.

.   .   .

Bars have happy hour. The advertising department has crazy hour, and it's setting in now. "About 4:30 in the afternoon, this place is Looney Tunes," says display ad manager Ollie Rodman. The salespeople, having carefully cultivated an air of professionalism all day while they were out making calls, hit the front door of the building and instantly drop their guard. Back home in the ad department, surrounded by people who understand the pressures, their pent-up energy erupts into jokes, usually at one another's expense. "The jokes are flying thick and fast," Rodman says, "and none of us is sacred."

Something about working at a newspaper seems to encourage freewheeling banter. People in every department mention the openness as one of the things they like best about their jobs, and the accompanying cynicism as one of the things that can be hardest to take. From the pressroom to the ad department to the newsroom, people talk about the ease of being able to say whatever they want, whenever they want, to their co-workers, and the strange looks that can result when they accidentally continue that behavior "outside."

Mailroom supervisor Bob Pritchard says that his department's version of craziness comes from the essential tedium of its task: inserting papers or advertising circulars into other papers or circulars and bundling them, or, more accurately, loading and watching the machines that do the inserting and bundling. "It's boring," Pritchard says, "and if you stay with a boring job long enough, it's twice as bad."

If the job is so boring, how do the 170 full-time employees in the mailroom amuse themselves? Pritchard offers a simple answer: "They screech and yell and talk all day long. The name of the game is to give the other guy the business." Although he acknowledges that the teasing can sometimes veer into meanness, he says it's not as bad as it may sound to an outsider. Occasionally, he says, one of the company's top executives will enter the mailroom, hear the shouting, and leave in a hurry, thinking he's walked into some kind of problem. Pritchard shrugs. "That's just the usual noise."

Each department considers its own brand of noise as unique as the qualities required for professional success. Nowhere is this pride of place more apparent than in the advertising department. Rodman not only thinks that the late-afternoon craziness is the best possible way to release tensions, he also wonders whether a person who couldn't participate would be capable of successfully selling ads. "Not everybody's made for sales," he says. "You have to be a character in this business."

Eamon Galvin, back with Marilyn Won from their appointment at Lafayette Place, pipes up, "Speak for yourself, Ollie."

Catching the spirit of the afternoon, Rodman makes a quick comeback. "If you've met anyone here who's really normal," he tells Galvin, "I want to know who it is."

• • • •

It's almost time to leave, but company controller John Mullin is still crunching numbers. He can wax eloquent about the human side of newspapers, but when he really wants to see how things are going, he turns to the numbers.

Number-wise, it's been an average day. The *Globe*'s 2,500 employees, not to mention the 600 employees of its subsidiaries, have worked various shifts that are recorded in various parts of the computer program that keeps track of payroll. Mullin designed the original payroll program in 1963, nine years after he arrived at the *Globe*. With modifications, the same program ran for twenty-two years; he felt a little nostalgic when it was replaced last December. But who could have foreseen in 1963 that payroll would be $86 million by 1985?

Who, come to think of it, could have foreseen how fast all the departments would grow, and how much of their work would be computerized? Back in the '60s, when Mullin began automating the various financial operations, he and a few other people were creating programs pretty much on their own. Now the *Globe* has an information services department with seventy-five employees who operate, program, and maintain the company's computers. Thirty of them spend most of their time developing software. All told, more than 700 computer terminals are scattered around the building. Even the people who don't have terminals make regular use of the reports, maps, and other printouts the computers produce.

Within Mullin's domain, eighty employees use computers to keep track of the nearly 60,000 accounts the *Globe* is likely to bill this month. If this June follows the usual pattern, 55,000 of those will be "transient advertisers," people whose only dealings with the *Globe* involve buying a classified ad or two. Some of those accounts are known in accounting department lingo as "regular transients," people or companies that do business with the newspaper six or seven times a year. Mullin hasn't settled on a name for the rest of these accounts, but he likes the sound of "truly transient."

On the news side, operations have been computerized since 1978. The wire services feed their stories into the computer instead of printing them out noisily on teletype machines. Reporters type their stories directly into the computer; editors edit them on the computer and then send them to another computer that does the typesetting.

Display ads are ordered on a computer, and some are composed electronically as well. In an airy, glass-enclosed room across from the composing room sit eight machines whose potential the *Globe* is just beginning to explore. An operator sits at one of these terminals with an ad on the table in front of him. He traces the ad with a light pen and—*poof!*—the same design appears on the computer screen.

199

Then he can change the type styles and sizes, reverse the black-on-white to white-on-black, set the copy in odd shapes, or play around in a hundred other different ways. He can also create an ad design from scratch, directly on the computer screen. The machines can't yet produce artwork other than simple line drawings, but Steve Taylor, director of information systems, says that's coming. He sees a lot more than advertising artwork in the *Globe*'s computer future.

The big word at newspapers these days is *pagination*, a catch-all description for any system that creates a newspaper page electronically. In a pure pagination system, the page—stories, headlines, photos, ads and all—would be put together on the screen of an editor's terminal and go directly from there to a plate destined for the printing press. A few newspapers are already using some version of pagination. Taylor says that every new operation the *Globe* computerizes moves it one step closer to that goal. The timing depends in part on labor contracts because pagination would eliminate many of the jobs now needed to guide the pages from the newsroom to the presses.

Computers have already made inroads in many of those operations. Nearly every piece of production machinery the paper has bought in recent years involves a computer, and some are completely under computer control. Printing color photos, for example, requires computers to scan the original, decide how the colors should be balanced to compensate for the vagaries of printing on low-grade paper, and alter the input accordingly. Computer-driven lasers etch the plates that go on the printing presses, and computers adjust the amount of ink applied to each column of each page.

Computer involvement doesn't end once the paper is printed. The mailroom has a new computer that directs particular bundles of papers into particular bins and ejects them at a particular time onto the proper loading dock for their destination. Another computer program contains—or will, when operators finish typing the information from hundreds of thousands of index cards into the system—the names of all *Globe* subscribers, along with their delivery history and any special instructions. A printout could tell one of the 4,000 carriers, for example, to leave the paper on Joe Smith's back porch and watch out for the Doberman.

Not to be forgotten in the inventory of computer functions is electronic mail, which allows users to communicate with anyone in the system without picking up the phone. Then there's the ordinary stuff like word processing, which allows the *Globe* to keep in a computer, among other things, a form letter to send to people who complain that the ink comes off on their hands when they read the paper. The letter, complete with refund offer, reads in part: "Ink rub-off is the number-one quality complaint from our customers, and we at the *Globe* are very concerned."

John Mullin marvels at all the computerization, but then he marvels at a lot about the newspaper business. Nothing— not thirty-two years at the *Globe*, not seven children and six grandchildren, not the college degree he finally got around to four years ago, when he was fifty-five—has reduced his capacity to view the world with amazement. Most amazing of all is the fact that he, an accountant who likes his numbers straight and clear, has stuck with an industry that stands so many of the principles of good business on their heads.

"What an industry!" he says with fond dismay. "We manufacture a new product every day. We don't know for sure what labor or materials or assembly are going to cost, or what profit we'll collect." For example, he says, consider a night when an explosive news story breaks. The people in the newsroom might rewrite and redesign the front page several times. They're creating a better product. But they won't charge any more money for it, and the improvements won't necessarily make more people buy it.

"If we put out a twenty-six-page paper it costs a quarter, and if we put out a 112-page paper it costs a quarter," Mullin says. "What an industry!"

5:00 P.M.

You can get close to the players, but you've got to remember who you're working for.
— Larry Whiteside, baseball writer

If Barbara Huebner hits all the lights right on her way to work, her coffee—always large, always black, always from Dunkin' Donuts—is still hot when the 5:00 news meeting begins. She carries the cup into the conference room, picks up a pile of budgets from the table, and settles into a chair against the wall. Lifting the lid, she takes a cautious sip. Victory.

Huebner is a copy editor on the national desk. When the meeting ends, she will take the dummies for the pages from three to the end of the U.S./World section, decide which stories and photos go on which pages, and determine the size of the photos and headlines. The stories will go to other copy editors, who will edit them and write head to fit Huebner's specs, and then to the "slot," or chief copy editor, who will review the others' work before shipping it off to be typeset. The dummies, on which Huebner draws lines to show where the various elements should be pasted on the page, will be brought to the composing room by college "co-ops," or editorial assistants.

In order to determine which stories from the world outside New England go on page three, however, Huebner must first know which ones will run on page one. The rest—along with the jumps of the front-page stories—are hers. That's why she comes to this meeting: to hear what stories are available and what importance the top editors place on them. If a story almost, but not quite, makes page one, she'll know it's a good candidate for page three, the lead U.S./World page. The foreign editor will make the ultimate decision.

"What's the book look like?" Ben Taylor asks no one in particular as the editors take their places around the conference table. He wants to know how much space is available for news.

"Huge," Ellen Clegg replies, sitting down opposite Taylor.

"How about the Neighborhoods page?" he asks. "Room for two fifty-twils and a forty?" Taylor is checking on whether the local desk's planned team police package—Pam Cox and George Smith's story on reactions at the three housing projects, another intern's story on another project, and a City Hall reporter's story updating the proposal—will be able to run together as planned.

Clegg nods as deputy managing editor Helen Donovan starts the meeting. Managing editor Tom Mulvoy is in his usual spot, but executive editor Jack Driscoll is missing, having left moments ago to deliver a commencement speech. Because little has changed since the 2:30 session, the rundown of available stories moves quickly.

"We're still in 'go' mode on secrets," national editor Royal Ford begins. As they listen, the others shuffle through their budgets, the lists of stories each department is offering. The budgets, which the editors keep in the computer and print out before the meeting, name each story's writer and slug (always in capital letters), describe it in one or two sentences, and list its length and any other pertinent information. The national budget, for example, describes the Ronald Pelton story this way:

"SECRETS. Kaplan/Robinson. Many of the 'secrets' U.S. is trying to protect in Pelton case can be dug out of specialty journals and even old press reports. Linked—and buttressed by Globe sources—they provide a pretty complete picture of U.S. undersea spying operations. LONG."

The budget also mentions two related stories. The first is listed this way: "PELTON. wires. Closing arguments in spy trial of former NSA technician with jury expected to get case in late afternoon or Thursday. 30." The designation "wires" means that the *Globe* will use a wire service account of Pelton's trial in Baltimore because the newspaper does not

203

have its own reporter there. The "30" means that the story is thirty typewritten lines long on a computer screen. The other story—"POLLARD. wires. Accused spy Jonathan Pollard, wife, plead guilty to spying for Israel; others to be named in espionage ring"—relates to Pelton only because it involves another spying case. Its budget entry ends with "WATCH," meaning that because the story is still developing, the night editors should watch the wires for new versions.

In addition to the spying stories, Ford is recommending three others for page one: The story on opposition to tax reform ("It's not coming from where you'd expect," Ford says), which Tom Oliphant is trying to finish in time to catch a plane back to Washington; David Chandler's story on the latest personnel shakeups connected with the explosion of the space shuttle *Challenger* ("The broom is continuing, but in a bigger way," Ford says); and Washington reporter John Robinson's story on a national "workfare" program for which Massachusetts is the model ("One of very few programs in Washington these days to which 'expand' is being applied with any popular enthusiasm," Ford has written in the budget). In each case, Ford's comments are designed to convince Donovan and Mulvoy, who together will choose the front-page lineup, of the importance of the stories.

Ford knows that all four stories are unlikely to make page one. Only six stories usually run on the page, and no one wants them all to be from Washington; there's Boston, New England, and the rest of the world to consider. But each day, each editor who supervises a department lists on the budget as many potential front-page stories as he thinks he can justify. If the other departments are having a slow day, each one figures, maybe my people can sweep the page.

In fact, although the other editors have submitted long budgets today, they have recommended only three other candidates for page one. The foreign desk is pushing Phillip Van Niekerk's story on the ban on public meetings in South Africa. The Metro desk offers two prospects: Jim Franklin's story on the controversy surrounding the local Paulist fathers, and Steve Marantz's feature on the Roger Williams Mint.

Business editor Lincoln Millstein, who likes to get business stories on the front page whenever he can, says he has nothing that belongs there today.

After the group has discussed a few of the day's more offbeat stories—they're especially fascinated by the one about the chambermaid who married J. Seward Johnson and then, when he died, fought his children and won $300 million from the Johnson & Johnson fortune—and looked over the selection of photos that Gerry D'Alfonso has tacked to the corkboard on the wall, Donovan announces her preliminary front-page picks.

"Secrets, shuttle, South Africa, Paulists," she says. She proposes that they "tease" the Pollard story from Pelton—in other words, run a head shot (head-and-shoulders photo) of Pollard with a cutline saying he has pleaded guilty and referring readers to the page where they can find the full story.

While everyone is writing down Donovan's first picks, she adds, "We'll look at nukes, sex ed, and Switzler." "Nukes" is a wire story reporting that radioactive contamination from the Chernobyl nuclear plant has spread farther, causing more evacuations. "Sex ed" is Peggy Hernandez's story on the proposed pregnancy-prevention plan for Boston public schools. "Switzler" is State House reporter Bruce Mohl's follow-up on the gubernatorial candidate who announced that he had lied about his past. Taylor listed SEX ED and SWITZLER under "Metro front" (the front page of the Metro section) on his budget, but when he read the list aloud, he recommended them for special consideration for page one.

Mulvoy, who has been silent throughout the meeting, asks Donovan, "Did you consider taxes or training?" Those are two of the national stories Ford recommended.

"Yes, but there's just too much," she answers. As the others rise and collect their papers, Mulvoy and Donovan agree that any of those nine stories—the seven she suggested, the two he added—could be strong front-page candidates. The Pelton story is the only sure thing. In the next forty-five minutes they'll read the others and compare their merits. Decision time is 6:15.

•   •   •

The sex education story Donovan and Mulvoy will read is not the real thing. It's a "top" Peggy Hernandez has sent from her terminal at City Hall to give the editors an idea what the beginning will look like. After a day of switching back and forth from that story, which she refers to as the pregnancy prevention story, to the teacher evaluation story, Hernandez is still having trouble spending more than five minutes on one subject before another intervenes. About an hour ago, one of the many people she talked to today finally offered her a copy of the pregnancy-prevention proposal, which turned out to be fifty pages long. She made her last trip to the School Department building to pick it up. While she was there, she checked one more time on the school bus drivers' contract (no news) and heard about yet another story, something about a court hearing involving special education services in the schools.

Her editor, Fletcher Roberts, advised her to finish the teacher evaluation story, which sounded less important, and then write the sex ed story. Save the bus drivers for tomorrow, he said, or maybe you can do it for Sunday. Hernandez banged out something on the evaluations and finally, about 4:45, started reading the pregnancy memo. Just then the telephone rang. It was the Globe Corner Bookstore, which also serves as the newspaper's downtown office for deliveries, saying one of her morning sources had dropped off a package for her. The caller said she had fifteen minutes to get there before the office closed.

Feeling overwhelmed, Hernandez called Roberts for advice. She knew perfectly well she had to go pick up the package, but perhaps a miracle would happen and Roberts would tell her not to bother. "It's either nothing or something powerful about the teacher and principal evaluations," she told him. "So find out," he said.

The bookstore wasn't far. On the walk back to City Hall, Hernandez saw that the information in the package would, indeed, help her with her teacher evaluation story. But first she had to write the top of the sex ed story so that the editors could see what it was about. She did that, then returned to the evaluations story and finished it. Then she switched back to the sex ed story, interrupting her writing now and then to take calls from Roberts, who was editing the evaluations story and had questions.

Now, free at last to concentrate on a single story, she hunkers down in earnest before her terminal. Even as she writes, she knows, Donovan and Mulvoy are looking at the top she sent, judging whether the story is worthy of the front page. But she's got to screen all extraneous thoughts from her mind, she's got to . . . Suddenly she stops typing. She's just remembered that she forgot to tell Roberts about the fourth potential story, the one about special education.

• • •

Leads are the topic of the hour. The writers are writing them, the editors are reading them, and the writers and the editors are trying to find compromises. In many ways, the straight news leads are easiest. If a writer can't find an unusual way to present the information in a news story, he doesn't have to worry; the information in the story is its own justification. In stories that tend more toward the feature end of the spectrum, however, readers don't really *need* to know the information. Compelling writing is the only thing that will keep them reading.

Larry Tye has decided to stick with a straight news lead. Until an hour ago, he didn't even expect to have a story in tomorrow's paper. He had worked all day on a piece on tooth implants for the Monday Sci-Tech page, only to learn that Sci-Tech was overcrowded and his story would have to hold for a week. He didn't mind; he would have had trouble meeting the deadline anyway.

With that pressure off, Tye started thinking about the story he'd given up when tooth implants came along. It was about a *New England Journal of Medicine* report comparing the services offered by for-profit and nonprofit hospitals. The editors had decided to use a wire story on the subject instead. But when he heard that he didn't have to finish tooth implants right away, Tye decided to look at the Associated Press version of the hospital story. He didn't like it and said so to his editor, who checked with the national desk and then gave Tye the go-ahead to write his own. To his astonishment, within an hour he was able to reach both the director of the study and the chief dissenter.

Tye wrote this lead: "For-profit hospitals typically charge higher prices and offer less care for the poor than community, nonprofit facilities, according to a report in today's *New England Journal of Medicine*." Not deathless prose, he reflected, but informative enough, especially if he added a second paragraph summarizing the study's other findings. The writing was much more straightforward than the approach he'd been using in the tooth implant story, but in his two months at the *Globe*, Tye had learned that the editors value reporters who can tailor their writing to the subject at hand.

While Tye was deciding that straight was the way to go, Steve Marantz was deciding that it was all wrong for his story. He really was interested in the local mint that's making the New York subway tokens, but for the first few hours after he returned, nothing he wrote seemed to capture the place. An hour ago his editor, Barbara Meltz, came by and confirmed his suspicions: The first forty lines, all he'd written at that point, didn't sing. Try being more descriptive, she suggested.

Descriptive? What should he describe? Marantz stares into space, trying to make his mind a blank so that pictures of the mint can form. He remembers the noise of the machine that stamped out the tokens, the steam that rose from it, the jerky way the raw brass moved as it began the trip that would eventually take it to the turnstiles of New York. The other vivid picture in his mind is of the mint's owner scooping up handfuls of the finished tokens. He'd like to put that scene in the story, but not as the lead. He's guessing that Joe Runci's photo of the scene turned out well, and if the editors choose to run it, Marantz doesn't want the lead and the photo's caption to be redundant. He'll stick with the presses. He turns to his keyboard, deletes everything in the lead except the dateline, Attleboro, and starts rewriting.

"Several thousand of the newest New York City Transit Authority subway tokens began their long journey yesterday

under a steamy blanking press at the Roger Williams Mint."
Fair enough, he tells himself; now let's get descriptive. "A
wide spindle of brass unwound into the machine, lurched
under the impact of punchers, and dropped its raw booty into
a cart." Okay, now he's rolling. He's just remembered a
thought that struck him as he looked at the finished tokens
heaped in the cart: That's a lifetime worth of subway riding.
Maybe he can get that idea into the next paragraph.

Every day at least one candidate for the front page causes
its writer more than the average amount of agony. Today that
dubious distinction belongs to Jim Franklin, whose story on
the Paulist fathers has attracted suggestions from so many
people that he's finding it impossible to satisfy them all. At
first, determined to screen out unsolicited advice, Franklin
chose to lead with what he considered most important and
newsworthy: The archdiocese had threatened to oust the
Paulist fathers if they didn't stop allowing women to preach at
Mass. But his editor, Fletcher Roberts, came back from the
2:30 meeting with a different idea. He had read Franklin's
lead aloud at the meeting, and at least two editors had
strongly suggested that it be changed. The news, they said,
wasn't that the archdiocese had demanded compliance; the
news was that the priests had acceded to the demands and
banned women from preaching. Try making that the lead,
Roberts advised.

Like the Paulist fathers, Franklin didn't give in right
away. Roberts stayed, trying to convince Franklin of the wisdom of the editors' recommendations. Their conversation
drifted across nearby desks, where other writers, without listening to the words, immediately recognized the tone. Each
had had similar talks with editors often enough to hear the
silent message being delivered to the writer: The big guys have
good reasons, and complying with them won't hurt your
chances of making page one.

"But the threat is the most unusual thing," Franklin said.

"Okay, but their bowing to the threat is newer," Roberts
replied. "It supersedes the earlier news."

"I don't know . . ."

"Try a lead that gets them both in," Roberts said. "And can you get to a quote sooner? You had a quote way down in the story . . ."

"From McGarry? 'The stakes are pretty high'?"

"That one."

"Yeah, that would be good for showing why they gave in."

Satisfied, Roberts turned to leave. As he did, he threw out one more suggestion. "Context," he said. "Does this signal some change in church policy?" He walked away, leaving Franklin staring at his screen.

By the time he saw Roberts heading into the 5:00 meeting, Franklin had fashioned a lead that contained both the threat and the response. He wrote that the Paulist fathers had stopped allowing women to preach at Mass after the archdiocese threatened to throw them out because of "complaints about liturgical abuses." When the editors' meeting broke up, Franklin closed the story. He knew that Tom Mulvoy and Helen Donovan would want to read it as they sized up the candidates for page one. He has glanced their way a few times in the last half hour, but from this distance there's no way to tell which story they're reading, or what they think.

Now Franklin looks up apprehensively; Roberts is approaching his desk again. Please, Franklin silently begs the patron saint of tired writers, don't make me change it again. The patron saint fails him.

"Another suggestion from the desk," Roberts says. "Not many people know who the Paulist fathers are, but they know the Paulist Center because it's right downtown. Can you focus the lead on the center?"

•   •   •

"I'd like to leave a message for Bud Collins. C-O-L-L-I-N-S," Bob Duffy shouts into the phone. The hotel operator in Paris either can't hear or can't understand him. *"Collins!"* he shouts again. "Tell him to call the *Boston Globe.*" Pause. "B-O-S-T-O-N G-L-O-B-E."

Duffy, the sports department's "backfield man," or chief copy editor, wants to ask Collins a question about his column on the French Open. When he's finished with that, Duffy will edit Bob Ryan's Celtics story, which is undergoing minor surgery right now. Ryan is on the phone from Houston with another editor. He's been looking over the story he sent a while ago from his portable terminal, and he's found some mistakes. At one point, for example, Ryan wrote "kind game" when he meant "mind game." The editors would probably catch the error, but Ryan's not taking any chances. Typos that form real words are notorious for their ability to sneak past copy editors' antennae and into the paper.

The sports editors have been taking inventory of tomorrow's section, and here's what they've found: In addition to Ryan's main Celtics story, they have in hand Mike Madden's story on Bill Walton, Ian Thomsen's story on Houston guard Lewis Lloyd, and Ryan's NBA Notebook, a collection of short items from Houston. Leigh Montville says he'll be done with his Celtics column in an hour. In Dallas, meanwhile, Ron Borges is nearly ready to hit a sequence of buttons on his portable computer and send his story on the Irving Fryar press conference. Will McDonough is at his desk, writing about the odd man out in Boston sports these days, Bruins coach Harry Sinden.

Dan Shaughnessy and Larry Whiteside are at Fenway Park. Whiteside is putting together a Red Sox notebook and getting ready to cover tonight's game against Cleveland. Shaughnessy is writing about Jeff Sellers, a twenty-two-year-old Californian called up from the minors to pitch for the Sox tomorrow night. Shaughnessy has also been working on a piece on pitcher Sammy Stewart, who talked with Shaughnessy at length about his two children, both of whom have cystic fibrosis. Stewart's love for his children was so touching, Shaughnessy told sports editor Vince Doria, that at times during the interview, Shaughnessy felt near tears.

Now he just feels frustrated. A photographer was supposed to meet the Stewart family at home today for a picture, but somebody messed up. Stewart says he was there at the appointed time; the photographer says *he* was there. But they never met, no picture was taken, and the Sox leave after tonight's game for a week-long road trip. Shaughnessy's only option, other than holding the story for a week, is to hope that Stewart's family attends tonight's game, and that a photographer can meet them when it's over. That may be wishful thinking.

Meanwhile, assistant sports editor Don Skwar and night editor Ken Fratus are looking over the layout for the front page of the section. Because the "windows" where color photos will go had to be positioned in advance for production purposes, there's not much room for last-minute changes. Ryan's Celtics story and Montville's column—nobody's sure what it's about yet, but he's known for pulling off last-minute miracles—will run at the top, on either side of a small color photo of Celtic Bill Walton that will tease some of the stories inside. The Sox–Indians story, with a large color photo that will have to be taken in the first inning and rushed back, will occupy the middle.

The current candidates for the two bottom spots are McDonough's Bruins column and the story about Irving Fryar of the Patriots, who held a news conference in Dallas today to defend himself against allegations that he had gambled on games. "That's a good place for the Fryar story," Skwar tells Fratus, "unless he says, 'Oh yeah, I did bet on games.' " Checking his terminal, Skwar sees that Borges' story on the news conference has just arrived over the phone lines that feed into the computer system. He opens it, reads the lead, and tells Fratus, "It's right where it belongs."

As soon as Skwar closes the Fryar story, Duffy opens it. He clicks his cursor quickly through the words on his screen, changing a spelling here, a comma there, but mostly deciding that he likes the story fine. Then he rereads the lead and pauses for a long time. The first sentence begins, "Irving Fryar is willing to bet he knows why he has become the target of an NFL probe into alleged gambling on football games." Using the word *bet* is clever in this context, but Duffy wonders if readers will perceive it as a cheap shot. Maybe he'd better take this one to the top, to Doria. Come to think of it, he ran into another question of taste in the NBA Notebook that he wanted to ask Doria about.

Doria, too, stops for a long time after he reads the lead

212

about Fryar. He reminds himself that he likes to give his writers the freedom to take risks, even if that means occasional failures. He reminds himself that he has long refused to edit the section to appeal to some imaginary lowest common denominator of readers. He remembers the times he's told the writers: If you use some obscure reference that only 20 percent of the readers will understand, but those 20 percent will really get a kick out of it, that's okay as long as it doesn't slow down the other 80 percent.

But none of those reminders seem to matter this time. Doria and Duffy review the issues. One: Gambling is a serious charge; it's nothing to joke about. Two: Fryar says he's innocent, but "willing to bet" makes him sound guilty. Three: The *Globe* shouldn't risk appearing to gloat over Fryar's embarrassment. Four: Relations between the newspaper and the Patriots have been strained since the paper broke a story about drug use on the team a few months ago.

The whole conversation has taken only a minute. Duffy proposes that the sentence would not suffer if "thinks" were substituted for "is willing to bet." Do it, Doria tells him.

Duffy's other question involves a quote that appears in the NBA Notebook column. After the Celtics won a game, forward Kevin McHale said, "We hug so many guys, people could think we're fags." Pretty offensive, Duffy and Doria agree—but, then again, it was McHale, not the writer, who said it. The paper isn't squeamish; sometimes profanity or items of questionable taste help convey the sense of a story. In the same column, for example, a player offers this praise of the referees in Game Four of the championship series: "I don't think anyone came away from that game saying, 'I got screwed.' " Duffy has already decided to leave that quote alone. The idiom is fairly widely accepted, and part of the column's point is to portray the players' personalities, speech patterns and all.

As for the McHale quote, Doria finds it an easy call. The statement isn't funny, it would definitely offend a lot of people, and it's a "loose item"; it doesn't advance any particular story. Get rid of it, he tells Duffy.

•   •   •

From the Fenway Park press box, high above home plate, the infield is the surreal green of the tiny trees in model railroad sets. Angled walls of shatterproof glass frame a living diorama: gray-uniformed shapes mingling in the visitors' dugout, white-uniformed shapes warming up on the field with motions that look, from this distance, somehow theatrical. The thick glass distorts the ball's trajectory. Instead of sailing smoothly through the air, the white dot seems to stop and start, stop and start, lurching toward a waiting glove as if its jerky rhythm had been drawn by some clumsy cosmic animator. As the ball staggers and stumbles and the players field and spit, figures in street clothes prowl the edges of the scene, wielding notebooks as their talismans. Now they converge on a television crew that has converged on a single uniform. Now they scatter to the dugouts and the bullpens, each seeking the angle that will distinguish this game from all the others.

Larry Whiteside has done as much field prowling as he needs tonight; it's time he started writing. His portable terminal awaits him at his usual seat in the U-shaped press box: front row, right side. On the long blue counter that extends around the U to his left, and on the identical blue counters in the two rows that rise behind him, sit terminals of various sizes, shapes, and stages of technological development. Pay phones line the platform behind the last row of orange plastic seats, but almost no one dictates stories by phone anymore. The press box regulars have phones at their seats. They're useful for the inevitable conversations with editors, but the receiver has a more important purpose: It fits into a hole in the terminal so that copy can be transmitted over the phone lines.

Whiteside's first task is to write his Red Sox Notebook, the equivalent of the Celtics Notebook now being edited back in the newsroom. Some days he gets the items simply by cruising around looking for tidbits—he usually gets to Fenway three hours before the 7:30 game time—but today he had a plan. The Sox had invited a local high school star to the park tonight, the first step in an effort to woo him away from college football and into pro baseball. Whiteside talked to the

kid, and to the Red Sox vice president who's interested in
him. That part will be easy to write. With a short item updating the injured list and another about the upcoming road trip,
he'll have a column.

A road trip for the Sox also means a road trip for Whiteside or fellow baseball writer Dan Shaughnessy. "You're in
and out of town like a rabbit," Whiteside says. "Some days I
think it's great to have a job so many people would kill for.
Other days I'd gladly let them have it." Baseball writers face
both the deadline pressure of individual games and the cumu-
lative pressure of the relentless schedule. This year, in the
twenty-seven weeks from early April to early October, the Red
Sox will be idle for a grand total of nineteen days. More than
eighty games will be played away from home. Even with two
writers to share the burden, it's a tiring routine.

Still, in Whiteside's opinion, covering baseball beats covering football, where writers watch one game a week and
spend the other days either rehashing the last game or looking
ahead to the next one. He'd rather lose himself in the nightly
routine: File the Notebook. Start the game story before the
game begins. Fill it up with the stats and other information
from the handouts in the pressbox, the quotes collected down
on the field. Once the first pitch is thrown, write a running
log of the plays. Transmit an unfinished story to the newsroom after the third inning, the fifth inning. Try to get it all
there by 10:20 and the "flash lead"—a quick announcement
of the winner—by 10:30, when the last copy is supposed to
leave the Sports department. If the lead doesn't arrive by then,
the editors may write their own, just for the first edition. Run
to the locker room for post-game interviews. Run back to the
pressbox to craft a more complete story for the later editions.
File again. Maybe out for a beer. Home.

Somewhere in there, he might have time for a meal at the
clubhouse, where the Red Sox staff and management eat. The
food is free, but the *Globe* sends a check every month to cover
what its people eat in the clubhouse and drink at the bar in
the pressbox. "Everyone's a lot more careful about freebies
now than they used to be," Whiteside says. "We try to main-

tain a distance. All the reporters used to hang out in the clubhouse and eat and drink before a game, but now we don't. Now we work."

Maintaining a distance can be a neat trick in sportswriting, where the writer deals with the same people day after day after day. He must build contacts while avoiding entangling relationships, cultivate sources without risking compromise. Inevitably, he will like some players better than others. Inevitably, a player he likes will screw up, and he will have to write about it. Inevitably, he will see that player tomorrow, when the bruising words are in print.

Sportswriting tolerates opinion to a much larger degree than does most newspaper writing. "Some people would maintain that a game story is a news story and must be a paragon of objectivity," says sports editor Vince Doria. "I don't. Sports revolve around differences of opinion—I like the Sox, you like the Yankees. That needs to be reflected in our stories. People want to know not just what happened at the game but also what the writer *thought* about it." Whiteside, actually, is one of the *Globe*'s least-opinionated sportswriters. The proof, according to him, is that he receives far less mail from opinionated readers than does Shaughnessy, who in turn gets less than did Peter Gammons, the baseball writer who recently left the paper. Whiteside says that he includes his opinion in stories when it seems to fit, but mostly he aims to convey the insight that comes from years of watching baseball. He wants his readers to sense what he perceives as the *Globe* sports credo: "We're thorough, we're fair, and we have fun."

Most fun of all is covering a team that's winning, and the Red Sox are winning now. It's been a great year for Boston sports: The Patriots made it to the Super Bowl, the Celtics are in the playoffs again, and now the Red Sox have a 36–15 record, their best start since the 1946 team that won the pennant. But covering a winner creates its own problem: how to portray the excitement that surrounds the team without crossing the line into boosterism. Fawning does not become a newspaper, not even a team's hometown paper. So Whiteside tries to play it straight, always mindful of the advice he got

216

from a teacher in 1959: Give 'em something they can't get in the box score.

"A real fan can read a lot in the box score, so that's a challenge," he says. "A box score can say there was a line drive, but it doesn't say that a fan touched it or that it snaked around a wall. It doesn't say what anybody said or what anybody felt."

6:00 P.M.

I thought there was a secret handshake that investigative reports know, but if there is I haven't learned it yet.
—Christine Chinlund, reporter for the Spotlight team

Managing editor Tom Mulvoy hasn't said a word in half an hour. He sits at a terminal in the middle of the newsroom, drinking coffee and reading potential front-page stories. Not far from his elbow, three tiny televisions mounted on the next desk simultaneously play the three local newscasts. Mulvoy ignores them. "Competition is not the be-all and end-all of my night and morning," he's been known to say. Night editor Ellen Clegg does watch the newscasts, in stolen moments between reading stories and talking with copy editors. She watches, she says, not because she wants the *Globe* to follow television's lead, but because television creates a thirst for more information, more detail. People look for that detail in their morning paper.

Mulvoy reads on. Around the newsroom, knots of reporters come together, then disperse. The intercom blares as the switchboard pages people who aren't at their desks. Editorial assistants rush by, bringing photos from the library, taking dummies to the composing room. To Mulvoy's left, copy editors call to one another. They rarely use the word *story*, referring to each by its slug.

"Have you seen Switzler yet?"

"C'mon, let's *move* that copy tonight!"

"Bob, would you store heroin for a minute so I can format it?"

"Am I willing? I don't think willing is part of this job."

"See if we have any file art on the Paulist Center."

218

"Is mint any good? You might like yearbook."

Still Mulvoy silently reads. Then, at 6:20, he rises and walks toward the conference room. A small group of editors follows him. The session is almost too brief to be called a meeting. Everyone knows his or her part and performs it with dispatch.

Mulvoy announces the front-page lineup: "Secrets, nukes, South Africa, Switzler, taxes, and Paulists." Victor Lewis runs down page three, the lead U.S./World page. David Chandler's story on the latest changes at NASA is definite, as is a wire story in which the Soviets say that President Reagan's intention to stop complying with SALT II jeopardizes plans for another summit. One of the wire services is promising a story on a meeting about a potential chemical weapons ban, and Lewis wants to run that if it comes. If it doesn't, he has some staff-written Washington Notes (items, sometimes amusing, that are worth only a paragraph or two) and his pick of wire stories and photos to fill the remaining space.

Now that he knows that "Switzler" and "Paulists" are the only local stories going on the front page, Ben Taylor can assemble a list for the Metro front. He names five stories: The mint that makes subway tokens, the pregnancy-prevention plan, the judge's ruling on physical punishment therapy for autistic children, the announcement of a new public housing development, and more backbiting in the Eighth Congressional District primary. The race would be big news anyway because local representation is at stake, but it's been getting more than the usual amount of national attention because one of the candidates is Joseph P. Kennedy.

As assistant managing editor for local news, Taylor considers it his job to set the tone for the newsgathering operations performed by about eighty people. To him, that means not only upholding certain standards of quality but also "aggressively pursuing page-one opportunities." When a local story with front-page potential is passed over by Mulvoy or whoever is the final arbiter that day, Taylor faces a decision. Should he schedule the story for Metro front tomorrow or hold it, hoping it can make page one the next day?

With the pregnancy-prevention story, the answer was easy. Because the proposal was made public today, holding the story would diminish its timeliness. Actually, however, the memo was written last week and became public today only because Peggy Hernandez asked for it, so the time peg really isn't that strong. But even if the story could be reshaped to look fresh tomorrow, it would be unlikely to make the front page because it lacks the key element of novelty. A sex education program for seventh-graders that *doesn't* call for distributing birth-control devices just doesn't pack the same punch as a program that does. The story still has impact; readers will want to know what their children will be taught. But the program simply isn't that different from dozens of others in dozens of other cities and towns. It does, however, have a wonderfully euphemistic title: Life Planning Education.

The decision on when to run the mint story was a little more difficult. It has no specific time element; the mint stamped out New York subway tokens today, and it will stamp them out tomorrow. Conceivably, the story might make the front page another day if Taylor held it. He heard several people saying they liked it during the last hour's reading marathon. He decided, however, that although the story is written in a way that maximizes its interest, the subject isn't compelling enough to make the front page except on a slow day—and no one wants to hope for a slow day. Besides, the mint story has a good photo, and none of the other stories on the page has a photo at all, unless someone digs out a file head shot. If he doesn't run the mint story tomorrow, the Metro front will be hurting for art.

Mulvoy used many of the same criteria as Taylor in choosing the front-page lineup. Tax reform, apartheid, and the Chernobyl nuclear accident are continuing news stories of such magnitude that each new development deserves consideration for page one. The Switzler followup belongs out front, Mulvoy decided, because they played the original story there this morning, and a lot has happened since the candidate's announcement yesterday that he had lied about his military record. As for the story about Ronald Pelton's alleged spying, if Mulvoy had had any doubts about its significance—

and he didn't—they would have been eliminated by the paper's dealings with the government in the last week.

As Mulvoy sees it, the only surprise on tomorrow's front page will be the story about the Paulist fathers' agreeing under pressure to stop letting women preach at Mass—and even that follows an unofficial *Globe* formula that encourages putting something unexpected out front as often as the hard news allows. Though he downplays the importance of competition, Mulvoy acknowledges that one reason he likes the Paulists story is that he's unlikely to see it on television or in "our only competition in town." Because nothing particularly newsworthy happened at the Paulist Center today, the story isn't an automatic front-page pick. It does have a good ending, in which a woman who has been active at the center says she's willing to wait a little longer for women to win a larger role in the Catholic Church, but she adds, "I'm not convinced we don't need a revolution."

Mulvoy enumerates the other reasons he chose the story for the front: "This is as Catholic a community as you'll find, the third-largest archdiocese in the nation. Women on the altar is much more a generic issue than just something at one church. The Paulist Center is on a major thoroughfare—everybody's seen it—and it has a history of being ahead of the curve on social awareness."

That last point coincides with Mulvoy's views on the newspaper's role in society. Once it may have been enough for a paper to hold up a mirror to the community and say, "Here, readers, here's what your world looks like today." But it seems to Mulvoy that that's not true anymore. Now, he says, a newspaper must not only reflect the world as it is but also must try to interpret that world for its readers while keeping an eye on the future. What do today's events portend for tomorrow? If tax reform is running into trouble, what does that mean? If it passes, how will it affect the average taxpayer? How will that taxpayer's reactions affect American business? How might the business response affect the international economic climate?

Mulvoy calls this kind of questioning "being proactive about issues," and it's one of his aims for the *Globe.* Being

221

proactive requires a level of consistency that's difficult for a newspaper, especially on subjects like arms control where change happens at a glacial pace. It requires an understanding of what the readers want but also a willingness to let reporters and editors "follow their noses" to stories that will surprise readers with their impact. It requires an expanded version of what editors have long called news judgment, the sixth sense that lets a journalist smell a story and the insight that shows him or her how to get it.

To Mulvoy, news judgment, like so much about journalism, embodies a contradiction: Though the essence of news is novelty, the essence of news judgment is "acknowledging that in life and politics, there's precious little new under the sun." Each day's events are unique, yet they follow patterns that point an experienced reporter or editor toward the next development. Fortunately for journalists' sanity, the element of surprise endures, especially when it comes to readers' responses. "Ideally, a news story that makes the front page always sets off a reaction," Mulvoy says. "The trick is that you can't predict who it will come from or what it will be."

Surprise, however, has no place in a newsroom when it comes to deadlines. The necessity of meeting deadlines should go without saying, but Mulvoy considers it his duty to remind everyone now and then. Reporters and editors can get so involved in trying to make one story or one page layout achieve perfection that they forget to think of the paper as a whole. It's Mulvoy's job to nudge them. So today, when the lineups for pages one and three and the Metro front are settled, Mulvoy ends the session with a reminder. "Let's try to stay with those decisions for the first edition," he says as the editors make a beeline for the door. "We've got a big paper, and we've got to get it out."

•   •   •

Ed Doherty has flipped through the available photos three times without finding what he's looking for: something spectacular for tomorrow's front page. As managing editor for graphics, he designs the page each evening before he goes home. The *Globe* prides itself on running strong front-page art, often designing the page around a large feature photo simply because its composition is interesting. The practice both distinguishes the paper from others and opens it to criticism from people who favor a more traditional news slant. "A typical front page includes oversize wistful photographs of the seasonal foliage," one critic recently wrote about the *Globe* in a national magazine.

Right now Doherty might welcome a foliage photo. With some photographers in Houston for the basketball playoffs and others scattered around New England doing assignments for future editions, tomorrow's paper has come up short. A college intern took a photo of windsurfers on Dorchester Bay that's not half bad, especially considering that today is the intern's first day, but it just isn't front-page material. Having watched the feast-or-famine cycle of stories and photos run its course for more than thirty years, Doherty wastes no time cursing fate. He's seen worse days than this one, and somehow a paper always rolls off the press at midnight. (How that happens can be a mystery even to the people doing the work—hence the label "the daily miracle.") He passes the windsurfing photo along to Bill Harting, who's laying out the Metro front, and starts looking for a wire photo for the front page. Since none of the stories has strong art, the wire is his only choice.

If Stan Grossfeld were in the newsroom instead of in Houston, he'd be groaning. He'd be saying that with fifteen photographers out combing the earth, the paper should not have to lead with wire art. Grossfeld, the *Globe*'s chief photographer, is a vocal proponent of strong front-page art. "A good photo that will interest people should be on page one every day," he says. "We need to mix it up, to run not just car bombs in Beirut but local news and slices of life. I really believe we have to bend over backward to get good news and humor into the paper." As for people who criticize the *Globe*'s feature photos, Grossfeld dismisses them as "old jaded newspaper people taking shots." The mail, he says, shows that average readers like a change of pace; "they like pretty pictures sometimes."

As Grossfeld sees it, New Englanders live in a unique region, and the photos in the paper should reflect that

223

uniqueness. "We've got the mountains, the sea, the four seasons," he says. "A scene that looks one way today could look completely different next week because of the light, the way the trees grow. When we take a picture of that scene, we just want people to stop and look and appreciate it."

The *Globe*'s openness to features is both a blessing and a burden for photographers. The blessing is the knowledge that if they take a good photo that doesn't relate to a story, it will be used, and probably played well. The burden is having to maintain the standard, having to be constantly alert for features, even while driving to and from other assignments. Grossfeld once worked at a paper whose photographers stayed in the office if they didn't have an assignment. ("Why?" he'd ask. "There are no photos in the office.") At the *Globe*, the photographers head out, whether or not they have a specific destination. "If you see a butterfly and you shoot it well, the picture will get into the paper," he says. "That's freedom."

Some days good feature pictures seem to be everywhere. Some days, like today, they're nowhere, or no one is free to find them. Many of the best features are what Grossfeld calls gifts—they're great and they're there, and the photographer need only have the good sense to accept them, even if it means showing up a little late for that head shot at the State House. One of Grossfeld's favorite "gifts" came while he was sitting atop a cliff overlooking the ocean in Maine, trying to work up the courage to visit a couple whose son, a former *Globe* photographer, had died in Vietnam. As Grossfeld sat watching the tide come in, two hands appeared from below and grasped the top of the cliff. "I thought, what the hell is this?" he recalls. "I didn't say anything for fear I'd scare the guy and he'd fall off." The climber turned out to be Spider Dan Goodman, who'd been getting publicity for his illegal ascents of tall buildings. "I got the picture," Grossfeld says. "That's a gift."

In addition to a willingness to accept the gifts, a good photographer must be skilled in light and patterns and human emotion, must be willing to do research and cut through red tape and sometimes bluster ahead on sheer nerve in order to capture the desired image. "Editors and readers don't know what you went through to get a picture, and they don't care," Grossfeld says.

The path from idea to finished photo can be a tortuous one. When *Globe* photographer David Ryan decided to document the reconstruction of the Statue of Liberty, for example, he couldn't just hop a plane to New York with his cameras. First he had to make about thirty phone calls and write a dozen letters to line up the proper permissions. Then he had to persuade the paper to take out a million-dollar insurance policy on him. Then he had to get to the island, climb the scaffolding, and hang off the side while it swayed in the wind. Level with the lady's collarbone, he shot the head shot to end all head shots, complete with a construction worker caressing the statue's battered nose.

Although the finger that clicks the shutter is the photographer's, Grossfeld sometimes wishes his photos could have twenty credit lines to recognize all the people who helped the image reach the page. Last week, for instance, looking for a new angle on the Celtics, he decided to take a color picture from the ceiling of Boston Garden. Since no one is allowed in the rafters, he needed to station a camera up there and devise a system of operating it from below. He went to one of the *Globe*'s carpenters, who built a platform with a lock to keep the camera from falling. A company electrician designed a remote-control system that would let Grossfeld trip the shutter by radio. That worked fine, except that other people's radios kept setting off Grossfeld's camera.

After collecting suggestions from the photo department, the electrician attached a wire that dangled from the camera's shutter release to the floor. Grossfeld could put the wire in his pocket and, while watching the game, calmly click the shutter whenever he wanted. The best part, in his view, was that none of the other photographers could tell when he was taking a picture. "I considered being really arrogant and sitting there eating popcorn," he says.

The cooperation didn't end with the design of the remote-control system. Grossfeld had mistakenly loaded the wrong kind of film into the camera, adding precious processing time to a deadline color system that was still experimental

225

at best. But a darkroom technician changed the chemicals and pushed the film through, the Sports department tried to finish its other work early to clear the decks, and the operator of the machine that makes the color separations changed the size at the last minute so as not to cut off a player's head. It seemed unfair to Grossfeld that the only name listed under the photo was his.

All the cooperation in the world, however, can't create a photo from thin air. Though he doesn't like it any more than Grossfeld would, Doherty has chosen an AP photo and started designing a front page that puts it smack in the center. Other than a small photo of the Paulist Center and head shots of Pelton and another accused spy, Jonathan Pollard, it's the only art on the page. He needs it to separate the stories.

The photo Doherty has chosen was taken at Wright-Patterson Air Force Base in Ohio. Like all wire photos, it came to the *Globe* courtesy of laser beams and telephone lines. Using this photo as an example, the system works this way: An AP photographer took the photo and printed it in the usual way in a darkroom in an AP bureau in Ohio. An editor there wrote the cutline and then put the photo into a transmitter. Rollers slowly fed the print into a metal box. By the time the print rolled out the bottom of the box, its likeness had been transmitted to newspapers all over the country.

Inside the transmitter box is a laser beam that scans the photo and cutline two millimeters at a time, determining how gray or white each area is by how much light it reflects back. The transmitter then sends that information over the phone lines as variable frequencies. When the frequencies reach the receiver boxes stationed at the *Globe* and other newspapers (for which the newspapers pay as part of their rate for subscribing to the AP), another laser picks up the impulses. Each impulse "tells" the laser how much light to direct at each section of the photo-sensitive paper mounted inside the receiver. The more light hits the paper, the darker gray that area will be on the finished print. As the laser exposes one section of the paper at a time, the print slowly emerges from the receiver.

The black in a wire photo usually isn't as black, or the white as white, as in a regular print from the darkroom. A wire photo is also on thinner paper, about the thickness of typing paper. Otherwise, a photo transmitted over the wire looks much like any other photo. The *Globe* photographers in Houston have been using the same technology to send photos of the NBA playoffs back to Boston on deadline.

At first glance, the photo Doherty has chosen for the front page seems to show a human fly. Actually, it's a pilot wearing sophisticated, and very heavy-looking, headgear designed to let him see outside the plane in darkness or rain, and to aim weapons just by turning his head. When Doherty laid the photo on the corner of his desk for a while, nearly everyone who passed stopped to ask what it was. If he can't give readers a photo with strong artistic or news value tomorrow, at least he can pique their curiosity.

.   .   .

Chris Chinlund is riding the subway back to work, feeling frustrated. She's riding the subway because she doesn't have cab fare, and she doesn't have cab fare because, after a morning in which everything went wrong, she rushed off four hours ago to a meeting at which even more things went wrong. The person who was supposed to tell her about the meeting had forgotten, and by the time she found out about it she was so late that she didn't have time to go upstairs and cash a check. She borrowed $5 from her editor and spent it on a cab ride into the city, leaving her with only enough for a subway token to get back to Dorchester. Well, she thinks, welcome to the glamorous world of investigative reporting.

Chinlund joined the Spotlight investigative team three months ago, after writing for the *Globe* for more than four years. "There's definitely an image of glamor associated with this kind of work," she says, "but it doesn't feel as true once you're inside it." In fact, the job so far has been a little intimidating. When Chinlund moved downstairs from the newsroom to the Spotlight office, the team—which consists of another reporter, an editor, and a researcher—had already started work on a series exploring medical malpractice.

Chinlund joined in and has been diligently reporting on the issue for three months, but she still doesn't feel caught up.

It's a humbling feeling for an experienced reporter, and it's magnified each time she looks at the wall next to her desk, which is covered with awards the team has received since its inception in 1970. (Spotlight's two Pulitzer Prize certificates hang in a glass case upstairs.) She's always thought of Spotlight as intense, serious, and feared by politicians with something to hide. Only about twenty newspapers in the country have permanent investigative teams, and she wants to help this one live up to its reputation.

In addition, Chinlund hasn't yet shaken the classic reporter's guilt over not having stories in the paper regularly. Three months is an average time for an investigative project to take, and she knows that no one is expecting her byline to appear more often. But seeing her stories in print a couple times a week has always been her reward for the hard work of reporting. It feels strange to go home every day with nothing concrete to show, and frightening that her usual worrying about a story ("I take my work home in my head," she says) can now continue for three months instead of three days.

On the other hand, the opportunity to take more time with stories was one of the main reasons she accepted the coveted invitation to join Spotlight. As a regular reporter, she'd never felt free to follow every last lead. "In my personal philosophy, you can't report too much," she says. "But in this business, because of the time pressures, there is a thing called over-reporting, and I've always done it." On Spotlight, she reasoned, she'd be able to dig as far into stories as any reporter could hope to go. She'd learn more about how to pursue sources and angles, and how to organize three months' worth of notes. And she'd have the opportunity to work with Gerry O'Neill, who had been one of the original Spotlight reporters and had now returned for his second stint as editor.

O'Neill says that the team's mandate is "to uncover malfeasance." The misdeeds don't have to be political, he says, but they often are. "Frequently checks and balances in government don't exist where they should," he says. "There are excesses, and people are victimized, and no one is doing anything about it. It sounds a little pompous, but I truly believe it's a newspaper's function to wade in in those instances and put the facts before the public. If we didn't, they'd never be known."

That mandate applies not only to Spotlight but also to the whole paper; Spotlight simply has the advantage of time. In fact, O'Neill considers time the only real difference between the jobs of an investigative reporter and any other reporter. "Any good reporter operates the same way," he says. "You vigorously pursue sources and accuracy, and you try for precise, lively writing." Chinlund, who acknowledges that a certain mystique surrounds investigative reporting, has been surprised to find the differences so few. "It turns out it's just hard work like anything else," she says of her new job. "There are no particular skills you need to be an investigative reporter that any good reporter doesn't already have."

Investigative reporters do, however, have to work together more closely than most reporters are accustomed to working, and they must be willing to do what O'Neill calls the "dog research," or tedious detail work, that tells them whether they're on the track of something big. Chinlund says Spotlight gets "tons of tips" from readers, other reporters and editors, and team members' own reading and observations. The trick is knowing which tips will lead to a good story and knowing when to abandon an idea that isn't panning out.

O'Neill says it's difficult to define what convinces him that a particular story is right for Spotlight. "I go on instinct and experience," he says. "I need to have a feeling at the beginning that there are strong possibilities, that there are good sources available and good information to be had." Once he's decided to pursue an idea, O'Neill gives it two or three weeks to prove its merits. He and the reporters come at the issue from various angles, looking for statistics, looking for people affected by the subject—looking, in short, for "a critical mass of material, something they can't take away from us." They're waiting for the moment he calls "the definition of exhilaration," when they look at the information they've collected and say, "That's it! We've got it!"

The series on medical malpractice sprang from observations O'Neill made after he left Spotlight to start the *Globe*'s Sci-Tech section in 1983. With the malpractice "crisis" constantly in the news, O'Neill became interested in the way doctors, lawyers, and insurance companies were blaming one another. The doctors accused the lawyers of driving malpractice insurance premiums out of reach by charging exorbitant fees and pursuing frivolous claims. The lawyers accused the insurance companies of trying to make up for bad investments by gouging doctors. The insurance companies accused the lawyers of encouraging worthless suits that resulted in huge jury awards.

Like many story ideas, this one began as a question: What about the patients? From that question sprouted more questions. How many incompetent doctors are practicing in Massachusetts? Who's supposed to stop them? Is there any truth behind the finger-pointing by doctors, lawyers, and insurance companies? Are patients suffering? What kind of change is needed?

The questions multiplied in a quiet corner of O'Neill's mind. Then this year, after he'd returned to Spotlight, he and the reporters started looking for answers. "I'd heard about repeat offenders who continually don't measure up, yet nothing is done," he said. "What we needed was a way to show that a small percentage of hard-core incompetent doctors were causing a disproportionate number of payouts by insurance companies." Team members read everything they could find about malpractice around the country. Then they went to the state insurance commission, which kept statistics on payments. After much compiling and analysis, they had what they were looking for: figures showing that 3 percent of the doctors insured by the state's largest malpractice insurer accounted for almost one-third of the malpractice lawsuits.

That was the exhilarating moment of "We've got it!" But it was only the beginning of the work. They checked how many cases were settled out of court and how the dollar amounts of those settlements had changed over the years. They studied one hundred cases in one court to determine the kinds of malpractice alleged and the kinds of injuries patients

230

sustained. They used a computer to analyze information on malpractice suits and disciplinary problems filed by all 21,000 of the state's doctors.

They found patients who couldn't get help, and doctors who had been sued repeatedly but had never been disciplined by the state medical board. Most of the patients were willing to talk for the record. Most of the doctors weren't, not even for Linda Matchan's sidebar about the devastating effects malpractice suits have on doctors. "Usually I'm surprised that some people will talk to us, and glad that they do," O'Neill says. "I'm seldom surprised when they don't."

The team has been putting together stories and sidebars and charts that would run on five consecutive days. The portion of the series dealing with the medical board is Chinlund's responsibility. The deadline for her first draft was noon today, and she made it with only minutes to spare. If any day were going to lay the glamorous image of investigative reporting permanently to rest, this would be it.

First there was the matter of the photocopying. She had piles of documents to copy this morning, but the Spotlight researcher was too busy to do it, and after asking one of the newsroom's editorial assistants for help, she learned that they're not supposed to do things that are technically the Spotlight reseacher's job. Chinlund decided to do the copying herself. Sometimes when she's under pressure, a routine task helps her relax. It didn't this time, though; she had to go to four copying machines before she found one that worked.

The confusion left her with just a few hours to finish her first draft, prepare questions for her afternoon interview, return several bulky containers of documents to a lawyer downtown, and find out whether the medical board was meeting. She was supposed to be at the lawyer's office at 1:00, but it was nearly 2:00 by the time she finally tracked down someone who told her that the medical board was in fact meeting—at 2:00. She raced off with cab fare borrowed from O'Neill, dropped the documents with the lawyer, and arrived at the meeting half an hour late.

After the meeting had dragged on nearly three hours, the board voted to go into executive session, meaning that everyone but board members had to leave the room. Reporters sometimes object to executive sessions if they don't think the reason given or the procedures followed are in line with the state right-to-know law, which safeguards public access. This time, however, everything seemed to be in order. Chinlund wouldn't have been inclined to object anyway, for two reasons. First, a staff member had promised to come out and tell her when she could return to the board room. Second, she wasn't that interested in the meeting itself. She had come mostly because she wanted to interview the chairman of the board afterward, to seek his comments on several cases the Spotlight team had been looking into while researching the malpractice series.

Later, on the subway, she told herself that she should have known what would happen. No one remembered to let her know when the executive session ended, and Chinlund missed the one item on the agenda she'd cared about, the board's actions on doctor discipline. When the meeting broke up, she sat down with the board chairman. Four staff members sat with them, which isn't the ideal way to conduct an interview. Reporters usually try to talk with an interview subject alone, to minimize distractions and the possibility that the interviewee will put on some sort of front for the onlookers. But when she asked the chairman about a particular case, he answered readily, and Chinlund could feel elation replacing the frustrations of the day.

Then the inevitable happened. A staff member interrupted the chairman, reminding him that cases under investigation could not be discussed. The interview ended soon after that, and Chinlund left with her notebook nearly empty. The blank pages are cold comfort as she rides the subway back to work.

7:00 P.M.

I tell people I put together puzzles for a living.
—Barbara Huebner, layout editor

At Symphony Hall in Boston, reviewer Tony Tommasini watches concertgoers at the $250-a-ticket tables raise their plastic stemware in champagne toasts, waiting for the Boston Pops' world premiere of "Liberty Fanfare." At the Opera House, critic Richard Dyer, fresh from his pre-performance swim, is settling in for *Tosca*, an opera he's reviewed in so many productions that he can't remember when he didn't know it by heart. At Fenway Park, the Red Sox have taken the lead in the first inning, and Joanne Rathe's color film of a safe call at second base is on its way back to the *Globe*. In the press box, Larry Whiteside is typing up the action, looking for connections to the quotes he collected before the game.

Back on Morrissey Boulevard, a phone rings in the Sports department. A man wants to know who on the Red Sox has made the most errors. A phone rings on the city desk. A little girl doing her homework wants to know the capital of Kentucky. The hotline from the composing room rings on the copy desk. "Damage control," someone answers.

Tom Oliphant finishes his tax reform story and bolts, hoping to catch the shuttle to Washington. The editors know he'll call later to see if they have questions. Peggy Hernandez makes one last call to her editor, who has run out of questions on her pregnancy prevention story. She straightens her desk at City Hall, checks her appointments for tomorrow, and heads home. All around the newsroom, other reporters are hoping to do the same. But a few reporters—and a few of the editors who arrived before 10:00 this morning—still have work to do.

Pam Cox sits beside Dave Morrow as he finishes editing her first *Globe* story. Morrow explains his reasons as he trims a phrase here, substitutes a word there. He tells her that she and fellow intern George Smith, who wrote the story with her, need more practice with organization and attributing quotes, but that basically they're on the right track. Cox flashes a relieved smile.

Ed Doherty has decided that he likes his second dummy for the front page better than his first. Both played the secrets story at the top and the "human fly" picture in the middle, but below that the stories seem about equal in importance; none cries out to be played higher than the others. He shows the second dummy to deputy managing editor Helen Donovan, who wonders aloud whether the Paulists story deserves the play it's getting—lower right-hand corner, boxed, with a photo. She and Doherty and managing editor Tom Mulvoy decide that it probably does. At any rate, with so little art on the page, they haven't many alternatives.

•   •   •

A bicyclist died in an accident today. The police released the cyclist's name to the media as part of the accident report, but now the victim's family is on the phone to the newsroom, asking that the name not be published. Family members have been unable to reach some of their relatives, and they don't want the relatives to read about the death in the newspaper before hearing about it from the family. Would the *Globe* please withhold the name?

Calls aimed at influencing the content of a newspaper come more often than readers might imagine. In some ways, editors welcome them. They want readers to think of the paper as an approachable, participatory product, not a cold, distant institution. In addition, people involved in a story sometimes bring up issues that reporters and editors hadn't thought to consider. But requests to change a story are nearly always difficult for editors. No reference books exist to offer an answer, the way a dictionary settles a spelling dispute. An editor or group of editors must decide each ethical question individually, and there's no guarantee that when they see the story in print tomorrow, they won't wish they'd said no instead of yes.

Such calls can wreak havoc when they come on deadline. It's difficult for the callers to understand that although they won't see the paper for twelve hours or more, the editors have little time to talk if the presses are to roll on time. As a result, an editor may get exasperated with a caller who doesn't understand the pressures, and the caller may get exasperated with what he perceives as arrogance on the newspaper's part. Fortunately, most such calls come during the day, when the ombudsman is available to take them.

But the biggest problem created when a reader wants to influence the content of the paper is that sometimes an editor may understand the caller's position, even sympathize with it, but still believe that the tenets of good journalism require the paper to do the opposite of what the caller wants. Take, for example, the prominent person who is arrested for drunk driving and doesn't want his name in the paper. His fear of damage to his reputation doesn't change the fact that a prominent person's activities are news because of his prominence. And his prominence, in turn, doesn't change the paper's policy of printing the names of people arrested for drunk driving.

Or take a more delicate case, that of a man who wants to be mentioned in the obituary of another man who has died. The two were homosexuals, longtime live-in companions, and the man calls to point out that he was in effect the deceased's closest relative because their relationship had alienated his companion's family. But the paper has already received the obituary information from the funeral home, which got it from the man's family, and it includes no mention of the friend. The friend points out that he played a large part in the dead man's everyday life, whereas the family did not. He wants recognition of his importance. The *Globe* received such a request recently and, though the editors understood why the caller was upset, they decided to stick with the paper's policy that all obituary information must come from the family.

Questions about obituaries have been arising more frequently with the spread of the disease AIDS. So far, the
Globe's policy has been to mention AIDS in an obit only if the
deceased was a prominent person whose cause of death is well
known and would naturally be of interest to readers; or if, like
Rock Hudson, the person wanted his or her death used as an
example to help fight the disease; or if family or the funeral
home lists the disease as the cause of death. Because the
actual cause of an AIDS victim's death isn't the disease itself
but some other ailment caused by the immune deficiency,
AIDS is rarely listed. The paper does not go digging for the
true cause of death if the one listed seems to hint at AIDS.

As the AIDS question shows, ethical goblins can lurk in
any corner, assuming new forms as the world changes. To an
outsider, some of the questions that cause fierce debate in a
newsroom may seem like much ado about very little. In the
grand scheme of things, what difference does it make whether
a certain piece of information is published or not? To journalists, it makes a lot of difference. They believe that a newspaper's job is to find information and pass it along to readers. If
a paper passes along only selected parts of that information—
if instead of "Here's the way your world looks today," it tells
its readers, "Here's part of the way your world looks; somebody didn't want us to tell you the rest"—it's not doing its
job. In addition, each time a newspaper withholds information, its credibility is undercut. Not only the newspaper's
employees but also some of its readers know the whole truth
and know the paper isn't reporting it.

Tomorrow's paper has already caused more than its share
of ethical wrangling because of the government's objections
to the Ronald Pelton story. The question of withholding the
name of an accident victim isn't a matter of national security
like the Pelton story, but still it's not an easy call. The reporter
who wrote up the accident has gone home, so night editor
Ellen Clegg consults the editor who handled the story. They
talk about how horrifying it would be to open the paper and
find out that a relative had died. They wonder if withholding
the name might be futile, since other newspapers or television
or radio might report it anyway. Though each medium aims

to act independently, some of the pack mentality lingers. For example, if several newspapers agree to hold a story until a certain date for what they consider a legitimate reason, but one paper breaks the embargo and publishes the information early, the rest will publish it as well. Once the cat's out of the bag, the reasoning goes, there's no use keeping the bag closed. The same logic applies when one newspaper gets a good story. The others jump on it. They want their readers to know it, too, even if that means the person involved has to tell his story to two dozen reporters in twenty-four hours.

Clegg turns the brief discussion of the cyclist's death to the most important question: How badly would the story be hurt if the name were eliminated? Not very, the other editors agree. Reporting on local accidents is part of the paper-of-record function. Newspapers report accidents because they happened, and because people who saw the accident or were stuck in the resulting traffic jam might want to know the details. Some accident stories also have advisory value, pointing out a dangerous intersection or the perils of bicycling on a certain road. None of those functions relies on the victim's name. Clegg decides not to use the victim's name, and to insert a paragraph in the story saying that the family wanted the name withheld until all relatives were notified. The decision made, she reopens her nightly note to the day crew and adds a paragraph congratulating the copy editor who took the family's call. She knows it's not always easy to be sensitive on deadline.

That issue settled, Clegg turns to another ethical question that's come up, this one involving a photo. Photos can cause even more public outcry than stories because they graphically bring the world to the breakfast table—complete with unpleasantness that readers may not want to hear about, never mind see in black and white over their English muffins. One might expect a television picture of war or famine to generate more complaints than a newspaper picture because it's close up and in living color, but it also blinks off as quickly as it appeared. A newspaper picture endures until a reader discards it, giving him plenty of time to hone his outrage.

Photos showing real or imagined harm to people or animals are almost guaranteed to provoke a strong response. Just let a paper publish a photo of, for example, a dog in a comical pose behind the steering wheel of a car, and the letters and calls begin. The windows in the car are closed; how is the dog supposed to breathe? What kind of person would do that to an animal? The depth of readers' feelings for animals often surprises editors. The revulsion caused by photos of bodies does not. But sometimes death is the news, and a photo that shows the whole scene, including but not focusing on the body or bodies, is the only honest photo to take. Sensationalistic photos do, of course, make it into print in various newspapers, burning themselves into many people's minds as the rule rather than the exception.

Although blood and violence have become commonplace in television newscasts, many newspapers have grown more reluctant to publish photographs that graphically show death. The editors must be so sure of the photo's merits that they're ready to defend its news value against the inevitable response. A few weeks ago, for example, the wires sent a photo of a Korean student who had set himself afire and jumped out a window as a protest. It was a horrifying shot, and the *Globe* debated whether to use it. Chief photographer Stan Grossfeld said yes; the photo was *supposed* to be upsetting, he said. Most of the editors, however, said no, and the photo was not used. Many other papers ran it. A more famous example happened years ago, when a six-foot piece of fencepost was rammed through a man's chest in an accident in Dorchester. A *Globe* photographer took a picture as the man was unloaded from an ambulance; miraculously, he survived and recovered. The photo ran on the front page of the evening edition. Later the editors, feeling squeamish, moved it inside.

The photo raising questions tonight is stark but not bloody. It is an AP photo of the scene of a plane crash in which a radio traffic reporter died. The crash was in California, but the reporter formerly worked for a station in Boston. The photo shows the wreckage of the plane and the tractor-trailer it crashed into, and, off to the side, the backs of a police officer and a woman near a black bag on a cart. The

woman, who is kneeling, is the reporter's wife. The bag holds
his body. Beyond it, two men in suits stand with heads bowed.
Again the decision is Clegg's: Should the picture be run?
She picks it up and makes a circuit of the copy desk.
"This bother you?" she asks each person who looks up.
The answers are unanimous:
"Nope."
"It's fine."
"Sad, but not gross."
"Wouldn't worry about it."
Clegg examines the photo again. It's a good news photo,
packed with information. The body is not visible, and neither
is the wife's grief; she is seen from a distance, and her face is
turned away. The photo adds to the story without being un-
necessarily upsetting. Clegg gives it back to layout editor Barbara Huebner with the instruction Huebner had hoped for:
Run it.
Photos that intrude on people's grief can cause as strong
a reaction as photos that show death. Even reporters and
photographers who pride themselves on sensitivity acknowledge that they occasionally venture where they shouldn't, and
regret it later. These errors in judgment—added to the times
when reporters and photographers feel it's necessary to capture grief, as some did after the explosion of the space shuttle
Challenger—stick in the public memory and further tarnish
the media's reputation. (Reporters usually come out about
even with used-car salesmen in polls measuring respect, or
lack of same, for various professions.) Newspaper people
tend to blame television for the intrusions and vice versa, but
in honest moments most reporters will acknowledge that in
their zeal to show "the way it is," they sometimes get carried
away. They'll also point out, however, how much of what
people know, how much of what they talk about every day, is
available to them only because of the media.
"You've got to be persistent, but that doesn't mean you
shouldn't be sensitive to people's grief," Grossfeld says. "If a
kid is hit by a car, there's no reason to shove a wide-angle lens
in the mother's face. The law says you can because she's on a
public street, but your sensibilities say you don't."

239

Hard thinking about the effects of an upsetting photo is in order both before and after it's shot. Grossfeld says he's taken photos he regrets, but he also says that people who call to complain about a published photo of themselves often call back later, asking for a print. And if the photo is of a public figure caught doing something he wishes he hadn't, all bets are off. "I mean, Nixon probably didn't want to be photographed leaving the White House in disgrace, but that's news," he says. "Tough luck."

· · ·

Jim Franklin and his editor have finally arrived at a lead they both like for the Paulists story. It looks much like the last one Franklin wrote except that it refers to the Paulist Center rather than the Paulist fathers, in order to anchor the place in readers' minds. Tom Mulvoy says he'll write the headline, as he sometimes does for front-page stories. "Two lines of 18 drop," Ellen Clegg calls to him. She wants an 18-point head below the main head, for which specifications—two lines of 36-point type, each twenty-three picas wide—have already been typed into the computer. Two columns would ordinarily be twenty-five picas wide, but because the box cuts into the space, Clegg figures he'll need additional lines to say anything meaningful.

Even after years of experience, few editors can predict which headlines will be impossible and which will nearly write themselves. The main head on the Paulists story, luckily, turns out to fall into the latter category. Mulvoy writes "Paulist Center bows to church's threat" and hits the "head fit" button. The computer compares the point size and letters he's typed with the available space and quickly flashes its verdict: The headline will fit into the space. Before computers, editors counted headlines manually, which meant more than simply counting the number of letters in the words. Because an uppercase *M*, for example, takes up so much more space than a lowercase *i*, a counting system had to be developed that took each letter's width into consideration. Lowercase letters were each counted as one unit, except for *m* and *w*, which counted one and a half, and *f*, *l*, *i*, *t*, and *j*, which counted one-half.

240

(To further complicate matters, *f* and *j* received a whole count in some typefaces.)

Each space and punctuation mark also had a value, as did each uppercase letter: one and a half for most of them, two for *M* and *W*, one for *I* and *J*. Counting uppercase letters was more important in pre-computer days than it would be today because nearly every newspaper then used "upstyle heads," headlines in which the first letter of each word is capitalized. Today many newspapers, including the *Globe*, use "downstyle heads," which capitalize the first letter only of the first word in the headline, and of any proper names. Downstyle heads, in other words, follow the same capitalization rules as ordinary sentences. They're considered part of a more modern-looking design.

When an editor writes a head and asks the computer whether it fits, the computer responds with more than yes or no; it also calculates how much too long or too short the headline is. Most computer systems calculate those measurements in picas, the usual newspaper unit of horizontal measurement, but the *Globe*'s system gives the results in *e*'s. For example, the information on Mulvoy's screen tells him that the second line of his head on the Paulists story—"to church's threat"—is three *e*'s shorter than the first line. That means he could fit three more letters the width of an *e* on the second line, or maybe two wider letters like *m* or *w*, or five or six thinner ones like *l* or *i*. Since the top line fits nearly perfectly, the shorter bottom line would leave the head looking unbalanced.

After checking the story to make sure the plural is accurate, Mulvoy adds an *s* to *threat*, so that the head reads, "Paulist Center bows to church's threats." The bottom line is still slightly shorter than the top, but not enough to create the archenemy of the layout artist, trapped white space. Now for the hard part: writing a drop head that, in two lines, explains who's making the threats and what the Paulists did to incur them.

When Mulvoy took up the Paulists story, he turned the secrets story over to Donovan. He has read it several times and so has she, but with a story this sensitive, another read can't hurt. Meanwhile, although they've relinquished control over the story, Washington bureau chief Steve Kurkjian and national editor Royal Ford are still sitting in Ford's office, not quite ready to believe that the story that spawned so much soul-searching is actually going to make it into the paper at last. If they leave, they might miss something.

Out in the the middle of the newsroom, Mulvoy's phone rings. It's the deputy director of the National Security Agency, and he has a request: "Please reconsider your decision to publish the Pelton story. We feel it contains details that shouldn't be printed." The agency has been trying unsuccessfully to reach executive editor Jack Driscoll. Would Mr. Mulvoy kindly give the request serious consideration and see that it is passed along to Mr. Driscoll? Mulvoy says yes. He can see a long night of phone calls ahead.

8:00 P.M.

The copy desk has saved my neck countless times.
—Richard Dyer, music critic

It's crunch time for the rim rats, a.k.a. the copy editors. All assignment editors are supposed to file their stories to the copy desk queues by 8:00, and now the computerized files—METRIM for the local, or metro, stories; WIRRIM for the national, or wire, stories—are bursting with copy to be read. For the next two or three hours, each person on the rim will wage solitary battle against the sneaky chameleon called error.

The rim rats inherited their unfortunate nickname from the horseshoe-shaped copy desks newsrooms favored before computers changed the scenery. The copy editors sat around the outside, or rim, of the desk, within easy reach of the chief copy editor, who sat in a center position called the slot. Without getting up, the chief could hand each copy editor typed stories to be edited. When the editors finished, they could hand the copy back to the chief to be checked.

Today the copy desk is as square as any other group of desks, and it conducts its business on computer terminals rather than pieces of paper. But the pre-electronic vocabulary lingers. The chief copy editor is still called a slot—there's a local slot and a deputy local slot, a wire slot and a deputy wire slot—and the rest of the copy editors still sit "on the rim." Only other copy editors, however, usually have the nerve to use the term "rim rats."

All editors are anonymous to readers, but many copy editors are anonymous even within the newsroom. While assignment editors work during the day, meeting with reporters and one another in sessions that quickly make their personalities known, copy editors work at night, rarely dealing directly

243

with writers. Some copy editors take the job hoping to become assignment editors. Others want to stay on the desk, preferring the quiet company of words to the ego clashes of the daytime scene. Whatever their reasons for being there, all copy editors—not only in the news section but also in business, features, and sports—share a feeling for language that's difficult to describe. Copy editing isn't easy to do, but it's a lot easier to do it than to generalize about it.

Tonight copy editor Bill Buchanan is reading the wire story about the traffic reporter who died in a plane crash, and something is tugging at his memory. Wasn't the same reporter involved in a crash when he worked in Boston? He checks the library under the reporter's name and finds that he was right. In 1964 the traffic helicopter in which the reporter was riding lost power and dropped into Boston Harbor. The reporter, who had his leg in a cast from a skiing accident, swam ashore. If Buchanan remembered that, some other people out there will, too, or will at least recognize the incident when they read it and say, "Oh, *that* traffic reporter." Buchanan adds a paragraph about the earlier accident to tonight's story.

If the story had been written by a staff reporter instead of a wire service, changing it would have been more complicated. Copy editors, although they are charged with keeping errors out of the paper, are not supposed to make major changes in the content of a staff writer's work. Assignment editors, the ones who have worked with the reporter on the story from the beginning, do that. If a copy editor gets a story he thinks has a major problem, he must first check with the editor who handled the story. If that editor agrees that it needs more work, he might call the reporter himself, or ask the copy editor to do it.

If the assignment editor isn't there, another editor on the city desk might be willing to take responsibility for the changes. Otherwise, the copy editor must call the original editor, and/or the reporter, at home. In the rare cases where all of those efforts yield nothing and the copy editor still believes that the content of the story needs work, the slot will decide whether the copy editor should forget it or go ahead.

These rules, which can seem annoyingly confining to a copy editor, are designed to protect the writers—and, through them, the readers. A writer who works with his editor on a story, the logic goes, deserves to go home knowing how that story will look in print. Every reporter has had the experience of opening the paper to find a story that bears his byline but does not, thanks to some overzealous editor, include a single sentence the way he wrote it. No writer who's survived that experience wants to repeat it. In addition, a story that goes through multiple editors can mutate like the first whispered phrase in the child's game of Telephone. The assignment editor may change a sentence just a bit, the copy editor change it a bit more, the slot tinker with it yet again. All of them have the best intentions, but soon the sentence—whether through an editor's misunderstanding or the writer's original lack of clarity—bears no relation to what really happened. Then the reader suffers, and so does the paper's reputation.

None of this means that copy editors lack authority. In fact, their province is a huge one. They're responsible for ensuring correct spelling and punctuation and grammar. (Did the student rack his brain or wrack it? Should there be a comma before the last *and* in a series? When is *convince* the right word, and when is *persuade*?) They make each story conform to the *Globe* stylebook. (When is a number spelled out and when written as a numeral? What's the proper name of the tunnel leading to the airport?) They hunt down errors of fact. (Did the writer promise five main points but list four? Was that make and model of car available in the year mentioned in the story?) They check to see that information remains consistent, both within a single story (is this guy "Andersen" at the end the same one who was "Andrewson" at the beginning?) and from day to day on a continuing story (yesterday's story said that the fire killed four people, but today's story says that it killed three). They must make sure that every sentence in the story advances its meaning, that none are simply stray ideas.

Then there's the ultimate question: Is this story as clear as it can be? Len Kelley asked himself that question a little while ago, when he was editing Peggy Hernandez's story about the evaluations of the city's teachers and principals. He wanted to be sure that readers clearly saw the contrast between the overwhelmingly positive reviews and the actual state of Boston schools.

Hernandez had included two examples: fifty-one seniors' being prohibited from graduating next month because they couldn't read at an eighth-grade level, and an overall dropout rate of 16 percent. Kelley thought the actual number of students who have dropped out might have more impact than the percentage. Tapping into the library's computerized files from his terminal, he found a recent story on the dropout problem. He read the story and then closed it on his screen, saving the statistics so that he could add this sentence to Hernandez's story: "Last year, 3,468 of the school system's 21,354 students dropped out." Then, because numbers are notorious for making fools of writers and editors, he checked to make sure that 3,468 is 16 percent of 21,354. Rounded off, it is.

Now Kelley is sending a message to an assignment editor. He has just finished reading a reporter's story about a minority-hiring effort among Boston corporations, and Kelley isn't sure that the body of the story supports the contention made in the lead. The lead says that the chairman of a group of business executives "has accused civil rights leaders of using false data" to support their claim that little progress has been made in minority hiring. Kelley doesn't see anything in the story that specifically justifies the verb *accused*. He wonders whether the reporter simply neglected to include all the information that led him to that conclusion, or whether the word *accused* is too strong to fit the circumstances. Luckily, the reporter is still in the newsroom. At his editor's request, he agrees to change the wording of the story to better support the lead.

Another copy editor is checking an atlas to make sure that the Irish cities mentioned in a story on gun-smuggling indictments are really in the counties listed. Another, noticing that the story about the witches protesting filming of a John Updike novel was written by a first-day summer intern, is checking the AP and UPI versions of the same story to

246

make sure that details of the filming and the book's plot are consistent.

Good copy editors, the people on the rim will tell you, are born, not made. People can be taught where commas go, but they can't be taught that mysterious feeling that sets off an alarm in a copy editor's head when something is wrong and won't let him rest until he finds it. The *Globe* usually hires only experienced copy editors, but every once in a while it brings an intern onto the desk. Then the slot and the people on the rim look at one other helplessly and ask the unanswerable question: How can we teach somebody to do this?

• • •

Jack Driscoll pulls into his driveway and hoists from his car a gigantic plant presented to him by the students at Essex Agricultural and Technical Institute, where he has just finished giving a commencement speech. The pot that holds the cactus plants and two dozen long-stemmed carnations is so big that he needs both hands to carry it. He leaves his briefcase and his daily stack of newspapers in the car.

As soon as Driscoll hears that Tom Mulvoy has called, he knows what's happening: another government attempt to halt publication of the Pelton story. He calls Mulvoy in the newsroom. As Mulvoy recounts his conversation with the man from the National Security Agency, Driscoll scribbles notes on the cover of the commencement program. "Tell JD Odom wants Globe withhold," he writes. JD is himself. Odom is Lieutenant General William Odom, director of the National Security Agency. "Words or sets of words open up area of violation of espionage law. Take up with counsel. If change, we'll go over again." At the bottom of the program he writes, "Some info not in pub domain. Can't tell what!"

A week's worth of frustration lies behind that exclamation point. It was exactly a week ago that the *Globe* decided to take Odom up on his invitation to the media. Come to us with your stories about national security, Odom and CIA director William Casey had invited reporters in a published interview, and we'll help you decide what's safe to print. But as Washington bureau chief Steve Kurkjian quickly discovered when he and two reporters met with Odom, the director

247

really wasn't free to help them. Federal law prohibited him from discussing details of national security operations, which meant he couldn't explain why the *Globe* shouldn't publish certain statements. "At some points I felt that was an unfair bind to put us in," Kurkjian says. "They brought us in to have an open discussion with a guy who was prohibited by law from doing that." Much of what they've heard from Odom and his staff in the last week could be summed up in those three scrawled words of Driscoll's: "Can't tell what!"

Now the agency is trying once again to keep the story out of print. Driscoll and Mulvoy have the same initial reaction to this latest request: Enough, already! It seems to them that the newspaper has gone out of its way to take national security into consideration. It has explained its position to the National Security Agency several times and has listened attentively to the agency's responses. "We've never gone this far with the government before," Driscoll says. "We wanted to show good faith." The reporters have made changes in the story at the agency's suggestion, chiefly to keep references to intelligence operations more general than specific. Kurkjian calls the result "a lesser but more defensible story." Now Driscoll is asking himself where all this good faith has gotten them. Right back where they started, it seems, with the government saying, "Don't print."

Before he gives the go-ahead order, though, he wants to make sure that nothing in the story has changed since the editors last decided, in consultation with their lawyer, to proceed. Driscoll's call to Dorchester lengthens as Mulvoy passes him to deputy managing editor Helen Donovan, who passes him to Kurkjian, who passes him to national editor Royal Ford. It's the same story the government saw before, they all tell Driscoll, the same one we agreed to run. Let's not back down now.

Driscoll is inclined to agree. But first he wants to make two more phone calls: to in-house lawyer Sal Micciche, to be sure they're not ignoring any legal issues, and to publisher Bill Taylor, to be sure he's still willing to go forward. The newsroom has been keeping Taylor posted on its dealings with the government, and Driscoll thinks it would be unfair not to tell him about this latest installment. The ultimate decision on publication, Driscoll and Mulvoy agree, will be Taylor's.

Deferring to a publisher is not something an editor does lightly. Newsrooms jealously guard their independence from all outside influences, and the publisher, though obviously an authority figure, is definitely "outside." In fact, the only other time Driscoll can remember seeking the publisher's okay was in 1971, early in the morning of the day the *Globe* was to start running excerpts from the Pentagon Papers. The *New York Times* had already gone to the Supreme Court with its contention that the papers, a secret history of American involvement in Vietnam, belonged in the public domain and posed no danger to national security. When the call from Washington reached Driscoll at 3:00 A.M., the *Globe*'s presses were already rolling with eight pages of material from the Pentagon Papers. Driscoll called Davis Taylor, and they agreed to keep going.

When Driscoll calls them tonight, both Micciche and Bill Taylor mention the parallel to that episode. Unlike the Pentagon Papers, the Pelton story doesn't purport to show government excesses or ethical violations. But the reaction from Washington is the same, and it seems clear to Driscoll that the government officials' purpose is to lay the groundwork in case they want to take future legal action against the paper. That's a sobering thought, but it's nothing they haven't already considered. Micciche and Taylor agree with Driscoll that the paper has thoroughly examined the issues, that most of the information in the story is public record, and that the rest is unlikely to harm national security. They support his decision to print the story. Driscoll calls Mulvoy back. "Let's do it," he says.

Mulvoy and Ford immediately join Donovan, who is working on a headline for the Pelton story. She's scowling at the terminal when they walk up, and soon their faces mirror her expression. Headlines are never easy, and the difficulty increases with the complexity of the story. How can seventy inches of copy be summed up in seven or eight words? It can't, of course, but that doesn't change the fact that a headline needs to be written, and that everyone at Donovan's terminal recognizes the headline's importance.

Most people don't read a newspaper the way they'd read a novel. They read *through* it, flipping the pages and stopping at whatever catches their eye. More often than not, what catches their eye is a photo or a headline. Only after being snared by one of those devices does the reader proceed to the body of the story. In the case of the Pelton story, the headline must summarize the complex information in a way that attracts readers, while at the same time steering clear of the national security entanglements the story's writers have worked so hard to avoid. Most reporters can recall a story on which they spent hours crafting the perfect careful wording for a sensitive point, only to have the headline writer unwittingly blare that very point in large type, in terms that tossed all that care out the window.

To further increase the stakes, the Pelton headline is the top headline on page one; it will set the tone of the paper for readers who pick it up or see it folded in a vending box. Although it's on top, however, the Pelton head won't be the biggest head on the page. "Biggest" means the head with the largest type, an honor usually reserved for the day's lead news story. Tomorrow Phillip Van Niekerk's piece on South Africa's ban on public meetings will carry three lines of 60-point type. Three other stories—tax reform, Chernobyl, and Switzler— will have 48-point heads, the same type size as Pelton's.

The page design is supposed to show readers that the Pelton story is different. The story will run at the top, it will run all the way across the page, it will be surrounded by a box, and it will have another head in 12-point type beneath the main head. Few readers will register those details consciously, but they'll get the idea that the story is important and perhaps realize, too, that it's being played differently from a straight news story. In design parlance, this sort of display is called an "overplay," which means not that the story is getting more play than it deserves, but that it's deliberately being played in an unusual position.

A good headline will make the Pelton story look natural in its lofty position; a bad head will make readers ask, "What is *this* doing here?" Mulvoy leans down to see what Donovan has written. "I like the top part," he says. Donovan, who was working on the main head while awaiting Driscoll's go-ahead on the story, has written this: "Pelton's 'top-secret' intelligence not so secret." It fits the space just about perfectly, and Mulvoy thinks that *secret* and *not so secret* play off each other well. If he and Donovan and Ford can come up with a drop head that logically follows, that line will do nicely.

Headline writing is a game of substitutions. The editor reads the story, determines the main point it's trying to convey, and chooses the key words necessary to get that point across. Then he or she strings the key words together in some sort of cause-and-effect sequence and keeps substituting shorter or longer words of similar meaning until the headline fits the space. Since no two words mean exactly the same thing, however, a particularly recalcitrant headline can sometimes require so many substitutions that it gradually loses its sense and its connection to the story. The only solution is to choose a slightly different focus and new key words, and start again.

Unlike most newsroom pursuits, headline writing lends itself to joint effort, much as crossword puzzles do. Instead of "What's a six-letter word for *anger* that starts with *e?*" a headline writer is likely to call out, "How can I say in five words that the tax bill is running into trouble?" And, just as the puzzler's neighbor may immediately know that the word is *enrage*, the editor's neighbor may immediately throw out a key word that casts the headline in a whole new light.

In a straight news story, the most important key words are usually verbs. News is action, and verbs are action words. The other headlines on tomorrow's front page, for example, include the verbs *bans* ("Pretoria bans events marking Soweto violence"), *surface* ("Obstacles surface to Senate tax bill"), *bows* ("Paulist Center bows to church's threats"), and *swirl* ("Accusations, turmoil swirl over Switzler"). But the Pelton story isn't about today's action at his trial. It's a portrait of the trial's background; hence the verbless headline. Actually, "Pelton's 'top-secret' intelligence not so secret" does have the implied verb *is*. Forms of the verb *to be* are usually dropped from headlines.

Donovan, Mulvoy, and Ford would like to get an active verb into the drop head, but first they have to agree on the subject matter. Donovan tries this: "U.S. claims a security threat, but many details already published." Three *e*'s under, and no one's in love with it.

Next try: "Highly successful operations believed compromised by accused spy's work."

That one sits on the screen for a while as everyone tries to pinpoint what's wrong with it. Finally Donovan ventures, "What the government is telling the press is a different agenda from what the story's about."

The next one doesn't get too far: "Despite U.S. warnings on security . . ."

Mulvoy chimes in: "Despite U.S. claims that security has been—could be? would be?—compromised, many details of intelligence data were published earlier." They all laugh; the head is obviously much too long. Thirteen *e*'s over, the computer tells them.

"*Despite* doesn't play off the main head right anyway," Mulvoy says.

Next try: "U.S. claims security has been compromised, but many key details are already known."

That one sounds okay, so they start fiddling with it. "Many key details have already been published." But that leaves out television, which broadcast some of the details. "Many key details already in public domain"?

Ford raises his fists in a silent cheer; he likes it. With the extraneous words taken out, it even fits. Together, the main head and drop head read this way: "Pelton's 'top-secret' intelligence not so secret. U.S. claims security compromised, but many key details in public domain."

"Go get Top Dog," Mulvoy tells Ford.

Ford returns with Kurkjian, who reads the head and says wearily, "Fine." The group exchanges relieved glances, then disperses. Mulvoy goes back to his office, which he left four hours ago, and packs up to leave.

. . .

While the headline-writing committee has been standing at attention around Helen Donovan's terminal, a reporter across the newsroom has been on the phone with Jack Driscoll. Driscoll called night reporter Bonnie Winston about an issue much smaller than national security—a six-week-old baby, to be exact. The baby was awarded an honorary degree at the Essex Agricultural graduation tonight because his mother, a nutrition major, had helped her class study the nutritional needs of unborn and newborn children. Driscoll thinks that the baby would provide an interesting angle on the brief account of the graduation the paper is running.

But the story, a four-paragraph item on page thirty-four, has already been typeset and the page pasted up. It's not important enough to change right away. Winston takes down the information and rewrites the story. The editors will substitute the new version of the story when the presses are replated for the third edition.

That done, Driscoll's sense of duty rears up again. He really should retrieve everything he left in the car and do a belated thorough reading of this morning's papers. But there's one more call he wants to make first.

For the third time in an hour, Driscoll dials the newsroom. He asks for Steve Kurkjian, the Washington bureau chief, whose existence for the last few weeks has been focused on the Ronald Pelton story and the troubles it's caused. When Kurkjian picks up the phone, Driscoll delivers his message quickly. Stop worrying. The story's going to run. It will be set in type any minute; we're not going to change it now. Go home.

9:00 P.M.

You can get pretty weird working at night.
—Bob Norling, makeup editor

The building is clearing out. The rooms where the night people toil glow like islands of light amid dark rivers of hallways. Custodians pad in and out of the shadows, collecting the contents of a thousand wastebaskets. On the top floor, bright lights glare down on rows of deserted cafeteria tables. Now and then a solitary soul rushes in, bouncing like a pinball from the coffee dispenser to the cash register and out the door.

Last call has come and gone in the circulation department, which has been selling subscriptions by phone, and it's fast approaching in the classified department, which will soon accept its last ads of the night. In the warehouse, a buzzer sounds as flat metal carts begin cruising the room's perimeter on a mechanical track, lurching around corners like riderless cars on a slow-motion roller coaster. Soon the carts will be loaded with rolls of newsprint, bound for the pressroom. The night superintendent should arrive there any minute; his press crew will join him at 10:30.

In the newsroom, the editors who orchestrated the daytime chaos have departed. A new kind of pressure, the final push toward deadline, consumes their successors. Within an hour all stories are supposed to be edited and gone. The hotline from the composing room rings shrilly and often with questions about stories' whereabouts. Between rings, the collective concentration muffles all but a few sounds. Someone groans. A fist hits a desk in frustration. "I'm up," a copy editor says softly as she finishes a story. The slot immediately assigns her another one.

254

Night reporter Bonnie Winston answers her third call about a story that's looking less like a story with each call. First someone from the city police department called to say that an officer had been hit in the head with a brick while trying to break up a fight among teenagers. Now a public relations person from the hospital is on the phone for the second time, telling her that the officer will probably be released tonight after being treated for head cuts. Winston checks with Ron Hutson on the city desk. As she expected, he tells her not to bother with the story. Police officers frequently receive minor injuries in the line of duty; the two agree that the paper needn't write up every one.

Though she wishes the officer no harm, Winston wouldn't mind having something happen that would give her a byline in tomorrow's paper. Chasing down small leads that get smaller tends to be the business of the night shift, and after a while a reporter starts craving a story she can sink her teeth into. Tonight, at least, Winston has been able to work sporadically on her Sunday story about the nurses' strike. And a few hours ago something happened that really made the night worthwhile.

Recently Winston wrote a story about an elderly woman who had traveled to South America to see Halley's comet for the second time in her life. The day after the story ran, a suburban teacher who works with learning-disabled children called the newsroom. Her students usually hate to read, the teacher told Winston, but they'd been fascinated by the story of the woman who had seen the comet twice. The teacher asked for the elderly woman's address so she could invite her to speak to the class.

Tonight the teacher called back to report that the woman had agreed to come to her class next week. Then the teacher told Winston something else. One boy in the class, she said, was more interested in the reporter than the subject of the story. He wanted to write Winston a letter about writing, and he was hoping that Winston would write back and tell him how she does her job. That's pretty hard to explain, Winston told the teacher, but she promised to answer the boy's letter

255

and to send him two things: the original version of a story as she wrote it, and the same story after it had been edited and copy edited. She wanted the boy to see that writing isn't a matter of sitting around while the words magically leap from your fingers; it involves hard work and lots of changes.

"It makes me feel good to know that someone, even if it is a bunch of little kids, is getting a charge out of what we do here," Winston said when her conversation with the teacher was done. "It may not happen every day, but when we write and connect, it makes all the difference in the world."

. . .

With a sigh of satisfaction, Barbara Huebner crosses off the last page number on a piece of yellow paper covered with penciled calculations and lists of story slugs. That's it. All the pages of national and foreign news have been laid out. She presents the last dummy with a flourish to an editorial assistant, who will take it to the composing room. Then she turns back to the yellow list, checking it a second time and cross-checking it with the budgets to make sure she hasn't missed a story.

She had a good scare a few minutes ago. She'd drawn the dummy for page three, the lead U.S./World page, and was halfway through assigning the headline sizes when she realized that she'd left out the Washington Notes. For a moment she succumbed to a wave of panic. It didn't matter that she'd caught the oversight early enough, didn't matter that she'd pulled herself out of worse holes plenty of times before. The Notes were two columns wide and 140 agates deep (an agate, the unit of vertical measurement the *Globe* uses, is one-fourteenth of an inch), and she was sure she'd never, ever fit them in.

Then the wave broke, and her sensible self surfaced in time to give her panicky self a lecture. The page had two strong pieces of art that would still look good if played slightly smaller, and one of the wire stories could definitely afford to be trimmed. So what's the big deal, the sensible voice said. Within minutes she had drawn a new dummy that included everything and probably, come to think of it, looked better than the first one.

256

At the afternoon *Globe*, where Huebner worked for a short time before it ceased publication, layout people were called "scribbly liners." At the time, she resented the implication that they scribbled without thinking. Now she knows that forging ahead with a minimum of deliberation can be the only way to survive some of these nights when the paper is huge. In fact, without her trusty lists and the help of assistant night editor Bob Cutting, tonight could have been a disaster. On the other hand, a big paper does reduce one source of tension because it has room for everything. Tonight she didn't have to agonize over which of two wire stories from faraway countries was more important, and she didn't have to spend time explaining her decision to other editors who advocated the opposite choice.

Her checks and rechecks of tonight's lists have revealed no major sins. The story about the Philippines and the story in which Secretary of State George Shultz talks about the Philippines probably should have run together instead of on facing pages, but that's a small problem she can fix in the third edition. For now, she's done. "Anybody need help?" Huebner asks the room at large. When no one answers, she bolts for the cafeteria. The man behind the counter greets her and starts making her tuna and Swiss on whole wheat before she orders it.

"The ship is sinking!" Bob Norling shouts. No one else in the composing room even looks up. Eventually another voice emerges from the background noise: "Anyone got a padded cell to throw that man in?" But Norling is already on the other side of the room, checking a page on which a story has come up short. "I'm getting this funny disastrous feeling," he mutters under his breath.

Norling is the makeup editor, the person who ensures that the pages look the way the newsroom intended. From 7:30 P.M. to 3:00 A.M. he's either traipsing up and down the stairs between the newsroom and the composing room or calling one from the other on the hotline. Upstairs, he checks with copy editors and layout editors to see how the copy is flowing and urge that it flow faster. Downstairs, he watches as headlines, photos, and stories, backed with sticky wax, are pressed onto ruled pieces of heavy paper called pasteup boards. (The ads were positioned on the boards earlier in the day.) From these pages, which are the same size as finished newspaper pages, plates for the printing presses will be made.

Tensions between the composing room and the newsroom are a fact of life at most newspapers. Only the newsroom can provide, or fail to provide, the material the composing room needs to put together the pages. Only the composing room can provide, or fail to provide, the polish that will display the newsroom's words and pictures to best advantage. The two groups see very little of each other. But on days when the paper is late, each is sure that it would have come out on time if only the other had been a little more diligent, a little more understanding.

Amid these tensions, Norling is a one-man demilitarized zone. He blends in with both groups, almost as if he were changing uniforms in the stairwell on each trip up or down. He's also a convenient target for both groups. When people in the composing room want to gripe about the newsroom, or people in the newsroom want to gripe about composing, they see Norling as their personal pipeline. He's heard enough griping to know there's some truth on both sides. "I'm the guy between," he says. "It's a helluva spot."

Norling sometimes sounds as if he had spent his eight years as makeup editor creating metaphors to describe the job. He calls himself a ramrod, pushing the pages through with one eye on the clock; a bridge, connecting the night editor with the production supervisor; a schoolmarm, obsessively checking the smallest detail. When he's tired of those, he turns to cowboy metaphors, then military similes. "I feel like the point man in an infantry squad," he says. "I'm out there taking it from the left and from the right. It's good because I'm never bored; time just flies. It's bad because time flies too fast."

One night Norling took his blood pressure after each of the four editions and found, not entirely to his surprise, that it was zooming progressively heavenward. He consulted a doctor and gave no thought to quitting. "I've been meeting deadlines for thirty-six years," he says. "Why stop now?" He's even grown accustomed to driving the seventy miles home to New Hampshire at 3:00 A.M., though at first he lived in fear of falling asleep at the wheel. Now he follows a familiar routine: Arrive home between 4:00 and 5:00 in the morning. Have a snack, play with the cat, read the paper. (The irony of relaxing with the very thing that causes his stress does not escape him.) Go to bed at 6:00 A.M., get up at 1:00 P.M., and have five hours free before it's time to head to work again.

Unlike Norling and his newsroom colleagues, the composing room is on deadline all day long. The fifty people on the "lobster" shift (the nickname for any shift that overlaps night and day) and the eighty people on the day shift must meet deadlines for pasting up each day's classified ads as well as the early sections of the Sunday paper. They spend much of their time dealing with display ads, which can require complicated coordination of type and art.

A photo equipment store, for example, might want an ad that shows twenty cameras and lists descriptions and prices. Unless the store has an ad agency that supplies a finished ad ready for pasteup, someone in the composing room will have to cut out all the little camera photos and pieces of type and assemble them into the proper design by a certain hour, so that a proof can be sent for the store to check. The ad cannot be pasted onto the page until the composing room receives a "release," a green sheet from the salesperson signifying that the ad has been approved. The composing room saves every ad for three months, in case the advertiser wants to run it again.

In 1979, 500 people worked in the *Globe*'s composing room. Today the staff is half that size and shrinking. The reason is computers. In the beginning, newspapers, like all printing operations, set type by hand. A compositor would pick pieces of metal type out of a case and place them, one letter at a time, into a hand-held composing stick. Then came the Linotype, a machine that cast a line of type in a one-piece slug. As the operator pressed keys on a keyboard, molds of individual characters dropped from a storage case into the line. The machine then forced molten metal into the molds, which were returned to the storage case as the finished metal slug was ejected. At the height of the Linotype era, the *Globe* ran seventy or eighty machines with one operator at each.

Today the work of all those machines and operators is done by two photographic typesetters. (The paper has three typesetting machines but generally uses one for news and one for classified ads, keeping the other as a backup.) The typesetters have no operators; therefore, their speed does not depend on the speed of a human. The machines can set hundreds of lines of type per minute. But they still need humans to maintain them and provide them with material to be typeset.

When the chief copy editor, or slot, reviews a story and hits the "send" button in the newsroom, the typesetter receives the information from the computer and begins sorting through its collection of character images to find the proper typeface. As it locates each appropriate character, a beam of light flashes through the image and is deflected by mirrors onto photosensitive paper. Lenses make the type larger or smaller. The paper is then developed mechanically, much as a photo would be, and one-column-wide strips of black type on shiny white paper emerge from the machine. At the *Globe*, the typesetting machines are in a room adjacent to the composing room. The type leaves the machines and feeds through holes in what everyone simply calls The Wall, dropping into waiting hands that slice it into individual stories and put it through the waxer.

The composing room's name is a relic from the days of the composing stick. Each time a new machine has come along—and some short-lived interim steps bridged the gap between hot type and "cold," photoset type—the people in the composing room have had to start training all over again. Some of the Linotype operators, for example, now sit at computer terminals and type in columns or reviews submitted by freelance writers who don't have access to the *Globe*'s computer system. Because a Linotype keyboard looked nothing like a typewriter keyboard, even the speediest Linotype operators had to be retaught how to type. "I give these guys a lot of credit," says Herb Blanchard, a composing room foreman. "Basically, their trade has been taken away."

Some of those who still have a trade know that its days are numbered. As newspapers march inexorably toward pagination, the ability to design and assemble an entire page on a computer screen, composing rooms all over the country feel the walls closing in. Reliable, affordable pagination systems haven't appeared as quickly as some industry analysts predicted a few years ago, but they're definitely on the way. The people in the composing room know that as more and more operations become computerized, their jobs will be needed less and less. Even Norling considers himself part of a dying breed of makeup men.

For now, however, the type must still be assembled by hand on pasteup boards, and that's what most of the 120 people on tonight's shift are doing. Each element on a page— each cutline, headline, photo, story, or ad—arrives individually. The page can go nowhere until everything called for on the dummy has been pasted up. If, for example, a copy editor upstairs turns away from a cutline for a moment to check the spelling of a name, then gets distracted and forgets to finish the cutline, the otherwise completed page could sit for hours in the composing room, awaiting that one element.

That's where the makeup editor comes in. Norling patrols the composing room, noticing which elements are missing from which pages and calling the newsroom to nudge them along. If the newsroom says that a particular piece of type has already been sent, Norling prowls around The Wall to see if it's just emerging from the typesetter. Union rules prohibit him from touching the type, but he can alert someone that it has arrived and is ready for pasteup. The goal is to achieve a constant flow of pages from the newsroom to the composing room to the engraving department to the pressroom. If the newsroom sent down all the stories at once, or the composing room held the pages until all of them were finished, the engravers couldn't possibly make the plates fast enough to let the presses roll on time. The weekday schedule calls for all news pages to be pasted up by 10:00 P.M., but usually it's more like 10:30 before the last piece of copy arrives.

Pacing his appointed rounds, Norling checks everything—not just the stories but also the crossword puzzle, the TV listings, the chess column, the comics. A month ago some Doonesbury strips ran on the wrong days, causing readers much confusion and the paper much grief. As for the crossword puzzle and chess column, managing editor Tom Mulvoy describes them as features with a low level but high intensity of interest. In other words, the cadre of chess-playing readers may not be large, but it's ferocious in its devotion to the column.

Making his usual stops tonight, Norling encounters the usual problems. A photo is missing a cutline. Another photo has a cutline but no credit line. A story needs to be re-output in a different measure (width). A headline is too long for the space. A byline says "byline" instead of the writer's name. A story on one page is two inches too long, a story on another page two inches too short. It's a lot easier to solve the first problem than the second, but not as easy as it used to be.

When the majority of news stories were written in inverted pyramid form—most important point first, then next most important, on down the line to trivia—the solution to a too-long story was simple: Just lop from the bottom. Today, writers' experimentation with story forms makes that approach dangerous. A writer may have put a surprise ending on a story, or saved a terrific quote for the last paragraph. The only way to trim is to read the whole story, or at least the whole last section, looking for sentences that can be eliminated without destroying the flow. If there's time, Norling will ask a copy editor to trim the story on a terminal upstairs and output a shorter version. If there's no time, and there usually isn't, he'll show a pasteup man which paragraphs to slice off.

Any number of factors can make a story come out the wrong size for its space—including, some editors theorize, a mysterious evil force that grabs copy in its teeth somewhere between the newsroom computer and the printed page. Among the more realistic possibilities, a layout editor might

262

read the dummy wrong, or an ad or photo might not really be the size drawn on the dummy, or an editor might make major cuts or additions during editing and neglect to recheck the length. When a pasteup man calls Norling's attention to a too-short story, Norling has several choices. He can ask the newsroom to send a longer version or, if that's not possible, to send another short story to fill the extra space. If it's just too late for substitutions, he can move an ad up and fill the resulting space with a "plug," or house ad. "But that's embarrassing," he says. Although the paper runs some house ads deliberately, to advertise special sections or programs, it tries to avoid running them just to fill space.

Norling keeps up a constant stream of lists and a constant stream of chatter, mostly to himself. "What a time for afterthoughts," he says as he hangs up the hotline to the newsroom. "Hey, those people upcountry aren't getting their money's worth," he says when he sees that two reviews for the Arts section won't be available until the third edition. "Wow!" is all he can say when he sees the disaster that has befallen page thirty-seven. For some reason, the person who drew the dummy thought that the telephone company ad on the page was a six-by-fifteen, meaning six columns wide (the full page width) and fifteen inches high. In fact, it's a five-by-eighteen. The page will have to be completely redesigned.

Norling yanks a blank dummy from his pile and starts drawing. The elements on the page—a nine-inch story and an eleven-inch story with a head shot—won't fit the reshaped space gracefully, so he'll settle for a utilitarian layout, fast. It's too late to move either of the stories to another page. The original layout called for running the longer story across most of the top of the page, with the head shot in the middle, and the shorter story in a box to its right. Norling scribbles on the dummy, then asks the pasteup man to put the photo at the top right and "back" the longer story in (start pasting from the end). When the type reaches the left-hand column, the first leg extends down eleven inches, leaving room for only seven inches of the shorter story. Norling points out two paragraphs to be trimmed and moves on to the next disaster. The man in the head shot will be looking off the page instead of at the

263

story, but that's a small minus compared with the big plus of a two-minute redesign that didn't require rewriting headlines.

The noise level in the room is rising as everyone tries to grab Norling's attention.

"Hey, Bob, where does this cutline go?"

"Where does sex ed go?"

"You gonna fix this head?"

"Two trims over here for you."

Barbara Huebner comes down to make sure that all the national pages are finished. Ellen Clegg comes down to see how things are going. A pasteup man studies the photo of the mint owner, which is slightly too tall for its space, and whips out his knife. "Let's give this guy a haircut," he says. On one side of the room, someone starts singing "On a Clear Day You Can See Forever." On the other side, another voice loudly launches into "Yes, We Have No Bananas." From the corner, someone yells, "Quiet! The Sox are winning!"

Eddie Franklin, the makeup man from the Sports department, strides around the pasteup tables, performing the same rituals as Norling. "Makeup may be appreciated here, but there's no use for it outside," Franklin says. "No one looks at the paper in the morning and says, 'Hey, great makeup.' " Norling, however, likes the sense of responsibility, likes being the last newsroom person to see the type before it goes into print. And if something big should happen after the night editor leaves, he's in charge of getting the news into the paper.

The call for silence in honor of the Sox had no effect. The next call does. "Megabucks!" someone shouts, and a hush falls as the winning lottery number is read aloud. For a moment the silence lingers, covering the room like an umbrella. Then it folds, and the torrent of voices streams back in. No one's a millionaire tonight. Norling dodges the clamor and makes for the hotline, tracking an errant piece of type. "Time to make the doughnuts," he says.

10:00 P.M.

We're all in the same lifeboat, so we'd better bail like crazy.

—Ellen Clegg, night editor

In the engraving department, across the hall from the composing room, a camera as tall as its operator is converting the last of tomorrow's news photographs into halftones. In an alcove nearby, an electronic scanner is "reading" Joanne Rathe's color slide of tonight's Red Sox game and separating it into four negatives, each a different color. From the room behind the camera, bursts of violet light mark the creation of the latest pairs of plates.

In these rooms and in the pressroom work some of the few people at a newspaper who truly understand how it's produced. Most employees in advertising, circulation, the newsroom, and other departments will admit somewhat sheepishly that, aside from their own role, they find the production of the paper as mysterious as the technology of the computers they use all day. Some of them prefer to preserve the mystery. Others vow that someday they'll make the time to join one of the tours the newspaper conducts for guests, just to find out "what those people do down there."

What the people in engraving do is act as translators. Instead of translating thoughts from one language to another, they translate artwork and pasted-up pages into forms the presses can accept. The front room, the camera room, exists because the presses recognize only black and white; their language does not include gray. A photograph creates varying shades of gray with varying amounts of silver. A drawing does the same with varying amounts of ink. But an offset press, the type used by most newspapers, knows only two commands:

265

ink or no ink. Without the operations that go on in the camera room, the presses would be able to print only stick figures and other line drawings. But with the giant-sized cameras, known as graphic arts cameras, doing the translating, the presses can print photographs as well.

When the editors in the newsroom choose a photograph for the paper, they mark it with a page number and crop marks and specify what size they want it to be. Photos are measured in agates (fourteenths of an inch), rather than inches or columns, both horizontally and vertically. An editorial assistant brings the photo to the camera room, where its first stop is a high white table called the scaling bench. There a proportion scale is used to determine how much the photo must be reduced or enlarged to achieve the desired size. If the photo is ninety-six agates wide, for example, and the layout calls for a photo forty-eight agates wide, the reduction will be 50 percent.

The camera operator then sets the percentage reduction on a big red-and-white-striped scale at the bottom of the camera and positions the photo on a board, called the copyboard, opposite the lens. After closing the glass cover and flipping the copyboard from horizontal to vertical, the operator is ready to take a picture of the picture. As in any photography, releasing the shutter allows light to reflect off the image, through the lens, and onto the film. Graphic arts photography, however, adds one more step. Before it strikes the film, the light is broken up by a screen divided into eighty-five lines per inch, both horizontally and vertically. The junction of each pair of perpendicular lines forms a dot on the negative.

The operator then develops the film in a small darkroom behind the camera's lens. On the finished print, called a halftone, all the dots are either black or white. The more black dots in a particular area of the halftone, the darker gray that area will appear; the more white dots, the lighter the gray. Although a newspaper picture appears at first glance to contain many gradations of gray, a closer look shows that the gray is an illusion created by clusters of black and white dots. The finer the screen used in the camera (the more lines it has

266

per inch), the harder it will be to see the dots in the finished picture.

Halftones of photos for both news stories and ads go from the engraving department to the composing room, where they are pasted onto pages along with type, and then back to engraving as part of the completed pages. This time their destination is the plate room, where more translating is needed. An offset press can't print from a pasteup board covered with cut-out type and photos; metal plates are the only language it understands. Getting from paper to plate requires a three-step translation.

First, one of the thirty engravers on the night shift puts a pair of pasted-up pages into a "reader," a machine similar to the transmitter used to send wire photos. A laser scans across the page, sampling its density a thousand times an inch in both directions — in other words, sampling areas a millionth of an inch square. The laser determines whether each of those tiny areas is black or white, then converts that information into digital signals that can be transmitted over a phone line. Steve Taylor, director of the *Globe*'s computer operations, describes the process this way: "The data for the entire page is turned into an enormous mishmash of ones and zeros," where black is one and white is zero.

In the second step, this mishmash is sent to three nearby machines called "writers," and three more at the satellite printing plant in Billerica. From that point through printing and distribution to drivers, the Boston and Billerica plants perform essentially the same operations.

The writer, like the reader, contains a laser. Using the information transmitted to it by the reader, the writer tells the laser how to attack each section of a thin piece of carbon-coated acetate positioned in the machine. For every one, or area that was black on the pasted-up page, the laser burns away the carbon, leaving that area clear acetate. For every zero it does nothing, leaving those areas black. The finished product, called a laser mask, looks like a full-sized negative of a newspaper page, with clear type on a black background.

Then comes translation number three, the one that will finally produce something the presses can understand. That

267

something is a plate, a thin piece of aluminum coated with a chemical called diazo, which decomposes when it is exposed to light. Two by two, the laser masks (which look like, but technically are not, negatives) are loaded into the platemaker and sucked into place by a vacuum. Like an ordinary photographic enlarger—though the exposure chamber of the platemaker looks more like an aquarium—the machine shines a light at these "negatives." The light cannot pierce the black areas, but it goes through the clear areas and strikes, instead of film, the aluminum plates, burning off the chemical coating in each spot it touches. Tonight each pair of masks stays in the platemaker a few minutes, long enough to produce four plates, one for each of the four offset presses scheduled for use.

The finished plates look like full-sized newspaper pages printed on sheet metal. They emerge jerkily from the platemaker, sliding down a hill of metal rollers like the ones grocery stores once used to move crates full of bags. As the plates chug around a corner on the wheels, two vise-like arms grab each one and crease it along the top, so that it will fit on the press. Then someone picks the plates up and hangs them on a series of hooks that are moving along the edge of the room on an overhead conveyer, starting them on their journey to the pressroom.

To an observer unfamiliar with offset printing, it seems impossible that these plates could produce a newspaper. The type on the plates reads left to right, like any type. Won't it come out backward on the page? And the type is neither higher nor lower than the surface of the plate. How will the ink know which spots to stick to?

Briefly, the answer to the first question is that it isn't the plate that does the printing. An offset press transfers the images from the plate to a rubber blanket and then onto the newsprint. (The images on the blanket are backward.) As for where the ink sticks, the platemaking process has left the exposed areas of the aluminum in a state described by the mellifluous adjective *oleophilic*, which means grease-loving— or, in this case, ink-loving. Those areas will attract ink and repel water, coming out black on the page. The unexposed, or hydrophilic, areas will attract water and repel ink, thus staying white.

The engraving department makes plates from 6:00 at night until 2:30 in the morning, processing at peak times about thirty-five pages an hour. It produces about 10,000 laser masks a month and more than 550,000 plates a year. Although the numbers sound impressive, the engravers, like their colleagues across the hall in composing, know that their jobs are on the endangered list. Pagination, the ghost of newspapers' future, may not be rattling its chains in the hallways yet, but it's not far off. And when it comes, when editors can design pages on their terminals and transmit the information directly to a printing plate, the word *engraver* will join *compositor* in the journalism history books.

Actually, the transformation of the trades has been going on for some time. "There used to be a five-year apprenticeship here," says engraving superintendent George Monroe, who worked his way into an apprenticeship after joining the *Globe* twenty years ago as an office boy. "You needed that time to learn the work. You had to prove yourself, and skill was really recognized. A guy would get a reputation as the best cameraman in the city. But pretty soon that won't mean anything any more. A whole era will be gone."

To illustrate his vision, Monroe looks no farther than the electronic color scanner whirring in a corner of his department. Until the scanner arrived, the process of printing color gave the sharp-eyed craftsman his biggest chance to shine. He had to know how dots would combine on the plate to produce colors, know when and where to brush the plate with acid to "etch" the dots and make a particular area redder or less red. Now, Monroe says, the same man need only program those variables into a computer.

The advent of the electronic scanner has given wary newspapers all over the country a final shove into the world of color printing. Buying a scanner, though a major investment of both money and training time for its operators, eliminates the one step that made color impractical for deadline work: sending the color slide out for separations. The scanner separates a color slide the same way the eye perceives the scene photographed in that slide. The eye has three color receptors: one for blue, one for red, one for green. When the eye sees the scene, each receptor responds to its particular color and sends impulses to the brain, which combines the impulses to recreate the scene. In color printing, that function of the brain is performed by the press.

A scanner isolates the three primaries by directing beams of light at the slide through three filters: one blue, one red, one green. Each filter effectively subtracts that color from the scene, producing a negative that, when printed, will contain only the other two colors. The print from the red negative, which records the blue and green in the scene, is known as the cyan printer. The print from the green negative, which records the red and blue in the scene, is the magenta printer. The print from the blue negative, which records the red and green, is the yellow printer. The scanner also produces a black printer, which improves the contrasts among the colors. Cyan, magenta, yellow, and black are the inks used to print process color.

After the Sports department had looked through tonight's color slides from Fenway Park and picked the one it wanted, the operator of the scanner spent about twenty minutes programming it to do its job. Making the separations took only ten minutes. Now comes the hard part: lining up the four negatives perfectly and positioning them so that they exactly fit the "window" left on the page for the color photo. That process can take an hour for one color picture, and the front page of tomorrow's Sports section has two.

This painstaking work, known as stripping, still requires old-fashioned craftsmanship of the type Monroe reveres. Soon, he believes, people without a background in computers won't be much use in the production end of newspapers. Even as he mourns the dying of the crafts, however, he's confident that when pagination comes, the company will find new jobs for him and his staff. He could worry about that, too ("I don't want one of those jobs where you just sit in an office all day"), but there's no use letting the stress build up so far in advance. He can't imagine leaving newspapers, abandoning that high he gets when he walks through the pressroom at night and the

270

presses are thundering and everything is hectic and he's part of it all.

At any rate, the positive effects of the new technologies have far outweighed the negatives so far, in Monroe's opinion. Using a densitometer to measure the depth of blue in a picture may not seem as creative as saying, "I think the sky should be bluer," but it generally produces a better-looking newspaper. Consistency ranks up there with quality in the constellation of production virtues. "We want everything to look the same day after day," Monroe says. "That sounds boring, but that's what we want."

. . .

The game is over, the Red Sox have won, and Larry Whiteside has transmitted the first version of his story before dashing to the locker room. Back in the Sports department, copy editor Bob Duffy opens the story on his screen as soon as the computer tells him it has arrived. He doesn't have much more time to edit it than Whiteside had to write it, so he needs to get started. This first version is always a little rough.

Duffy clicks the cursor quickly through the story, looking for small glitches as he absorbs the overall idea. He changes *pain* of glass to *pane*. He eliminates a redundant reference to a player being on first base after a single ("Good place for him," Duffy mutters). Another sentence mentions "the wall in left field." He deletes "in left field," reasoning that there's not a *Globe* sports reader alive who doesn't know the location of "the wall," the green monster, at Fenway Park.

Other phrases give Duffy pause. Are they acceptable, or are they clichés? George Orwell may have advised writers never to use an expression they commonly saw in print, but sometimes the catalogue of ways to describe a baseball game seems uncomfortably finite. Even so, *veteran* is an adjective Duffy can definitely do without. Now that anyone who's done anything for more than a week is called a veteran, the word has lost its meaning. Whiteside has described one pitcher as a "veteran knuckleballer." Duffy changes the description to "300-game winner." Another sentence, in which a pitcher's transgressions "earned him an early shower," strad-

271

dles the line between okay and cliché. Duffy changes the phrase to "drove him from the mound."

Now he returns to the lead. He wasn't crazy about it the first time through, but he didn't want to change it until he'd read the whole story. Whiteside has written a three-sentence lead: "When it starts to happen like this, you can believe. These Red Sox really might be as good as advertised. It's a banner season any year when the Sox can come away with a 6–4 victory and a second straight series sweep over the Cleveland Indians." Overkill, Duffy thinks; let's not to make the World Series seem like an anticlimax. He deletes the first and third sentences and checks to see how the second sentence, alone, looks as the lead: "These Red Sox just might be as good as advertised." Not bad. The second paragraph explains that they beat Cleveland 6–4 Tuesday.

Wait a minute! Today's Wednesday, not Tuesday. Good thing he remembered that losing track of time is an occupational hazard of covering a team. Duffy might wish this story had contained fewer errors, but he knows how quickly it was written—and anyway, it's his responsibility to catch them. As one of his fellow copy editors likes to say, "We wouldn't have a job if everyone wrote perfectly."

• • •

The applause for *Tosca* echoes behind him as Richard Dyer strides out of the Opera House, letting his review take shape in his mind. After thirteen years as a critic, he can usually write a review like this one in less than an hour, but only if he's developed the theme by the time he gets back to the newsroom. It's 10:50 now. His deadline is midnight.

During the performance, Dyer scrawled a few key words on the program to preserve his impressions. The performance was good, he thought, but not as good as the elements in it. It seemed that everything, from the singers to the orchestra to the scenery, should have contributed more than it did. That theme will do for a start, he thinks as he walks toward the parking lot. Some writers can craft an entire piece in their heads while walking or driving, but Dyer can go no further than the general idea until he knows how much space he'll have. He's hoping, as always, for a lot.

Dyer has been moving fast, but when he arrives at his car he stops short. While he's been watching Tosca stab Scarpia, his car has been broken into—again. He chose this parking lot specifically because the attendant said he'd be on duty until 11:00, but it's 10:55 and the place is deserted. His tape player, of course, is gone, along with his tape of *Antony and Cleopatra*. The thief must have yanked them out and put them in Dyer's gym bag, right on top of his wet bathing suit.

11:00 P.M.

A paper that's late is like yesterday's sandwich. Nobody wants it.

—William O. Taylor, publisher

The mechanical eye of closed-circuit television sweeps untiringly around the outside of the *Globe* building, filling the four screens in the security office with grainy scenes of tranquility. The doors are locked and quiet. In the parking lots, where by day drivers circle like vultures, car-shaped shadows huddle at the edge of a blizzard of white lines. Even the loading dock, which soon will resemble a shopping mall at Christmas time, shelters only a few murky human forms waiting for something to happen.

The peaceful exterior belies the activity within. Although the evening started smoothly, in the last hour one department after another has acknowledged the inevitable: The paper is going to be late. Maybe not outrageously late, maybe not late enough to cause major delivery problems, but late enough to require some soul-searching. If it were a game night in the basketball championships, everyone could pin the delay on Sports. But with the Celtics idle, the blame will have to be shared. The composing room has told night editor Ellen Clegg that too many pages came down at once. Thirty-five were still awaiting pasteup at 10:00, and though composing had finished them all by 10:45, engraving will be hard-pressed to make that many plates in time for the presses to roll at 11:30.

But Clegg's detective work can wait. For now, although the first edition isn't printed yet, she and the copy editors chalk it up to history and start planning for the second and third. The decompression period—the minutes after the last story has been sent, when copy editors munch snacks and trade horror stories—is ending as quickly as it began.

As the three local newscasts play on her desktop TVs, Clegg studies a stat, or photocopy, of the front-page pasteup, checking for errors and asking the local and national desks what they want to change. Unless a major error or news story has cropped up, the newsroom generally changes only the front page in the second edition. The company likes to limit the number of replated pages in the edition to six, and Sports usually needs five of them. The key to producing the first and second editions is speed. Since these editions go to readers farthest from the city, they must roll off the presses and into the trucks as early as possible in order to reach distant New England points by daybreak. With the third edition, which has more readers and circulates closer to the city, the editors can take more time. As many as thirty pages can be changed.

Bob Norling will supervise the revamping from his usual perch downstairs. Tonight the front page of the second edition will differ from the first edition's only in the lower left-hand corner, the Inside box, which "teases" several stories. Sports wants to include the final score in its "Red Sox keep on rolling" item, and Living has noticed that the wrong page number was listed in the description of Nathan Cobb's bowling banquet story.

At first glance, the front page won't look much different when the third edition rolls around, either. Same layout, same headlines in the same places. Only someone who made a word-by-word comparison would notice the differences. This is the fine-tuning stage, where a story is changed to add new information, background, or perspective. In the background category tonight is Phillip Van Niekerk's South Africa story, which clearly explains today's announced ban on events marking the anniversary of the Soweto student uprisings but does not, one copy editor has decided, give enough background on the uprisings themselves. Two sentences will be added to explain what happened on June 16, 1976.

Clegg crayons "2V" in red over the South Africa story on the stat, to show the composing room that a second version is coming. The story about the Chernobyl evacuations will be

"2V-ed" too; an editor is replacing the Reuters report from the first and second editions with a story from the *Los Angeles Times* wire. Although the two are similar, the foreign desk says that the *Times* story adds more perspective: why the latest evacuations are important, and what the Soviets' acknowledgment of them means.

Every change has a snowball effect, and Barbara Huebner is busy dodging the snowballs. When front-page stories like South Africa and Chernobyl change, their runover pages—the pages where the stories continue inside the paper—change too. And if the runover pages change, stories from the runover pages may have to move to other pages, and then those pages change, and other pages change because of errors or new information, and so on until the thirty-page quota of replates is swallowed up.

Huebner and local layout editor Bill Harting are dummying as furiously now as they were four hours ago, only this time they know it won't last long. They'll get done and catch their breath, and everybody will hang around the copy desk until the first fresh-off-the-press papers arrive from downstairs. Then, after they've all flipped through looking for errors, the weary exodus will begin. But Huebner isn't feeling sleepy yet. Maybe she'll stay until the *Herald* comes out. Her husband works there, and if she reads his paper they'll have more to talk about at breakfast.

● ● ●

Sitting at home in front of the 11:00 news, five newspapers spread out around him, Jack Driscoll realizes that he's no longer absorbing any of it. He is newsed out. Earlier tonight, sleep seemed an unattainable goal. Then, quite unexpectedly, he made his peace with the day.

It happened about an hour ago, when he went out to his car to pick up the newspapers and briefcase he'd abandoned there in the heat of the latest firestorm over the Pelton story. It was a beautiful night, clear and cool, and Driscoll stood in his driveway, drinking it in. As the smell of cut grass washed over him, he thought: That's it. We've done our best, and the story is gone. Finished. He opened the car door and stood there a moment longer, feeling like a man who is doing the right thing.

• • •

Twenty lines into his *Tosca* review and counting, Richard Dyer has almost forgotten that he'll be driving home tonight without a tape player for company. He came straight back to the newsroom without reporting the theft to the police. Doing that would have meant missing deadline, and deadline always means putting the rest of life on hold. Tomorrow will be plenty of time for dealing with the insurance people, especially since he knows the routine so well. One week his car was broken into three times.

Dyer could have taken a portable terminal and written at home or somewhere in the theater (the *Globe*'s rock critic sits with his terminal on his lap at concerts, typing away as the teenagers scream around him), or anywhere else he wanted, but he can't work in solitude. He likes the buzz of the newsroom, even in its reduced nighttime state. At the height of the season, when several critics sit until midnight pushing deadline together, he and dance critic Christine Temin often barter for space. If their reviews are running on the same page and Dyer's is coming up a few lines short, he "gives" the lines to Temin. If one of them is writing long and can't bear to cut, the other might relinquish some space.

But tonight Dyer is working alone, and he has been given all the space he needs—eighty lines. In the third edition, his review will replace a wire story and a rock review that ran in the first and second editions tonight because it was too late for those editions last night. Having expected to be confined to fifty lines, Dyer writes with gusto, reveling in the luxury of letting his thoughts spin out to their logical conclusions.

Like the Arts section's editor, John Koch, Dyer believes that arts stories are as important as news stories. (Koch goes so far as to say, "People are going to remember George Balanchine long after they've forgotten Jimmy Carter.") And like the news staff, the arts staff is always juggling far more events than it can cover. Koch says that few people—including, unfortunately, some who have the money to support the arts—

277

realize just how active the Boston arts scene is. He doesn't consider it the newspaper's job to crusade for improvement in Boston's arts image, but he wouldn't mind if the paper had that effect simply by showing readers the wide range of things going on.

Dyer says that arts reviews are not only *like* news stories, they *are* news stories—news stories on the arts. Readers may expect more stylistic flash from a review, but they also expect the Five W's. Most important of all, Dyer says, the critic must let his readers know immediately what he thought of the piece he's reviewing. In his nightmares, someone reads to the end of one of his reviews and then asks, "Did this guy like the thing or not?"

So Dyer tries to indicate his opinion early, then use the rest of the space to show how he developed it. With all those strictures, he says, "the form of the review can seem as limited and demanding as a sonnet." A few years ago, when the demands seemed too much to bear, he took a year off from reviewing to write for the Sunday magazine. Now that he's back and enjoying it, his critical eye occasionally detours from opera and classical music to something a little more "popular." A recent review of a glitzy, megaselling Hollywood paperback gave him the chance to write lines like these: "These characters spend most of their lives in horizontal positions, which inspires their creator to vertical prose. Their values are repulsive, racist, ethnophobic, homophobic and sexist." It was great fun to pull out the stops that way, but he feels more comfortable doing what he's doing tonight: hunching over his terminal in his striped shirt and madras bow tie, gently pointing out a weakness in a diva's lower-middle register.

•   •   •

As the delivery trucks are warming up, as the plates are being fastened to the presses, Ellen Clegg's phone rings in the newsroom. "I don't think that's the right headline for the Pelton story," Walter Robinson says.

Robinson is calling from Washington. He is the reporter who wrote the Pelton story, based on reporting that he and Fred Kaplan did. He tells Clegg that he couldn't sleep because he was worried about the story, so a minute ago he called and asked a copy editor to read him the headline. Now he doesn't know what to do. He knows it's late, he doesn't want to cause trouble, he realizes that on a story this sensitive the editors would be inclined to understate rather than overstate the headline. And for the most part he's been delighted with the way the paper has handled the story, sticking by him and Kaplan when the editors could easily have decreed that the government was making publication too dangerous.

But having said all that, Robinson still thinks that the main head and the drop head submerge the news. Both heads say that the secrets Pelton sold weren't so secret, but neither one hints at what those secrets were. To him, that's the point: The paper found out about the secrets, and now it's telling its readers as much as it can without harming national security. Couldn't the drop head maybe mention "risky U.S. operation in Soviet harbors"?

Clegg explains to him that four editors worked a long time to come up with those heads, that Robinson's immediate boss, Steve Kurkjian, approved them, and that everyone seemed satisfied that they'd laid the matter to rest at last. Although she's tempted to tell him not to rock the boat, she does understand how much he has invested in the story. She promises to call one of the editors who wrote the headline, and to have that person call Robinson in Washington. It's too late for the first and second edition, but maybe they can agree on a revised head for the third edition.

Midnight

We do all this work, and then we put it in the hands of a twelve-year-old kid.
—said by everyone, always attributed to someone else

In a candlelit café in Santiago, Chile, Pam Constable pushes back her glass of wine and closes her journal. Writing in the journal, trying to capture feelings and impressions and shades of meaning that don't seem appropriate to her news stories, has relaxed her as always, but what she really wants to do now is talk to her fiancé. She girds to do battle with the telephones.

Being a foreign correspondent is the life Constable has dreamed of since she drove cross-country in 1974, a brand-new college graduate looking for the newspaper that would give her her start. She worked in Annapolis and Manhattan and Baltimore before landing in 1982 at the *Globe*, where the Latin America correspondent quit only a few months after Constable arrived. Suddenly her dream was coming true—not in the part of the world she'd envisioned, but in a place that would give her a broader perspective on the poverty and social problems she'd been covering in the United States.

For three and a half years the job has been everything she'd imagined, and more. The chance to explore a new world, and to send glimpses of that world back home, is endlessly fascinating. She feels privileged, and never more so than when she meets one of the dozens of freelancers trying to make their way in Central and South America, much as Constable tried in the States years ago. They work as hard for their stories as she does, but they never know whether those stories will be printed, or when they'll next be paid. I'm incredibly lucky, she tells herself. She believes it. But sometimes

280

late at night, she'd give anything to have someone with whom she could share her day.

She wants to tell someone about the press conference the striking teachers held tonight, about how she looked at the bowls of cookies they'd set out and suddenly realized that she'd forgotten to eat all day. One hundred and fifty more students and ten more teachers were arrested in protests today, and a teacher at the press conference told the reporters that the government had ordered him to tear out and burn certain pages from history books. She wants to share that with someone, and to talk about the former senator who told her today, "What a horror, what a horror Chile has become."

Constable returns to her hotel and reaches her fiancé on the third try. As they talk, the operator breaks in periodically to tell them how much money they're spending. There's nothing to do but laugh. So far this year, their phone bills have totaled more than $3,000.

• • •

The last plates are being locked onto the presses. The mailroom crews eye the clock warily, waiting for the avalanche of papers they must strap into bundles for the long journey into first-edition country. Below them, backed up to their designated loading doors, the drivers, too, are waiting, listening for the sound that will tell them that the bundles are on their way.

At midnight, when every plate is in place, the press runner enters a booth at the center of the pressroom and pushes a button. With a roar that extinguishes conversation and with a shudder felt from cellar to roof, the monstrous machines begin to roll. They groan like beasts reluctant to leave their slumber, pulling the long ribbons of newsprint slowly at first, then faster and faster as men run alongside, shouting commands and making adjustments.

The pressmen shout to one other as naturally as if they were speaking in normal tones. For them, shouting *is* normal. When all the new machinery is installed, the space at the center of the pressroom will be enclosed as a "quiet room," where the pressmen can escape from the constant noise. At first, says Jim Malnati, a pressman for thirty-nine years, the crews resisted the idea that they needed refuge from the rumbling. Now, he says, anyone who spends any time in the press runner's quiet glass booth finds it difficult to leave.

Each plate made tonight in the engraving department has been wrapped around a cylinder on one of the presses. As the plate cylinder rotates, it meets a rotating roller dampened with water. The water sticks to the non-image areas, the areas that will be white on the finished page, because of the chemical with which those parts of the plate were treated. Then a roller covered with ink rolls over the plate. The areas dampened with water resist the ink, but the other areas—the areas that will be type and pictures, which have been treated to accept grease and resist water—welcome the ink and hold it there until they contact another spinning cylinder covered by a rubber blanket.

The plate transfers the inked images to the blanket, which in turn transfers them to the passing stream of newsprint. The arrangement of plates on the cylinders has been carefully planned so that each press will produce a collection of same-sized sheets that, after the press cuts and folds them together, will form a newspaper, first page first and last page last.

As the tachometer in the control booth moves up toward 10,000 papers an hour, the pressmen fiddle with the ink and water balance and the register of the color photos, until all the images seem to have the right amount of ink in the right places. The 500 or 600 papers printed during this adjustment process won't leave the building. As soon as the press runner is satisfied, he puts his finger on the button and leaves it there, pushing the speed to 60,000 an hour. The noise pounds louder and faster, faster and louder. It vibrates through the room until each person in it feels as if he is running uphill, listening to his heart slam a wild spiraling rhythm in his chest. Then the press runner flips a switch, and the papers cascade toward the mailroom.

The presses will run for an hour, then stop to be replated for the second edition, run for another hour and stop again to replate for the third, the edition most of the 514,000 readers will see tomorrow. Later, if anything else needs changing, they'll stop for a final replate. Between this plant and Billerica, 590,000 papers will roll out into trucks, bound for stores and vending boxes and, eventually, canvas bags slung over the handlebars of thousands of bicycles. By the end of the week, 7 to 10 percent of those papers will have come back to Dorchester, unsold. They'll be bundled and sent to a mill that will use them to make rolls of fresh white newsprint, which in time will ride the carts to the pressroom again, ready to become another batch of Globes.

A pressman's work doesn't end when the presses start rolling. He must keep watch over his assigned reel, which holds three 1,800-pound rolls of paper for the monster to swallow. Every twenty minutes, a roll runs out. Before that can happen, the pressman must guide a new roll into position so that the press can grab it and start it spinning as fast as the expiring roll. When the old roll gets down to its last inches, the machinery slices it off and quickly shoves the new one into running position, picking up its end. With any luck, this process will continue in twenty-minute intervals for the next four and a half hours.

•   •   •

Managing editor Tom Mulvoy, who was asleep when Ellen Clegg called him, dials her number in the newsroom to report the outcome of his talk with Washington reporter Walter Robinson. After Robinson had explained why the headline on the Pelton story bothered him, Mulvoy agreed to call the other people who had helped write it. As Clegg had already discovered, however, none of them was home. Mulvoy called Robinson back, and eventually they agreed that it would be wiser to leave the headline unchanged than to risk further problems by fooling with it.

That's good news, Clegg tells Mulvoy. After she's assured him that all is well in the newsroom, they say goodnight. He'll be back in nine hours to start a new shift.

The front page of the *New York Times* has emerged from the wirephoto machine, and Clegg scans it, looking for stories the *Globe* might have missed. Nothing jumps out at her. An editorial assistant drops a proof of the third-edition front page on her desk, and she scans that, too. All the changes

283

seem to have been incorporated smoothly. Clegg continues writing her note to Mulvoy and his two deputies, letting them know how the night went.

Then her phone rings. "I've been thinking," Walter Robinson's voice says. "If the headline wasn't clear, that could mean the *story* wasn't clear. Maybe I should change the second graf."

They talk for a while, the weary editor and the weary reporter too hyped up to sleep. Eventually, as Clegg hoped he would, Robinson decides that since no one can find his editor, and since the new front page has already been pasted up, he'll leave the story as it is.

"Good night, Robby," Clegg says.

When she looks up, the newsroom is almost empty. Piles of scrap paper cover the desk; piles of paperwork await her in her office. She heads for it with a groan, leaving Bob Norling in charge. By the time he's wrapped up his shift and the long drive home, early-rising readers will be picking the paper from their front steps. As the readers scan this morning's news, the first reporters will be arriving in the murky newsroom, ready to hunt down tomorrow's.

News summary on page 2
Telephone 929-2000
Classified 929-1500
Circulation 929-2222

The Boston Globe

Open wide, say blah
Thursday – Mostly cloudy, 70
Friday – May rain, 60
High tide – 10:54 a.m., 11:01 p.m.
Full report – Page 42

Vol. 229; No. 156 THURSDAY, JUNE 5, 1986 120 Pages • 25 cents

Pelton's 'top-secret' intelligence not so secret

US claims security compromised, but many key details in public domain

By Fred Kaplan and Walter V. Robinson
Globe Staff

WASHINGTON – In a crowded federal courtroom in Baltimore, only carefully selected, elliptical references have been made to the top-secret communications intelligence Ronald W. Pelton is accused of selling to the Soviet Union for a paltry $35,000 in cash.

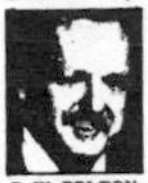

R. W. PELTON
Accused spy

Thirty-seven miles away in the nation's capital, top US intelligence officials have emerged from the silence that shrouds their agencies in secrecy to threaten reporters with prosecution for publishing articles about the intelligence that can be assembled, for the most part, from unclassified technical manuals, pre-trial statements in open court and even from past news reports.

In the two cities, the government appears to be making contradictory arguments: Prosecutors in Baltimore have asserted that Pelton sold a treasure trove of intelligence data to the Soviets that destroyed a successful intelligence program. But officials in Washington have warned that even general press speculation about the program may alert the Soviets to things they do not know.

Obscured under this extraordinary security blanket, according to sources, is the program the Soviet Union is undoubtedly aware of because of the information it gleaned from Pelton, but one which could prove embarrassing to the United States if it were to become publicly known.

According to the sources, the program involved the use of US Navy submarines, creeping into Soviet waters at great risk, to facilitate eavesdropping on an undersea communications system – an underwater replay of the U2 overflights of the Soviet Union that became a deep embarrassment to the United States in 1960 when one of the reconnaissance planes was shot down and its pilot, Francis Gary Powers, was captured.

With the help of a high technology device, identified by Pelton in trial testimony this week as a "recording

SECRETS, Page 16

PLEADS GUILTY

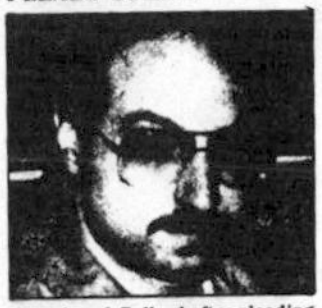

Jonathan J. Pollard after pleading guilty to selling US secret documents to Israel. Page 15 AP PHOTO

Obstacles surface to Senate tax bill

Talk of passage more guarded

By Thomas Oliphant
Globe Staff

WASHINGTON – The great Senate tax reform steamroller has hit its first big bumps in the road.

The road still leads on most maps to passage by the Senate – which formally began consideration of the massive measure yesterday – of a drastic revision of the nation's income tax laws and a compromise with the House that produces a measure President Reagan will want to sign.

However, the euphoria that erupted after the Senate Finance Committee dramatically reversed field and approved a bill slashing individual and corporate rates and eliminating scores of deductions and other tax breaks last month is gradually being replaced by more guarded prognoses.

Here are the latest problems:

- A groundswell has developed against the Senate Finance Committee's proposal to end the deductibility of annual contributions of up to $2,000 to individual Retirement Accounts as one of the major tradeoffs for its lower rates (two rates of 15 and 27 percent in place of the current system of 11 rates up to 50 percent).
- The Republican leadership's strategy, backed by President Reagan, of pressing for quick passage without amendments in the interests of avoiding a legislative marathon has been attacked by senators in both parties. Sen. Alfonse D'Amato (R-N.Y.) went so far as to accuse Majority Leader Robert Dole of Kansas and Finance Committee chairman Bob Packwood (R-Ore.) yesterday of approaching "Gestapo tactics" in their methods.

House and Senate Democrats, prompted by the success of a pilot welfare-to-jobs project in Massachusetts, launched an effort yesterday to adopt a similar program for all 50 states. Page 6.

- Problems are also emerging between the so-far-separate tax revision and budget deficit reduction efforts in Congress. The Senate tax bill was written so that it raises well over $20 billion in its first two years and loses an equivalent amount the following two years before becoming "revenue-neutral" over the long term. These estimates have drawn criticism from Budget Committee leaders who do not want to see that revenue bulge applied to 1987 deficit reduction targets in place of the modest tax increases they have recommended.

TAXES, Page 24

A SPECTACLE

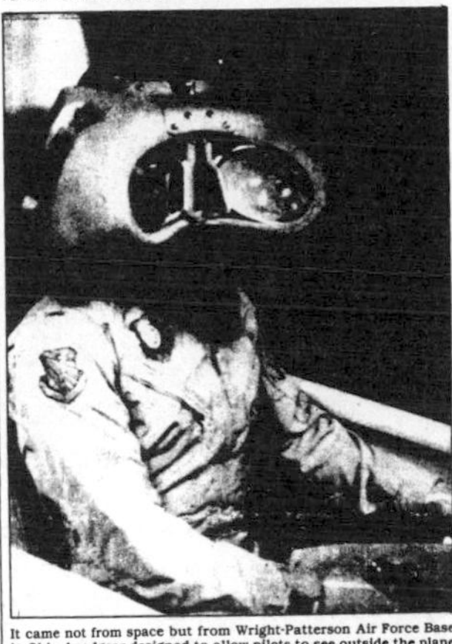

It came not from space but from Wright-Patterson Air Force Base in Ohio, headgear designed to allow pilots to see outside the plane despite darkness or rain. Helmet encloses television receivers linked to outside cameras and also contains controls for plane's weapons system, allowing pilot to aim by a turn of the head. AP PHOTO

Pretoria bans events marking Soweto violence

By Philip Van Niekerk
Special to the Globe

CAPE TOWN – The South African government yesterday banned for the rest of this month all meetings to commemorate the 10th anniversary of the Soweto uprisings of June 16, 1976, in which hundreds of blacks died.

The action came as civil rights and antiapartheid organizations formed a common front to oppose legislation before Parliament granting Louis le Grange, the minister of law and order, wider powers.

The Soweto anniversary is viewed by antiapartheid groups as a highly emotional event, and countrywide protest meetings and a national general strike have been planned to commemorate it.

Meetings later in the month to celebrate the 31st anniversary of the signing of a document that lays down guidelines for a postapartheid society – the Freedom Charter – have also been banned.

The charter was signed by the now-outlawed African National Congress, and the anniversary of its signing has become an annual protest event.

The decree forbidding all meetings from June 4 to June 30 was declared by Le Grange yesterday under the terms of the country's Internal Security Act. He said the ban was "deemed necessary for the preservation of public peace."

The government has already banned outdoor meetings except when authorized on an individual basis, although the restriction is frequently defied. The new decree extends the ban to indoor meetings connected with the two anniversaries and says exceptions will be allowed only when specifically authorized by Le Grange or a local magistrate.

Several black political organizations yesterday said privately that they would go ahead with the protests anyway.

The ban went into effect as a national civil rights organization – the Ad Hoc Committee Against New Repression Bills' – was formed representing a wide range of organizations.

The bills opposed by the organization will give the minister of law and order power to declare martial law in any area he wants

SOUTH AFRICA, Page 23

Soviets say 60,000 children evacuated

Chernobyl radiation reportedly spreading

Reuters

MOSCOW – Radioactive contamination from Chernobyl has spread north from the Ukraine, and at least 60,000 children have been evacuated from a danger zone in the neighboring republic of Byelorussia, Pravda reported yesterday.

The report was the latest in a series from the official press showing that danger from the April 26 accident was not limited to the 18-mile emergency zone around the Chernobyl nuclear plant from which 92,000 people were evacuated.

Soviet officials, who have listed 25 dead, had previously reported no serious threat to health outside the Chernobyl zone. But on Tuesday for the first time they said 18,000 people suffered respiratory problems and some spat blood after the accident, which was the world's worst nuclear accident.

Pravda, the Communist Party newspaper, yesterday quoted government officials in the Byelorussian republic as describing extensive evacuation and protective measures in districts south of Gomel, a city 90 miles north of Chernobyl.

It spoke of an 18-mile danger zone "on Byelorussian territory" and the existence of "dirty spots" outside it.

Specialists at Western embassies said the wording was vague but it implied a danger area extending well beyond the original zone, which runs only about 9 miles into a rural area of Byelorussia.

Diplomats said they did not take Pravda to mean a new 18-mile zone had been imposed in Byelorussia but rather that some population centers beyond the

NUCLEAR, Page 23

Paulist Center bows to church's threats

Liturgical practices challenged; women out as preachers at Mass

By James L. Franklin
Globe Staff

The Paulist Center in downtown Boston has discontinued allowing women to preach at Mass after the Boston Archdiocese threatened to oust the Paulist Fathers because of complaints about liturgical abuses.

Leaders of the Paulist Center said this week that they agreed to end what they describe as "liturgical adaptations" and to follow a strict interpretation of the sacramentary, the guidebook for the celebration of Catholic worship.

But Rev. Michael McGarry, CSP, director of the Paulist Center, said the staff and members of the Paulist Center Community are discussing how to continue preaching by lay people, for example at prayer services before or after Masses, which he called traditional forms of devotion.

"We assured the archdiocese we would follow the sacramentary closely because the stakes are pretty high," Father McGarry said. "The ongoing vitality and outreach of the Paulist Center are important to us."

Although technically a chapel, the Paulist Center is listed in the Boston Catholic Directory as the third church in the nation's third largest archdiocese and is well known for

PAULISTS, Page 22

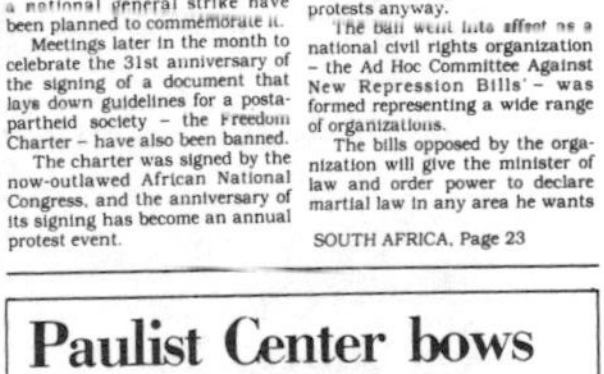

The Paulist Center on Park Street in downtown Boston. GLOBE STAFF PHOTO BY WENDY MAEDA

Inside

Today: Calendar

Red Sox keep on rolling

First-place Boston downed the Indians, 6-4, last night for their fifth straight win and ninth in their last 10 games. Page 53.

American Pop: Bowling banquets

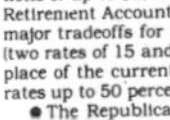

The bowling banquet is an annual sign of spring, as certain to occur as is winter's snow to melt. Ritualistically performed after 30 or so weeks on the hardwood, it brings together lobbers and speedballers alike, people who eagerly party anyplace there's room for some tables, a dance floor and a bar. Living, Page 81.

US OK's human interferon use

The US government approved a type of human interferon yesterday as a treatment for hairy cell leukemia, an uncommon but deadly form of cancer. The substance is the first so-called biotherapy – a medication produced by the human body – to be approved as a treatment. Page 12.

Guide to features

Accusations, turmoil swirl over Switzler

By Bruce Mohl
Globe Staff

Republican gubernatorial candidate Royall H. Switzler yesterday had to fend off accusations that his embellishment of his military record continued after 1980, both in an interview he gave a newspaper reporter last year and in statements he made on the House floor.

Many of his supporters rallied behind him and said he would weather the political storm set off Tuesday when he corrected inaccuracies about his Army rank and service affiliation that he had allowed to appear in old political brochures and political journals.

But as the latest in a series of controversies that have rocked GOP candidates, his revelations only accentuated the serious problems facing the Massachusetts Republican Party.

"I think it says the Republican Party is in even deeper trouble than you thought it was," said Jack Flannery, a Republican political consultant. "Whoever wins the [Republican gubernatorial] primary in September wins the dubious privilege of getting creamed in November."

Gregory Hyatt, Switzler's rival for the GOP nomination for governor, was accused two months ago by a former client of having been fired for poor performance last year, a charge he denies. In a previous controversy involving a Republican candidate, John Lakian of Westwood was found to have embellished his background in his 1982 bid for the gubernatorial nomination.

A July 1985 article in the Natick-based newspaper NewsWest that surfaced yesterday indicated Switzler had said he had been a Green Beret in Vietnam, an adviser to a South Vietnamese battalion and had seen "activity" against the Viet Cong.

Switzler had said on Tuesday that he had never been a Green Beret and that he had only visited

SWITZLER, Page 14

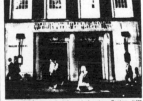

METRO/REGION

Comics 40,41
TV & Radio 43.
Classified 44

Mint owner David Kilmartin indulges in hands-on activity with transit tokens.   GLOBE STAFF PHOTO BY JOSEPH RUNCI

Mint concludes its token assignment

By Steven Marantz
Globe Staff

ATTLEBORO – Several thousand of the newest New York City Transit Authority subway tokens began their long journey yesterday under a steamy blanking press at the Roger Williams Mint. A wide spindle of brass unwound into the machine, lurched under the impact of punchers, and dropped its raw booty into a cart.

Several steps later, the cart was filled with finished tokens of glistening brass and steel, each valued at $1, a lifetime's worth of subway riding.

David Kilmartin, owner of the mint, inspected the tokens, scooping handfuls out of the cart. "I feel like Midas," he said.

Kilmartin's mint may well be described as having a golden touch. On Monday, the New York City Transit Authority announced it had completed a switchover to the new tokens. Yesterday, Roger Williams was minting the last of those tokens, 50 million of them at a cost of $5.75 million to the authority. That contract is one of many transit, casino, and commemorative coin contracts that make it, in the estimation of industry experts, the nation's largest private mint.

Yet, despite employing 110 workers in a 100,000 square-foot plant, the mint is by choice "a well-kept secret," Kilmartin said. He cited two reasons for maintaining a low profile:

• The mint is a manufacturer's manufacturer, producing collectibles, commemorative coins, key fobs, and jewelry for
MINT, Page 33

Judge reinstates punishment therapy

Overrules state agency, says school can resume practices

By Jean Dietz
Globe Staff

ATTLEBORO – A Bristol County Probate Court judge yesterday overruled the director of the Massachusetts Office for Children and reinstated the use of a controversial physical punishment therapy in the behavior modification program at a school for severely disturbed youths.

Judge Ernest Rotenberg granted a preliminary injunction sought by the Behavior Research Institute and families of 62 students. The state plans to appeal, according to Mary Kay Leonard, director of the Office for Children.

Finding that Leonard acted "in bad faith" in a series of decisions involving treatment programs at the institute, Rotenberg also set up a procedure to determine individual programs of the clients by petition of parents and guardians to the court.

Rotenberg accused Leonard of playing "Russian roulette with the lives and safety of students," adding her "unsubstantiated orders [are] based on no medical foundation."

Following his decision, parents of students from Massachusetts, New York and New Jersey called on Gov. Dukakis to fire Leonard for interfering with treatment programs.

"Responsibility for her actions belongs with the governor. We've already spent $110,000 in legal fees just to protect our children from her directives," said William Martin, a New York stockbroker whose 18-year-old son attends the school.

The Office For Children has licensing jurisdiction over the Providence-based institute because students live in group homes in southeastern Massachusetts.

The state began to investigate the institute's procedures following the death of a 22-year-old, male student from New York who died last July while undergoing "white noise" therapy.

The therapy, which involved placing a helmet with special earphones on his head while his hands and feet were tied, called attention to other physical aversives used at the institute, including

JUDGE ERNEST ROTENBERG
Says official acted in bad faith

spanking, muscle squeezes, cold showers and water vapor sprays.

The institute endorses the use the punishments as well as rewards to curb harmful or self-destructive behavior.

Critics say the punishments cause the students extreme physical harm.

Last night, Leonard said she was disappointed but "not surprised" by Rotenberg's decision.

Philip Johnston, human services secretary, said that the decision was "extremely unfortunate" and that he was disturbed that Rotenberg's decision included "personal comments" about Leonard, whom he called "a decent, competent and caring public servant."

James Dorsey, press officer for Gov. Dukakis, said "Mary Kay Leonard is responsible for protection of the rights of children in Massachusetts. She has done an outstanding job. It is difficult to understand how her aggressive advocacy to protect children following a mysterious and terrible tragedy involving the death of a child at the institute could be construed as endangering children."

Families spoke openly of their resentment toward the office after Rotenberg read his 28-page decision.

After announcing her intention to
INJUNCTION, Page 31

Boston schools ready pregnancy prevention plan

By Peggy Hernandez
Globe Staff

Boston school officials yesterday recommended a pregnancy prevention program for seventh-graders to begin next year that would not include the distribution of birth control devices.

The prevention program, titled "Life" Planning Education," would be phased in over a two-year period and reach 1,300 seventh-grade boys and girls in eight schools.

"The focus of the proposal will clearly be an interventional preventative program and does not contain in any component the directive, requirement, or permission to dispense birth control information or devices in the middle-school level," Deputy Superintendent Rudolph F. Crew said to Superintendent Laval S. Wilson in a memo dated May 22.

The proposed program, expected to cost $75,000, was forwarded to the School Committee with the signed approval of Wilson, Crew and Deputy Superintendent James F. Walsh. The first year of the program would be devoted to staff and parent training and curriculum development, Walsh said in a memo. The second year would see the start of classroom instruction and a job program that would complement the curriculum.

The proposal does not recommend any specific schools for the program. Sixteen middle schools, however, have volunteered for the program: the Barnes, Cleveland, Dearborn, Holmes, Irving, Lewis, Mackey, McCormack, Rogers, Roosevelt, Shaw, Taft, Thompson, Timilty, Wheatley and Wilson.

The School Committee is being asked to vote on a proposed curriculum at Tuesday's meeting. If approved, the proposal would be submitted to a private foundation for funding consideration.

The life planning program was prepared by a committee of students, parents and representatives from the School Department and community agencies. It comes a little more than a month after a citywide health task force recommended establishing health clinics in four middle and high schools.

The task force recommended that the clinics dispense contraceptives to students.
PROGRAM, Page 33

INSIDE

• The Boston City Council yesterday rejected a proposal that would have given subpoena power to the Internal Investigation Commission. Page 38.

• About 40 self-described witches marched in protest to the possible filming of a movie based on "The Witches of Eastwick," in the Bay State. Page 44.

• The Massachusetts Department of Mental Health has assessed its three largest bus contractors a total of more than $40,000 for poor performance. Page 88.

Metro/Region news on pages
29-39, 42, 44, 75, 88

8th District opponents criticize Kennedy remarks on foster care

By Andrew Blake
Globe Staff

Several candidates in the 8th Congressional District race yesterday directed some of the sharpest criticism of the campaign at Joseph P. Kennedy 2d over a statement he made Tuesday on gays and foster care.

They accused him of being muddled on the issue at best and of lacking credibility at worst. One of his opponents, Sen. George Bachrach [D-Watertown], remarked: "I don't know what the hell Joe's position is. He is trying to appeal to both sides, and that is an absolute impossibility."

In January, Kennedy said sexual preference should not be an issue in choosing foster parents, but in March he said he agreed with Gov. Dukakis that foster children should be placed in a traditional family. At a forum Tuesday night sponsored by the Massachusetts Gay and Lesbian Political Caucus, Kennedy basically espoused the current state position, which virtually bars gay and lesbian couples from taking in foster children.

But after being peppered with hisses and heckling from the audience, Kennedy was asked a direct question on the issue from the floor. In response, he said he opposed.

EIGHTH DISTRICT, Page 35

New homes vowed for old West End

By Andrew J. Dabilis
Globe Staff

In the 1960s, most of the old West End neighborhood in Boston was razed, forcing 3,000 families out of their homes to make way for a parking lot, a state office building, luxury high-rise apartments and lots of commercial buildings.

Yesterday, Gov. Dukakis, Mayor Flynn and a host of legislators and other officials stood next to the state building and a dusty parking lot on New Chardon Street and said they want to bring residents back to what Flynn called "the new old West End."

Dukakis proposed building 400 units of housing on the lot for sale to middle-income families, those making $18,000 to $35,000. He said asking state-owned land would reduce the cost and a combination of townhouses and high-rise condomin-

iums could be built.

State housing officials said they hope the Legislature will earmark funds from a $225 million housing bond for the project, or use money from a $100 million Home Ownership Opportunity program proposed by Dukakis.

"We remember the old West End as one of the finest, the most integrated and stable neighborhoods in America, and it was destroyed," Dukakis said. He said it was done in by an urban renewal mentality that razed most of the old brick buildings and narrow streets.

Dukakis said the wave of recent condominium conversions and new housing construction in Boston had attracted mostly the affluent. "Where do the nurses who work at Mass. General, the clerks, and the families live?" he asked.

WEST END, Page 35

DIP OR DUMP

Windsurfer seems to be losing grip on his mode of transportation across Dorchester Bay yesterday.   GLOBE PHOTO BY RAY OWENS

LIVING/ARTS

Deaths 86,87

A man of many roles

By Catharine Rambeau
Knight-Ridder Service

DETROIT – Donald McNichol Sutherland, serious sailor, former disc jockey and truck driver, political activist, the original Hawkeye Pierce (in the movie "M*A*S*H), fool for jazz and the Montreal Expos, father of five – leaned into a bowl of red lentil soup, wistfully inhaling the garlic from a nearby plate of Turkish food.

Although Sutherland often looks 40 instead of almost 51, his digestion, unlike his politics, has become more conservative with age.

The Canadian-born actor was taking a short break from his role as Father Koesler in "The Rosary Murders," which, depending on whose list you're reading, is somewhere around his 50th film.

Although he played a priest in 1970's "Act of the Heart," Sutherland said there's no resemblance between that character and Koesler's. "The ears are the same, but [Koesler] kind of resembles the guy in 'Klute.'"

This fall, Sutherland goes to India to make "Deathless," a film about the transmigration of souls. "It makes my hair stand on end," he said. He smiled suddenly and displayed his arm. He wasn't kidding.

Next spring he's off to China, Spain and England to make another picture, this one about Norman Bethune, the Canadian doctor who died in China serving as a surgeon with Mao Zedong's guerrillas. Sutherland has already done one TV show about Bethune, whom he much admires as a true Canadian radical.

As an actor, Sutherland has avoided typecasting by attempting roles with a wide emotional and physical range. He has been a priest and a cop, a concerned father and an Army surgeon, an Italian fascist and a pot-smoking academic – and Casanova.

That has to do with his own ambition, said Sutherland. He believes it's possible to be a leading man who plays characters, and not fall into the trap of repeating himself because the audience expects a certain Donald Sutherland.

"An actor can define his career by saying 'I'm going to do this [film], and then I'm going to do this, so that I can then do this one,'" he said. "But then you have to define yourself in terms of what you perceive that your audience wants, which limits you even further. That's much too boring."

Sutherland believes he avoided the dilemma by thinking not in terms of what the films were going to do for him but concentrating instead on what directors wanted from him. It may even be that Sutherland's consistent professionalism – and his practice of refusing interviews while shooting – has occasionally cost him goodwill. Asked about persistent rumors that he is temperamental and arrogant, Sutherland doesn't take the question lightly.

"I know people say that," he said. "And I don't know why. I don't think it's true. It's difficult to be difficult, because the person I have to satisfy is my director. It's as if he's my lover, or I am his, and it's difficult for a lover to be intransigent – it's a contradiction in terms. I want to give him the best, but if he can't accept it, that's tough."

Of all the directors he worked with, Sutherland said that Federico Fellini, for whom he starred in "Casanova," was the best. "The best. Yep. It was like being in love, like having the most wonderful affair," he said. "He loves you so much, and he's so nice. To me. To other actors, he can be terrible. There are a lot of flaws in the English version of that picture, but it was a wonderful experience for me. We had a lovely time. He makes you cry."

SUTHERLAND, Page 83

Right up their alley

In spring, a bowler's fancy turns to the annual league banquet

GLOBE STAFF PHOTO BY JOHN TLUMACKI

Randolph Senior League table is laden with trophies and roast beef.

AMERICAN## AMERICAN POP

By Nathan Cobb

See the men sporting spiffy pastel jackets, the women sashaying past in dreamy coiffures created this very afternoon. See the bully-gully earnestly danced, long-neck beer bottles energetically opened, mounds of roast beef efficiently doled out. See the four-piece band segueing neatly into "New York, New York," the glitzy mirror ball rotating slowly overhead, the coveted Championship Jackets being presented. Why, everyone's having a heckuva time here at the annual bowling banquet. Can I get you a little something from the bar?

The bowling banquet is an annual sign of spring, as certain to occur as is winter's snow to melt. Ritualistically performed after 30 or so weeks on the hardwood, it brings together lobbers and speedballers alike, men and women who eagerly party in fraternal lodges, function facilities, country clubs, restaurants, hotels, anywhere there's room for

some tables, a dance floor and a bar.

"We'd never think of not having an annual banquet," announced Marjorie Harwood of Peabody, president of the Wednesday Morning Women's Bowling League, whose 100 members, ages 22 to 75, roll once a week, September to April, at Andy's Sunnyside Bowladrome in Danvers. As she spoke, Harwood was seated at a long, U-shaped table on the ground floor of the Danversport Yacht Club. The sun was setting over the Danvers River behind her, a three-piece band in matching red jackets was riffing lightly through a neo-Calypso version of "Mary Ann," and 90 other women had shown up in their Thursday best to choose between prime rib and baked stuffed shrimp.

One of them was Irene Pszenny of Danvers, who was commiserating with her teammates on finishing 19th in a 20-team league. ("Yes, but one of our girls – our captain – died," explained Madeleine Bacheller, who was seated across the table.) Pszenny bowls in four leagues, which means that she is deeply ensconced in the banquet circuit at this time of year. "The dinners are all the same," she an-

nounced as she wrestled with a large shrimp. "And they stay the same, too."

Fred Tortola concurs. Last week Tortola was seated at the head table at the silver anniversary banquet of the Waltham Senior Citizens' Bowling League, whose 140 weekly participants include three nuns, two deaf persons and a bowler with a wooden leg. Tortola owns the 60-lane Wal-Lex Recreation Center in Waltham where, by his own count, 75 winter leagues bowl weekly, from just after Labor Day through April. "Oh, God, I don't know how many of these things I've been to," he said as he surveyed the scene at the Pfc. Jim Sullivan VFW Post in Waltham. "Hundreds? Thousands? Anyway, they really don't change much from year to year. The format is set. It stays the same."

And just figure the numbers. There are approximately 130 candlepin bowling establishments in Massachusetts, according to the Massachusetts Bowling Association. (There are some 40 tenpin facilities in the state, though most of these also feature candlepins.) They represent somewhere in the neighborhood of POP, Page 83

FASHION## FASHION | JULIE HATFIELD

Laced for success

Attention, Adidas! Roll over, Reebok! Nudge on out, Nike! There's a new athletic shoe company vying for the lucrative position of No. 1 sneaker maker in the country. And the story of how it was formed may be as quirky as the design that makes its product unique.

The company is called Kaepa. And although it's relatively unknown hereabouts because its products have not so far been heavily marketed in Boston, it has been the No. 1-selling tennis shoe in Texas since 1982 and is one of the top sellers on the West Coast, grossing $30 to $40

million in total sales last year. It's a company that literally began on a shoestring – a broken one.

Kaepas – the name comes from a combination of Mikaela and Paula, the daughters of company founder Tom Adams – are shoes with split personalities that feature vamps that deliberately are split in two and laced with two separate laces, each with its own bow.

By being able to lace an athletic shoe over two separate parts of the foot, one can, in effect, fit the shoe to the arch, in FASHION, Page 83

Tom Adams and the unusual sneakers he markets.

GLOBE STAFF PHOTO BY TED DULLY

BOOK## BOOK REVIEW

Very Spenserian

Robert B. Parker: The plot isn't the point.

TAMING A SEA-HORSE, by Robert Parker. Delacorte Press / Seymour Lawrence. 250 pp. $15.95.
By Bob MacDonald
Globe Staff

Spenser to the rescue again. This time it's April Kyle, whom Spenser fans will remember from "Ceremony," in which our hero rescued April, a teen-age runaway, from the clutches of Boston's Combat Zone and delivered her to the haven of a high-class brothel in New York, a lesser of two evils.

Now, it seems that April has lost the relative safety of the brothel and gone to work for a pimp with the wonderful name of Rambeaux, downward mobility of sorts, with promise of an even worse future. Poor April thinks she is helping Rambeaux through the Juilliard School of Music. Spenser saves her, of course.

Along the way, the typical Spenserian plot: Spenser comes to aid of victim. Bad guys threaten Spenser. Spenser doesn't care. Tough guys lean a little harder; Spenser shows he's tough, too. Tough guys lean much harder; Spenser is joined by Hawk, his urban Tonto, BOOK, Page 83

Glossary

Agate: A vertical measurement of type or photos. One inch equals fourteen agates.

Art: Any element on a newspaper page that is not type. May include photos, charts, drawings.

Attribute: To explain the source of a piece of information in a story.

Beat: The area a reporter covers regularly. May be a geographic area or a subject area, such as education or crime.

Blanket: On an offset press, a rubber surface that covers a cylinder. The press transfers the page image from the plate to the blanket, and from the blanket to the paper.

Breaking news: News that is still developing and changing.

Brief: A news story of only a few paragraphs. Briefs are usually run together, in groups called packages.

Bright: A short, funny story.

Broadsheet: A standard-sized newspaper (as opposed to the smaller tabloid). Also, the name for the full-size pieces of heavy paper on which designers work.

Budget: A list of the stories each department is offering for a particular day's paper. The budget usually lists each story's slug and length and describes it briefly.

Byline: The writer's name as it appears at the top of the story.

Column: The vertical divisions on a newspaper page. The standard format is six columns per page. Also, a piece of writing that strongly shows the writer's opinion or personal style.

Composing room: The department that composes the pages by pasting photos and typeset copy onto pre-ruled heavy sheets of paper called pasteup boards. The composing room receives copy from the news and advertising departments and sends the pasted-up pages to the engraving department.

Copy: The material of a story or advertisement, as prepared by the writer.

Copy editing: Checking copy for accuracy, consistency, grammar, spelling, and style. This job is done by copy editors, whose place of work is called the copy desk.

Correspondent: A reporter who writes his or her stories somewhere other than the newspaper office. May or may not be a full-time newspaper employee.

Cut: A photograph or other illustration.

Cutline: The caption beneath a photograph or other illustration.

Dateline: Line at beginning of a story that shows its place of origin. Some newspapers also include the date in the dateline (for example, BOSTON, Dec. 2).

Deadline: The time when reporters must submit their stories to editors, or editors to the composing room.

Deck: Individual line of a headline. A three-deck head, for example, has three separate lines.

Desk: The collective term for the editors at the newspaper. May be general ("the desk") or specific ("city desk," "foreign desk," or "copy desk").

Downstyle heads: Headlines in which the first letter is capitalized only in the first word and in proper names.

Drop, drop head: A headline in smaller type, below the main headline, that elaborates on it.

Dummy: A sheet of paper divided into columns representing a newspaper page. Layout editors draw lines on the dummy to indicate placement of advertisements and stories. As a verb, *to dummy* is to diagram a page.

Edition: One version of a single day's newspaper. Different editions may cover different geographic areas (city edition, suburban edition) or different times of day (morning edition, afternoon edition).

Editorial: As a noun, refers to the unsigned, staff-written statements of opinion that run on the editorial page. As an adjective, distinguishes any news-related department or material from the rest of the newspaper.

Embargo: A restriction on when the media may release a piece of information.

Exclusive: A story obtained by one reporter and no others. Also called a scoop.

Feature: A story or photo whose primary purpose is entertainment rather than reporting a news event.

File: To send a story to the newsroom from somewhere else. A reporter may file using a portable computer or may dictate by phone.

Flack: A press agent or public relations person.

Flag: The large front-page type that bears a newspaper's name.

Folio: The line of small type at the top of a newspaper page that includes the name, date, and page number.

Followup, follow, folo: A story that reports new developments, or answers remaining questions, about a news event reported previously.

Futures file: A place where press releases and other tips to upcoming stories are organized by date.

General assignment reporters: Those who do not cover a specific beat; editors assign them to whatever story comes along. Also called g.a.

Graf: The journalist's abbreviation for *paragraph.*

Halftone: A reproduction of a photograph that converts the image into tiny black or white dots.

Handout: A press release.

Hard news: Breaking news written in a straight news style, as opposed to a feature style.

Hawker: A person who sells newspapers on the street.

Head shot, head cut: A photograph showing only the subject's head.

Hed: The journalist's abbreviation for *headline.*

Honor box: A newspaper vending box, so called because the buyer must be trusted not to take more papers than he pays for.

House ad: An advertisement that promotes the newspaper as a whole ("Read the *Bugle*") or a special section or event ("Come to the *Bugle*'s book festival").

Inverted pyramid: The classic form for a news story, in which the most important point comes first, then the next most important, and so on.

Jump: Continuation of a story from one page to another. As a verb, to continue to another page. Also called runover.

Jump head: The headline above the second part of a continued story.

Jump line: The line that says, "Turn to page so-and-so" for the rest of a story.

Justify: To arrange type into columns of a predetermined width, so that margins are straight rather than ragged.

Kill: To discard a story or section of a story. Also called spike.

Layout: The design or diagram of the elements on a page.

Lead, lede: The beginning of a story. In a news story, the lead is usually the first paragraph. In a feature, it may be longer. Also, a tip on a story ("I've got a lead that something's going on at the jail," a reporter might tell an editor).

Library: The place where clippings, photographs, and other reference material are kept at a newspaper. Also called a morgue.

Linage: Number of lines. Usually used with advertising.

Localize: To stress the local angle in a broader story.

Masthead, mast: A formal list, usually on the editorial page, of a newspaper's top officers and editors.

Mug shot: A head-and-shoulders photograph. Same as head shot.

Morgue: Newspaper library.

News hole: The amount of space in a newspaper filled by non-advertising material.

News peg, news hook: An element of timeliness that explains why a story is in the paper today, rather than yesterday or tomorrow. For example, the anniversary of an unsolved murder might be a peg for a story updating the investigation.

Offset: Printing process in which the page image is transferred from a plate to a rubber blanket and then to the paper.

Off the record: When said by a source, "off the record" means the reporter cannot use in a story the information the source is offering.

Op-ed page: The page opposite the editorial page, usually filled with opinion pieces by columnists.

Package: A group of related stories and/or photographs tied together by the page layout. As a verb, to group in layout.

Pagination: The process of designing a newspaper page on a computer screen rather than on paper.

Pasteup: The process of affixing type and other elements to a page.

Pica: A unit of measurement equal to one-sixth of an inch.

Plate: In offset printing, a piece of aluminum on which the image of a page is etched. The plate is wrapped around a cylinder on the press, where it picks up ink and transfers it to a rubber blanket.

Play: The emphasis given a story, as determined by placement on the page, size of headline, etc. ("My story got terrible play.") As a verb, to place a story. ("Let's play this one well.")

Plug: A story printed in an early edition to hold space for a breaking story (a concert or sports event, for example) that won't be completed until a later edition. Also, another term for house ad.

Point: A unit of measurement. One inch equals approximately seventy-two points. Used to measure size of type.

Puff, puff piece: A story so complimentary to the subject that it reads like an advertisement.

Queue: A person's own collection of files in a computer system.

Quote: The journalist's abbreviation for *quotation*, the exact words of a speaker.

Replate: To put a new plate or plates on the press in order to change something. Also, the version of the paper produced by this change.

Rim: The place where copy editors sit. When copy desks were horseshoe-shaped, the copy chief sat in the "slot," the copy editors "on the rim." The term has lingered.

Roto, rotogravure: A printing process in which the image is etched onto a copper plate. Because roto is more expensive than offset printing, most newspapers use it only for their Sunday magazines or special advertising sections.

Roundup: A story that reports several events with a common theme, such as traffic accidents or fires.

Runover: The remainder of a story that began on another page. Also called jump.

Scoop: To report a story that competing papers miss. Also, the story so reported.

Sidebar: A companion piece to a news story that elaborates on some point in the main story.

Slot: The place occupied by the copy desk chief. Also refers to that person.

Slug: A one-word name for a story, usually in capital letters, such as FIRE.

Source: A person or document that provides information for a story.

Spike: To kill a story or part of a story.

Standalone: A photograph that does not go with a story; it stands alone. Also called wild art.

Straight news: A description of the most basic way of reporting an event.

Stringer: A writer, not a full-time employee of a paper, who is paid per assignment.

Stylebook: A book that lists a newspaper's rules on spelling, capitalization, abbreviations, etc.

Sub: A story, or part of a story, that replaces earlier material.

Take: A page of copy.

Trim: To eliminate part of a story.

Upstyle heads: Headlines in which the first letter of every word is capitalized.

Wire services, wires: Press associations that send their stories to newspapers that have paid a subscription fee. The best-known wire services are Associated Press, United Press International, and Reuters. Some newspapers and chains of newspapers run their own wire services, selling their stories to papers in other parts of the country.

Index